MINOR LEAGUE BASEBALL TOWNS of MICHIGAN

Adrian to Ypsilanti

the teams & the ballparks of the Wolverine
State from the 1880s to the present

by
MARC OKKONEN

Published by Thunder Bay Press
Publisher: Sam Speigel
Book layout and assembly: Marc Okkonen
Photocopy work: Photographics (Muskegon, MI)
Typesetting: Sharon Tingley (Lake Elsinore, CA)

Printed by Dickinson Press, Grand Rapids, MI
Cover by Adventures with Nature, East Lansing, MI

ISBN: 1-882376-43-9

Printed in the United States of America

97 98 99 2000   1 2 3 4 5 6 7 8 9

FOREWORD

The original goal of this project was to identify and document the minor league baseball parks of Michigan's past and present. After several months of fairly exhaustive research in the Michigan State Library in Lansing, it became apparent that the necessary information to produce a comprehensive volume on this subject was simply nowhere to be found on a good number of these ball parks. Faced with the prospect of a finished reference work that would necessarily be full of unknowns and merely educated guesses, I decided to expand the scope of the subject matter to include summary histories of the teams that played in these parks. Now it became possible to provide a decent amount of historical information for each of the minor league cities that would also make for more interesting reading. In the end, the team histories became the primary focus of the research with the ballpark studies taking on a supportive role to wind up each chapter.

Minor league baseball had a long and cyclical existence in Michigan and elsewhere. Like batting averages, the history of professional league baseball is more about failure than success. It took some solid organization and the pure good fortune of riding a rare wave of public enthusiasm to allow any league to survive over a period of years. These ups and downs of popularity were impossible to predict, but the cycles are easy to define in examining the historical patterns over the last century or more. Clearly the Great Depression of the thirties coincided with one of the most difficult periods for minor league baseball. Conversely, the period from 1905 to 1915 was the "golden age" of league baseball, especially in Michigan. No less than eight minor leagues were represented by Michigan cities during that period, including 32 of the 43 towns included in this volume. For reasons that are difficult to define, league baseball suddenly lost its appeal around 1915. Perhaps it was the rising popularity of motion pictures, or the unsettling ripple effect of the emergence of the "Outlaw" Federal League. Ultimately, World War I further killed interest in the sport, but the U.S. was not yet involved in 1915. No one knows for sure, but the game's popularity rebounded in 1920 and enjoyed another period of modest success.

For individual franchises, minor league participation was equally risky business. Normal revenue from gate receipts was seldom adequate for financial survival unless the home team was in a volatile pennant race or on a winning rampage. Very often the team's survival hinged on voluntary financial support by well-heeled stockholders and much-publicized "booster" campaigns to urge citizens to rally behind the usually near-bankrupt franchise. The cities in leagues who were under the protection of the National Agreement stood a better chance of survival than the independents. The infamous reserve clause maintained some stability on team rosters and pre-established salary limits helped retain balanced competition. Owners with winning teams and outstanding players had to make difficult business decisions that often broke up their winning combination overnight and naturally alienated their fans. Making a profit or even just making ends meet usually required selling off the most popular players to the higher leagues at season's end. To continue a winning tradition through constant rebuilding was nearly impossible and as a consequence very few "dynasties" emerged in the minor league picture. But in the long run it helped the leagues to survive, as many member cities had a better chance to win an occasional pennant.

The most valuable and reliable sources for this type of research are the microfilms of the hometown newspapers. Fortunately, the State Library in Lansing has most of this microfilm under one roof. The coverage of local baseball varies from generous to pitifully scarce, depending on the particular newspaper's emphasis on sports. It can be a very frustrating and sometimes hopeless search to find the information needed and it can be a grueling test of one's patience and perseverance. Researching baseball in Cadillac proved to be nearly impossible. That particular city's historic newspaper, the Cadillac News, has to this day refused to microfilm past editions. Whatever their reasoning might be, they are committing the cultural felony of allowing the daily history of their community to decay into dust in original hard-copies that historians and researchers of all kinds are denied access to. I only hope that one day soon they will recognize their historical responsibility while there is still time.

Obviously, a treatise of this scope cannot be accomplished alone and accordingly I am indebted to countless individuals and local organizations for their assistance. Fellow members of the Society of American Baseball Research (SABR) in several Michigan towns have come to my rescue with vital local information and in some cases have performed research through their local sources to come up with needed answers. Personal visits to selected libraries, museums, historical societies, etc. in a number of towns on my list have brought mixed results. Response and cooperation has ranged from indifference to genuine enthusiasm for my project. In some communities, knowledgeable historians were nowhere to be found, while in others much of the needed information had already been documented to some degree. I have attempted to maintain a balanced coverage based on the relative extent of minor league participation in each city. But in some cases, the availability of information and photographs overstate or understate the city's rank as a minor league participant. A majority of the photos used were gleaned from newspaper microfilms, which excuses their barely acceptable quality. For statistical data on leagues, teams, and individuals, the old Reach/Spalding Guides have been invaluable. The more recent Encyclopedia of Minor League Baseball compiled by Lloyd Johnson and Miles Woolf has also been a godsend and a marvelous ready reference that provided basic facts that otherwise would have required tedious searching. The contributions of SABR minor league researchers Ray Nemec and Bob Hoie also deserve special recognition.

Despite the frustrations of the research and the prospect of only modest compensation from book sales, this project has been a gratifying labor of love. With the renewed interest in minor league baseball in Michigan and the potential for additional future participation by more of the state's communities with neglected traditions in professional league baseball, I can only hope that this effort to document those traditions will further reawaken fan interest and reinforce Michigan's renaissance as a desirable locale for minor league baseball.

SOURCES & CONTRIBUTORS

Adrian
Adrian Public Library

Battle Creek
Willard Library
Michigan Battle Cats

Bay City
Bay County Historical Society

Belding
Alvah N. Belding Library

Berrien Springs
Gary Land
Berrien County Historical Assn.

Big Rapids
Big Rapids Public Library

Boyne City
Boyne City Public Library
Robt. Morgridge (Charlevoix)
Geoffrey Reynolds (Garden City)

Cadillac
Cadillac Public Library
Cadillac Historical Society

Charlotte
Charlotte Public Library
Grace Morey

Detroit Area
Detroit Public Library
Jeff Samoray
Dick Clark
Ray Billbrough (Saline)

Dowagiac
Dowagiac Public Library

Evart
Evart Public Library

Grand Rapids
Grand Rapids Public Library
Dick Harms

Greenville
Greenville Public Library
Flat River Historical Museum

Hancock-Houghton-Lake Linden
Houghton County Historical Society
Van Pelt Library (Mich. Tech. Univ.)
James Kurtti
Gordon O'Rourke

Holland
Holland Public Library
Hope College Library
Randy Vandewater

Ionia
Ionia Public Library
Ralph Bartelt

Ishpeming-Negaunee
Carnegie Public Library

Jackson
Jackson Public Library

Kalamazoo
Kalamazoo Public Library
Kalamazoo Kodiaks
Dick Kishpaugh
Jack Moss
Bob Wagner

Lansing
State Library of Michigan
Bob Caldwell
Len Peterson

Ludington
Bill Anderson

Manistee
Manistee County Historical Museum

Marquette
Superior Views Gallery
Marquette Public Library

Menominee
Spies Public Library
Menominee County Historical Society

Mt. Clemens
Steve TenBrink

Muskegon
Hackley Public Library
Muskegon County Museum
Muskegon County Library
Ron Pesch
Jim Moyes

Niles
Niles Public Library
Steve Krah (Elkhart IN)

Owosso
Owosso Public Library

Port Huron
James Maywar

Reed City
Reed City Public Library

Saginaw
Saginaw Public Library
–Eddy Collection
Joseph Heitkamp
Craig Zanot

St. Joseph
Bob Gaunt (Lakeland FL)

Sault Ste. Marie
Bayliss Public Library

Tecumseh
Tecumseh Public Library

Traverse City
Traverse City District Library

Wyandotte
Bacon Memorial Public Library

Ypsilanti
Rich Adler

Out of State
National Baseball Library
(Cooperstown NY)
Ray Nemec (Naperville IL)
Bob Hoie (San Marino CA)
Larry Zuckerman (Sherman Oaks CA)
Ed Koller (N. Hollywood CA)
Lefty Blasco (Van Nuys CA)

TABLE OF CONTENTS

THE
MINOR LEAGUE TOWNS
OF MICHIGAN

ADRIAN

PROFESSIONAL LEAGUE MEMBERSHIP

YEARS	LEAGUE	HOME FIELD
1895	Michigan State	Lawrence Park
1909-14	Southern Michigan	Franklin Park

Like many Michigan towns of comparable size, Adrian was a hotbed of baseball in the 1890s and the early decades of the twentieth century. The strongest independent team to represent Adrian against other state teams and indeed out-of-state teams during this period was composed entirely of black players. The local Page Wire Fence Company organized the traveling team in 1894 and provided them with their own railroad car, an unheard of luxury even for white teams of the period. The Page Fence Giants played almost entirely on the road and proved to be an entertaining, winning, and profitable venture for about five years.

The all-black Page Fence Giants put Adrian on the baseball map in the mid 1890s. They were a popular and formidable opponent for hometown teams throughout the Midwest. Some of their players, including ace hurler George Wilson (center, holding ball), also played for Adrian's 1895 Michigan State League team.

Adrian native Rube Kissinger pitched for the Detroit Tigers in 1902-03. He began his professional career with Battle Creek in the 1902 Michigan State League.

When Adrian assembled its first bona fide professional league team for the 1895 Michigan State League, they profited from the success of the Page Fence Giants by adding several of its black stars on their roster, including founder Bud Fowler and the battery of pitcher George Wilson and catcher Vasco Graham. The new league team was organized by Adrian businessmen J. C. Buck, Len W. Hoch, and R. L. Taylor. Despite the disruption of twice rescheduling the balance of the season, Adrian finished with the best overall win-loss record. The team included future big leaguers Bill Carrick and Hall-of-Famer John P. Wagner, better known as "Honus."

Baseball immortal Honus Wagner batted .386 in 16 games for Adrian in 1895. Two years later he began his fabled 21-year ML career.

Pitcher Bill Carrick, who won 68 games for the NY Giants and Washington from 1898-1902, was also a member of the 1895 Adrians.

Adrian's next venture in professional league baseball commenced in 1909 when they joined the Southern Michigan League. This circuit was formed in 1906 and had included nearby Tecumseh through the 1908 season. Frank Reed was president and Arch Seager secretary of the newly formed Adrian Baseball Association. The field manager was Charles Cassel. Adrian barely escaped the league basement that first year, but the following year they finished a strong third under new manager Carl Vandergrift. Outfielder Billy Smith took charge of the team in 1911 and gave Adrian a league championship the following season. The 1912 champs were paced by pitchers Bob Troy and Walter Scott plus catcher Emil Huhn and outfielder Danny Jenkins. Huhn later had a 3-year ML career with the Newark Federal Leaguers and the Cincinnati Reds. Pitcher Troy had a brief tryout with Hugh Jennings' Detroit Tigers at season's end.

Charles Cassell was the manager for Adrian's first Southern Michigan League entry in 1909.

Detroit Tigers' owner Frank Navin hailed from Adrian and gave moral and financial support for his hometown teams. He donated used Tiger uniforms and brought his Detroit team to Adrian for exhibition games.

Emil Huhn, catcher for the 1912 club, later had a brief career in the bigs with Newark (FL) and Cincinnati (NL).

Billy Smith was a player and field manager for Adrian's 1912 pennant winners.

The City of Adrian went wild with excitement to celebrate their victorious 1912 season. The celebration carried over to July 18, 1913 when they staged an elaborate ceremony to officially raise the 1912 pennant at Franklin Park. The festivities included a mammoth automobile parade through downtown Adrian and other nearby communities. Among the dignitaries at the flag-raising were American League President Ban Johnson and Detroit owner Frank Navin, a native son of Adrian.

Outfielder Danny Jenkins was a standout among the 1912 champs. He also managed the team in 1913.

Outfielder Cecil Coombs hit 10 HRs for Adrian in 1913. The following year he had a trial with the Chicago White Sox.

Popular Danny Jenkins took over as field manager in 1913, but the Adrians were unable to repeat as champions, finishing a distant second to Battle Creek despite a 10-home run season by Cecil Coombs. Billy Cristall was picked to lead the team in its final season (1914) as a member of the Southern Michigan League but the Adrians were lucky to escape the cellar by only two

Carl Vandagrift was Adrian's manager in 1910. He later surfaced in the Federal League of 1914 as an infielder for the Indianapolis club.

A newspaper ad promoted the gala pennant raising ceremonies at Franklin Park in June 1913.

games. It was to be the end of the road for Adrian's six-year run as a minor league town. Independent teams represented Adrian in subsequent decades and one of the more notable baseball memories in the post-league years occurred in October 1923 when Frank Navin's Detroit Tigers played an exhibition game with the locals at Franklin Park. Unfortunately, player-manager Ty Cobb was a "no show," opting to attend the World Series games in New York. But all the other regulars showed up, including batting champion Harry Heilmann, who even pitched the ninth inning of a 17-3 Tiger romp.

Detroit Tigers' slugging out-fielder Harry Heilmann, fresh from a .403 season, accompanied the Tiger team for an exhibition game with the Adrian independents in October 1923 at Franklin Park.

THE PLAYING SITES

| ① | **LAWRENCE PARK 1890s (on Maumee St. immediately west of the Raisin River)** |

Extensive research has revealed very little about the features of the Lawrence Park facility, its creation or its demise. We do know that it was the principal home field of the 1895 State League club and other independent Adrian teams in the 1890s. As with most 19th century ballparks no known photo exists and only occasional descriptive comments are found in newspaper accounts. The Adrian Times & Expositor in May 1895 mentions the erection of a high board fence up to the NW corner of the diamond and a six-foot high canvas screen on the east side to obstruct the view of "freeloaders" on that end of the property. The grounds were adjacent to the properties of Major Cole and McFarlane and the park itself was on the property of T. Lawrence, hence the name Lawrence Park. Earlier accounts describe the existence of a race track on these grounds with its grandstand on the east edge of the property, facing west. In October 1879, the roof of the grandstand collapsed, killing 23 and injuring hundreds. The fairgrounds were subsequently relocated to the east side, but the Lawrence Park site continued to be used for baseball.

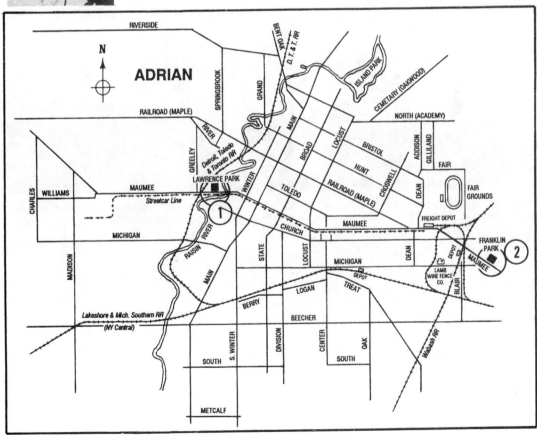

FRANKLIN PARK 1909-14 (on the north side of E. Maumee St.–just east of the Wabash RR crossing)

The original date of the construction of Franklin Park is unknown but it was apparently already in use when Adrian joined the Southern Michigan League in 1909. Modifications and enlargement were underway in the spring of 1909 to welcome the new league team. The field was further enlarged in 1910 and the center field scoreboard was relocated to the left field fence. Home plate probably was on the SE corner of the lot, since the new left field scoreboard obstructed the view of employees of the Lamb Fence Factory (to the west) who kept up with game action using a powerful telescope. In keeping with a trend of the times, a Bull Durham sign was erected on the outfield fence in 1911.

In early 1913, heavy winds blew down most of the outfield fence, including the Bull Durham sign. Since the previous location was seldom reached by the hitters (the tobacco company offered a $50 reward for hitting the sign), the new sign was relocated to a more reachable location to enhance its publicity value. Groundskeepers during the heyday of Franklin Park included Willie Teachout, Sam Pearly, and Andrew Parks.

Franklin Park enjoyed its most glorious day on July 18, 1913 when an overflow crowd jammed the field to view the raising of the 1912 championship banner, the first and only league pennant claimed by the City of Adrian. The day was complete when Manager Danny Jenkins crossed the plate with the winning run against Battle Creek. After Adrian dropped out of the Southern Michigan League in 1914, the field remained as the home of local and independent teams for decades. Another overflow crowd filled old Franklin Park in October 1923 to witness an exhibition with the Detroit Tigers. The final year of Franklin Park as a baseball field is uncertain, but according to Charles Lindquist's LENAWEE REFLECTIONS (1992), the Ace Drill Company currently occupies the site.

Franklin Park entertained an overflow crowd on June 18, 1913 with the hoisting of the 1912 SML pennant and a thrilling victory over visiting Battle Creek. This newspaper photo may be the only surviving image of the ball park.

BATTLE CREEK

PROFESSIONAL LEAGUE MEMBERSHIP

YEARS	LEAGUE	HOME FIELD
1895	Michigan State	Clark Driving Park
1902	Michigan State	Athletic Park
1906-15	Southern Michigan	Athletic Park
1919-20	Michigan-Ontario (MINT)	Athletic Park
1951-52	AAGBL (Girls)	Bailey Park
1995-	Midwest	C.O. Brown Stadium (Bailey Park)

Amateur and independent baseball flourished in Battle Creek in the decades following the Civil War. Jacob Weickgenant, the patriarch of local baseball around the turn of the century, and his brother John were pioneers in assembling numerous Battle Creek nines at various levels. Messrs. Mittenthall and Loftus managed the city's first entry into organized professional baseball in 1895 when Battle Creek joined the Michigan State League. The Adventists (as the locals were nicknamed) fared poorly on the field and at the gate. With a league's worst record of 14 wins vs. 40 losses, the franchise was transferred to Jackson in early August.

For the next six summers it was strictly independent baseball for Battle Creek, but Jacob Weickgenant, with the backing of William Woods and L. A. Davison, secured another franchise in the Michigan State League for 1902. Financial support from one of the local cereal companies resulted in an unusual team nickname, the "Cero Frutos." (The previous year's independent team had played under the name "Malta Vitas," another cereal brand). Unlike the dismal entry of 1895, the 1902 Cero Frutos were laden with talent and captured the league championship with a 53-31 W-L record. But their claim to fame was somewhat tainted, as the state league failed to complete a full season as scheduled. Among the star players on the Battle Creek nine were Ben Koehler, Claude Starke, Rube Kissinger, and Captain Harry Arndt. Koehler, Kissinger, and Arndt later distinguished themselves with brief careers in the major leagues.

Rube Kissinger, a star pitcher for the 1902 BC State League club, went on to join the Detroit Tigers.

Infielder Harry Arndt was one of the 1902 State League stars and also advanced to the majors for four seasons.

An 1886 local team called the "9 Spots" included some pioneers in Battle Creek baseball. TOP ROW (L to R): Ed Phelan, Eugene Farrell, John Gaines, Jerome Buckley, Robinson. FRONT ROW (L to R): John Whalen, John Weickgenant, Ed Clock, Jacob Weickgenant, Will Potter. Gaines was black and Jacob Weickgenant organized many local nines and leagues in later years.

In 1906, Robert Carroll assembled a franchise in the new Southern Michigan League and the Cereal City embarked on a 10-year saga of professional league baseball. A local promoter, George Black, was named manager of the new "Blackbirds" (later called "Crickets") but was replaced by Mo Myers and Joe Ganzell later in the season. The Crickets finished a distant fifth (of six clubs) and the fledgling league suffered financial losses but regrouped for 1907 with eight clubs. Led by pitcher Harry Steiger's 17 wins, the 1907 Battle Creeks surged to third place. By now the league had attained stability and became one of the more successful minor leagues in the country for years to come. The Crickets failed to produce a contender for the next four years, but in 1912 their fortunes took an upward turn. Under Manager Ed McKernan, Battle Creek finished a strong second, just two games behind pennant-winning Adrian. The following year (1913) Battle Creek baseball had its' finest season as the Crickets ran away with the SML pennant by a margin of nine games over runner-up Adrian. Ace hurler Rich Niehaus led the charge with a fine 24-7 won-loss record.

Battle Creek finished second in the final two seasons (1914-15) of the Southern Michigan League's existence. The first World War and fading attendance caused the league to close up shop after the 1915 campaign. Professional league baseball was essentially put on-hold for the duration, but in 1919 Battle Creek was ready to take another fling in the minor leagues. The SML never resurfaced, but the Cereal City was recruited into another new league, the Michigan-Ontario ("MINT") League for the 1919 season.

John Ray, field manager in 1909

Billy Earle managed the "Crickets" in 1910.

Robert Carroll, president of Battle Creek's first SML club in 1906

Thomas Moore was the '06 club's treasurer.

George Black, the 1906 club's first field manager

Sam Zigenbein infielder 1906

Ed McKernan took charge of the team in 1912.

Ex-big-league pitcher Eugene "Rubber" Krapp was the 1920 pilot of the MINT club.

Frank Shillinberger outfield 1906

Clyde Goodwin 1b-outfield 1906

George Southerton was president of the new MINT League entry and a one-time Southern Michigan Leaguer, the popular Danny Jenkins, was named field manager. The Battle Creek "Custers" finished a respectable fourth that year, led by Ted Kaylor's lofty .376 BA. The new field pilot for 1920 was former big league pitcher Eugene "Rubber" Krapp and the Custers barely escaped the league basement. 1920 was to be the last season of league baseball in Battle Creek for three more decades as their 1921 franchise was relocated to Port Huron. Cereal City fans had to settle for independent ball after that, but they had one last treat in October 1923 when the Detroit Tigers came to town for an exhibition game.

The 1920 MINT club's pitching corps included a local man, Herm McMillan (center). The group posed for the camera at Athletic Park.

League baseball of a different variety returned to Battle Creek in 1951 when the Racine Belles of the All-American Girls Baseball League transferred operations here. By this time, the new diamond at Bailey Park was ready and waiting. James T. Williams was the new owner and he hired one-time GR Herald Sports Editor Heinie Martin as general manager. A former New York Giant star and baseball Hall of Famer Dave Bancroft was named as field manager. Expectations were high for the new game in town, but a losing team quickly eroded fan interest and the franchise went into debt. A group of local backers assumed ownership for 1952 and hired another former big leaguer Guy Bush as the new field manager. But team fortunes plummeted from very bad to awful as the Belles soon found themselves deeply mired in the bottom of the standings. In the end, the two-year trial was a financial disaster and the girls' team moved to Muskegon for the 1953 season.

The popularity of Bailey Park's excellent baseball facilities kept the game alive in Battle Creek in subsequent decades. Battle Creek became the state's most prestigious site for semi-pro, amateur and scholastic tournaments, which very often were national playoffs. The success of these tournaments encouraged the city to replace Bailey Park's main ballpark with a state-of-the-art facility to be renamed C. O. Brown Stadium. As fate would have it, a renaissance of minor league baseball was about to begin in Grand Rapids after a 40-year drought. The response in the Furniture City exceeded the most optimistic expectations and Michigan suddenly became a "hotbed" for new prospective franchises. In 1995, the Midwest League relocated its Madison, Wisconsin team to the Cereal City and minor league baseball made a triumphant return with the Michigan Battle Cats, a Class A farm for the Boston Red Sox.

Key members of the 1952 Battle Creek Belles discuss game strategy at Bailey Park. (L to R): Rita Briggs, Marge Russo, Jo Hasham, and league all-star Sophie Kurys.

William L. Collins III, CEO of the 1995 Midwest League entry

The Battle Cats' first manager, Demarlo Hale

7

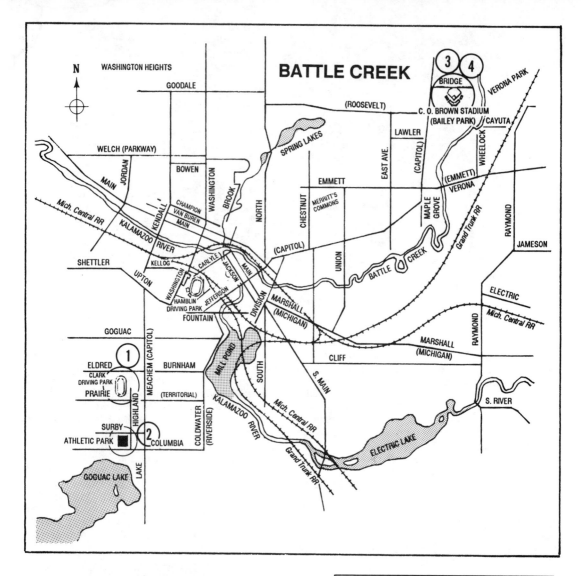

THE PLAYING SITES

① **CLARK'S DRIVING PARK 1895
(west of Highland between
Eldred & Prairie—north of
Goguac Lake)**

② **ATHLETIC PARK 1902-1920
(near the north shore of
Goguac Lake, west of
Highland between Surby &
Columbia—Fairview section)**

The Battle Creek Driving Club leased the race track owned by Walter Clark in 1895 and made significant improvements to the grounds. In addition to a new fence, the grandstand was refurbished—primarily for racing events. Although baseball is not directly identified with this facility, the new fence and grandstand made it suitable for staging professional baseball and very likely it was the DRIVING PARK mentioned as home field for the 1895 Battle Creek team of the Michigan State League. Since this is as yet unconfirmed, it is also possible that the baseball games were played instead at the downtown Hamblin Driving Park.

Built in 1897, the first game played at Athletic Park was on July 3 between the Battle Creek independents and the Jackson club of the Michigan State League. In 1901, the grounds were enlarged to cover an area of 380 x 400 feet. Athletic Park hosted its first professional league team in 1902 with the Cero Frutos of the Michigan State League. An experimental night game took place on September 4, 1904 when the local independents took on the Cherokee Indians. 25 arc lights were strung around the field on iron supports and a specially made large rubber ball was used in place of a regulation baseball. Quality baseball it was not, but a large crowd was highly entertained by the novelty.

8

In 1906, Jacob Weickgenant purchased Athletic Park from a group of local owners and immediately rebuilt and upgraded the facility for his new Battle Creek entry in the Southern Michigan League. A new fence was built 20 feet back from the old one, which squared off and enlarged the playing field. The original grandstand was remodeled and connected to the north stand. New bleachers increased the seating capacity to 2500. A new streetcar spur was added to improve access to the park. New Manager George Black also made the upgraded park available for local high school and college games.

In 1910, an attempt was made to secure downtown property for a new ballpark but in the end it was business as usual at Athletic Park. A spring windstorm in early 1920 badly damaged the outfield fences, but the stands and bleachers were spared from any serious ruin. After league baseball left Battle Creek in the early '20s, the field continued as a principle playing site for amateur and independent teams. But the emergence of equal or superior local ball fields closer into the city such as Post Park and Bailey Park eventually made the Athletic Park site obsolete. The property was turned over to the school system and became the site of the new Highland Junior High School.

An early postcard view of Athletic Park c. 1907

Local students gather for a May Day observance at Athletic Park in 1915. The outfield fence is clearly seen with numerous billboards, including Battle Creek Lumber's "elephant," which was probably a target for long ball sluggers.

BAILEY PARK 1951-52 (northeast section of city between Capitol and the Battle Creek)

③

The main baseball facility at Bailey Park was built by the WPA during the great depression of the 1930s. Under the inspired leadership of local baseball patriarch Arch Flannery, Bailey Park became the host facility for numerous state and national amateur and scholastic baseball tournaments. In 1937, the prestigious American Amateur Baseball Congress (AABC) chose Bailey Park as a permanent site for its annual tournaments (later renamed the Stan Musial World Series). Battle Creek teams have been well represented in these tournaments over the years, winning the championship on three occasions and finishing second in seven other years. Lights were installed in 1948. In 1951-52, the ballpark became home for the beleaguered Racine Belles of the All-American Girls Baseball League (AAGBL).

Action in the '52 Belles' home opener shows catcher Rita Briggs attempting to take a wild throw from Marge Wenzell that allowed South Bend's Betty Wagoner to score.

Belles' star Sophie Kurys hands Vice-Mayor Frank Wagner the opening baseball for the 1952 season at Bailey Park. Local baseball patriarch Arch Flannery is in the overcoat. Also in the picture are Building Commissioner Frank Murray and South Bend catcher Shirley Stovroff.

C. O. BROWN STADIUM 1995- (rebuilt version of Bailey Park's principal baseball facility)

④

By the early 1990s, the success of the Bailey Park baseball and softball complex (three baseball fields, eight softball fields), resulted in a complete overhaul of the main baseball park. With the prospect of more and more tournament activities and even the possible resurgence of minor league baseball on the horizon, the old park was renovated to meet the latest requirements. The new version was renamed for C. O. Brown, former president of the AABC. Finally in 1995, professional baseball made its return to the Cereal City with the arrival of the Michigan Battle Cats of the Class A Midwest League.

An exterior view of the new grandstand at C.O. Brown Stadium in 1995

The sprawling Bailey Park complex includes three baseball diamonds and eight softball fields.

An aerial view of C.O. Brown Stadium

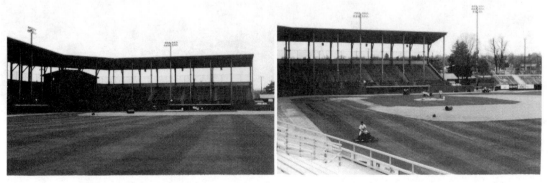

Ground level views of the grandstand from inside the stadium

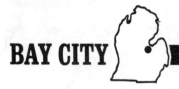

BAY CITY

PROFESSIONAL LEAGUE MEMBERSHIP

YEARS	LEAGUE	HOME FIELD
1883-84	Northwestern	Woodside Park
1888	Saginaw Valley	Athletic Park
1890	International (joint franchise w/ Saginaw)	Recreation Park (W. Bay City) (Sundays-Wenona Beach)
1891	Northwestern	Athletic Park
1893	Ohio-Michigan	Fairgrounds
1897	Michigan State	Athletic Park
1898	International	Athletic Park
1906	Interstate Assn. (dropped out May 15)	(no home games played)
1907-15	Southern Michigan	League Park ('07-'08) Clarkson Park ('09-'15)
1919-26	Michigan-Ontario (MINT)	Clarkson Park
1926	Michigan State	Clarkson Park

Up to the late 1920s, Bay City's participation in professional minor league baseball ranked close behind only Grand Rapids and Saginaw among Michigan towns. All three cities were charter members of the earliest minor league that included Michigan entries—the Northwestern League of 1883-84. The Bay Citys finished next to last in their debut season of league ball. The following year they fared better with 40 wins in 54 games, but failing attendance forced them to transfer operations to Evansville (IN) at the end of July. The league itself folded up shortly thereafter with Grand Rapids on top and Bay City/Evansville with the second best W-L record. The team included several members who later distinguished themselves in the higher leagues. The manager was William H. Watkins, who went on to manage the 1887 Detroit champions of the National League. "Watty" had a long career as a manager and executive in professional baseball mostly in Indianapolis. He spent his retirement years in Port Huron, MI, where he died in 1937. Other members of the 1883-84 Bay City team who later played and/or managed in the big leagues were Bill McGunnigle and Dave Foutz.

Bay City's Northwestern League team of 1884. Back row (L to R): David, Howard, Morrison, Captain Bill McGunnigle. Middle row (L to R): Turbidy, Porter, Manager W. H. Watkins, Dave Foutz, Cudworth. Front row (L to R): Crotty, Bignell, Robinson, Strauss.

In 1890, Bay City and Saginaw sponsored a joint franchise (called the "Hyphens") in the International League. Home games alternated between both cities. W. A. Pettapiece was president of the Hyphens, who had the best winning percentage when the league collapsed in early July. The following year, Bay City went it alone in the resurrected Northwestern League, which included Detroit and Grand Rapids. But again this venture failed to play out a full season as Bay City and Detroit dropped out on June 8 and the league itself folded on July 30. In 1893, Bay City entered the Ohio-Michigan League and once again the circuit failed after half a season. Yet another short-lived attempt at league baseball came in 1897 when Bay City survived into early August with a combination of an original franchise followed by a relocated Kalamazoo entry in the Michigan State League. The pattern of aborted league participation continued in 1898 when Bay City and Saginaw both joined a basically Canadian circuit, the International League. At least this time Bay City could claim a somewhat tainted championship with the best won-loss record when the IL collapsed in early July. For the next seven summers, Bay City settled for independent baseball, discouraged by the string of unsuccessful league ventures.

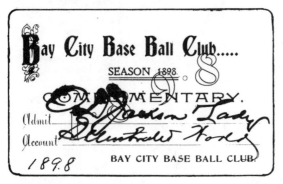

A complimentary pass for the 1898 International League club

Once the unsettling baseball wars brought on by the emergence of the American League in 1901 were resolved, the game's popularity had a dramatic resurgence. Minor league baseball regained its confidence and new leagues were launched, including the Interstate Association in 1906 by Emerson Dickerson of Grand Rapids. Bay City, Saginaw, and Flint were the Michigan entries along with towns in Indiana and Ohio. But barely after the season had begun, financial difficulties plagued the Michigan entries and Bay City dropped out in late May without having played a home game. Undaunted by yet another failure, Mr. M. Everett Taylor, a young promoter from Grand Rapids, managed to get a new baseball grounds erected near the fairgrounds on the city's east side and made plans to enter the new Southern Michigan League for the 1907 season. The SML had made a fairly successful debut in 1906 with six teams and elected to add new franchises in Bay City and Flint.

BASE BALL

AT NEW LEAGUE PARK TODAY

JACKSON
vs.
BAY CITY

GAME CALLED AT 3:30

A newspaper ad in 1907 mentions the new League Park, which was later renamed Clarkson Park.

Finally, after so many failed attempts, the 1907 Bay City league club managed to complete a full season, finishing in 5th place. Clyde McNutt's 1908 team finished dead last, but the new ballpark and a solid footing in the healthy Southern Michigan loop ensured Bay City's status as an established franchise for many more summers to come. In February 1909, the already legendary pitcher John Clarkson died in Massachusetts at the age of 48. Clarkson had pitched for Saginaw against Bay City in the old Northwestern League days. He married a Bay City girl and for a time he operated a cigar store in downtown Bay City after retiring from the game. His reputation and popularity in the community inspired Bay Cityans to rename their east side ballpark in his honor. An elaborate ceremony was staged in early 1909 to rechristen the field, with Clarkson's widow, family members, and friends in attendance.

Clyde McNutt, 1908 manager

Eddie Herr 1909 manager

Leonard "King" Cole pitched for Bay City in '09, went directly to the Chicago Cubs

Shortstop Nugent was Bay City's pilot in 1910

The 1909 Bay City Cardinals, under Eddie Herr, climbed to a more respectable 5th place in the SML final standings. Featured on that team were future major leaguers Dutch Zwilling and Miles Main. For the next three seasons, Bay City failed to seriously challenge for the championship and their future in the Southern Michigan circuit took a disturbing turn when they were unceremoniously dropped by the league in mid-season of 1912. The SML regrouped for 1913 and once again the Bay City club played out the full season, but finished in the basement, a full 23-1/2 games behind first place Battle Creek. Player/Manager Danny Jenkins, fresh from a pennant-winning 1912 season at Adrian, finally gave Bay City a league championship in the first half of 1914. Second half winner Saginaw, however, stole some of the 1914 glory by defeating Bay City in a post season playoff. But the 1914 club was easily the most talented group to represent Bay City to date. Joe Harris was the league's top batter with a .386 BA, followed by Coombs·and Mgr. Jenkins at .355 and .318 respectively. Danny's brother John Jenkins led all pitchers with a sparkling 23-4 record. The 10-year run of the Southern Michigan circuit came to an inglorious end in the summer of 1915 when the league disbanded, never to resurface. Bay City finished fourth in the shortened finale, but they again claimed the batting championship with Charles Connelly's .387. The World War I era saw the demise of many minor leagues across the map, but the "salad days" of minor league baseball in Bay City were yet to come.

In 1919, an eight-team circuit was formed consisting of four Canadian cities and four Michigan cities, aptly named the Michigan-Ontario (MINT) League. It was to be a higher level class B operation with Battle Creek, Flint, and Saginaw joining Bay City as Michigan's representatives. Billy Cristall was named to manage the locals, who finished a distant fifth in the final standings. In 1920 Cal Wenger, a veteran of the old Michigan State League, took the reins and fared no better. One bright spot in the 1920-21 Bay City lineup was a local boy, Hazen "Kiki" Cuyler of nearby Harrisville. Cuyler, of course, advanced to a Hall of Fame career as an outfielder in the National League from 1921 to 1938. The 1921 Bay City club, paced by pitcher Cy Boothby with 21 victories, finished in a tie for second place with Brantford and lost in the championship playoffs to first place London, Ontario, four games to two. In 1922 they slipped to fourth place but were on the verge of assembling the finest team ever to represent Bay City in organized baseball.

An experienced player-manager from the Central League, Charles E. "Punch" Knoll was Bay City's new pilot for the 1923 MINT League season. With a stable of talented hurlers and a hard-hitting lineup, Knoll brought Bay City two consecutive league championships in 1923-24. Although none of the 1923-24 Bay City roster were able to graduate to major league careers of any

Pitcher Cy Boothby was a big winner for the Bay Citys in 1921. 13 years later, he managed Muskegon in the failed Central League of 1934.

Baseball Hall-of-Famer Hazen "Kiki" Cuyler was arguably Bay City's greatest major league product. From nearby Harrisville, he played for the Bay Citys in 1920-21.

distinction, many were sought after for big league trials, including Bud Connolly, Spencer Harris, George Tomer, Joe Kiefer, Bill Mizeur, and Seraphin "Sep" Good. Most of the regulars hit well over .300 (the team BA was .301 in 1924) including 42-year-old player-manager Knoll, who had played in the big show for Washington in 1905. The pitching corps of Sep Good, Ovila Lahaie, Joe Kiefer, Heitzman, Zeigler, etc. was as formidable as any in the history of the MINT League. In 1925, team fortunes plummeted to a 4th place finish and they began the 1926 MINT season with an equally disappointing 10-18 record when the league collapsed and merged with the struggling Central League to start the season anew as the Michigan State League. Led by veteran infielder Bob Prysock (.370) and Al Bashang (.343), the Bay Citys feasted on the restructured league's pitching and batted .312 as a team. Pitching ace Sep Good chipped in with 19 victories as they proceeded to win the Michigan State League championship for 1926 by eight full games over runnerup Port Huron. But by this time, minor league baseball was losing its appeal and becoming a huge financial risk for most towns in Michigan. It was the end of the road for Bay City's long odyssey of professional league baseball as the MSL opted not to return in 1927. At least for Bay City it ended in a blaze of glory with three championships in its last four years of pro ball.

The 1924 Bay City Wolves, champions of the Michigan-Ontario League. It was the second straight pennant for the locals in the fast MINT League. Back row (L to R): Secretary Beckett, Hauger, Hendee, President W. I. Foss, Keifer, Schwartze, Tomer, Scorer Ken. Middle row (L to R): Hegedorn, Kimpling, Harris, Manager Punch Knoll, Heitzman, Lahaie, Prysock. Front row (L to R): Hughes, Mascot Foss, Ashley, Boelzle, Connolly.

Charles E. "Punch" Knoll, a veteran of the Central League, played with and managed the powerful Bay City champions of 1923-24.

THE PLAYING SITES

WOODSIDE PARK 1883-1884 (Woodside Ave. near the intersection of N. Lincoln and the RR tracks)

As with nearly all 19th century ball fields, no photos are known to exist and detailed descriptive features are equally scarce. We do know that Woodside Park was adjacent to the home of prominent merchant C. C. Rosenbury at 1400 Woodside Avenue. Which side of the Rosenbury residence it bordered on is unknown, but remarkably, the house still exists, and despite the vast changes in the surrounding neighborhood, we can speculate that it was on the south side of Woodside Avenue and probably north of the railroad tracks that once existed parallel to Woodside.

A current photo of the 1880s residence at 1400 Woodside of C. C. Rosenbury, a prominent merchant in the city when the NW League team played their games next door at old Woodside Park.

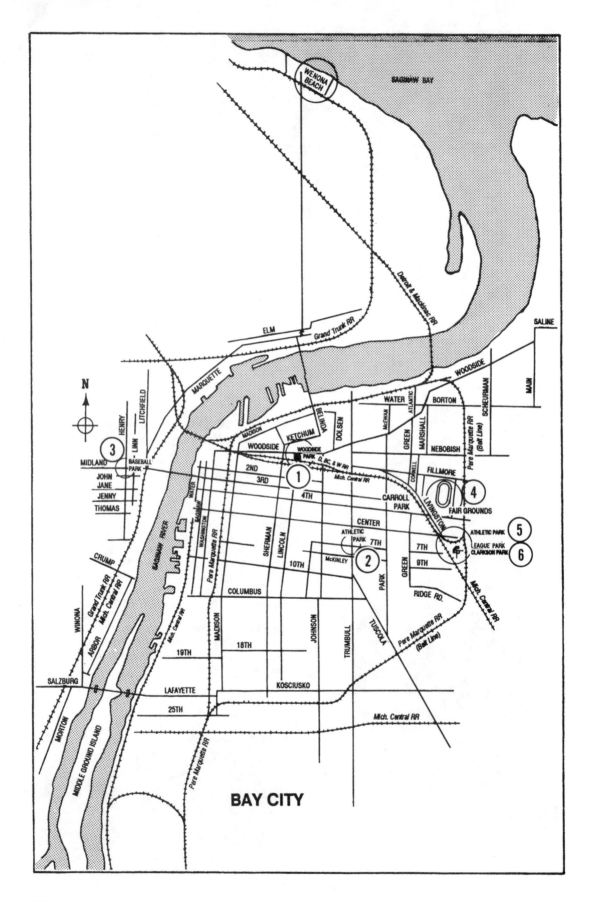

BAY CITY

ATHLETIC PARK 1888
(7th & Trumbull in the central part of the city)

This first edition of Athletic Park is a questionable entry as a minor league ballpark, since it only survived three years and was home to the Bay City entry in the 1888 Saginaw Valley League, an amateur or possibly semi-pro 3-team circuit with West Bay City and Saginaw. However, it was the home field for the best teams representing Bay City during the 1888-90 period. According to newspaper reports, it was a convenient location for patrons, being only two blocks from the streetcar line.

WEST BAY CITY SITE 1890-91
(Henry Street and Midland)
(also referred to as Athletic Park)

Bay City residents were left out in the selection of a home field for the joint Saginaw/Bay City entry in the 1890 International League. With half the home games played in Saginaw and remaining games to be played in West Bay City (still a separate city), local fans had to cross the river to the new park or travel downriver to Saginaw. Newspaper accounts place the main grandstand on the north end of the lot with a seating capacity of 600 to 700 people. Surplus dirt from grading of the playing surface was made into a bleacher embankment on the east side of the grounds. Sunday and some holiday games were played at Wenona Beach.

FAIR GROUNDS 1893
(Eastern edge of the city at Livingston & 4th)

The existing grandstand for horse races and other fair events provided seating for 2000 people. Presumably the ball diamond was laid out perpendicular to and east of the main grandstand. Although the next major ball diamond was to be built in the vicinity of the fairgrounds, newspaper accounts suggest that the fairgrounds itself was the playing site for 1893.

An 1893 ad for an Ohio-Michigan League doubleheader vs. Mansfield. Streetcar directions to the park are included at the bottom.

ATHLETIC PARK 1897-98
(immediately south of Fairgrounds)

It is unclear in newspaper descriptions exactly where this diamond was located. It may have been on fairgrounds property or possibly a bit further south where the future League/Clarkson Park was built. In any case, it was in this general vicinity and was sometimes referred to as Athletic Park, the third time this generic name was used for a Bay City baseball facility.

LEAGUE/CLARKSON PARK
1907-1926
(southeast of the intersection of Livingston & Center—east of the RR tracks)

19th century Hall-of-Fame pitcher John Clarkson played for nearby Saginaw in 1884. He met and married a Bay City girl and was a Bay City resident after his playing days were over. His death in early 1909 inspired the city to rename their new baseball park in his honor.

This location was described as "new" in 1907 and was referred to as League Park. Two years later (1909) it was renamed Clarkson Park and once again described as a new park (very likely the diamond itself was not new—only new refurbishments to the grandstand structure and other park features). In any case, this was the primary field for Bay City baseball for the next two decades and the last place where professional league baseball was played in this city. The streetcar service on Center Street made it a convenient location for all local residents. The place gave Bay City some memorable baseball teams and provided the city with a minor league tradition in its lifetime. After league baseball left for good in 1926, Clarkson stubbornly clung to life for three more years. A disastrous fire destroyed the grandstand in early 1927. Fully expecting an eventual return of league baseball, a new and modern grandstand to replace the old one was quickly erected. But the prospect of another professional league failed to surface. Meanwhile, fire insurance coverage had elapsed and, as luck would have it, the rebuilt grandstand was also consumed by fire in June 1929. With no insurance to cover the loss, the park was abandoned. A small supermarket currently occupies the site.

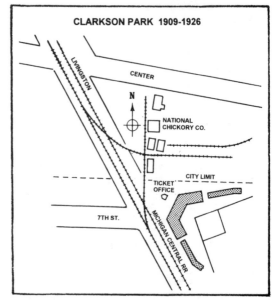

CLARKSON PARK 1909-1926

A postcard view of Clarkson Park's grandstand from the first base bleachers c. 1910

On July 9, 1924 the 1923 MINT League pennant was ceremoniously raised up the center field flag pole at Clarkson Park. Baseball Commissioner K. M. Landis was the honored guest at the festivities. Pictured in the upper right inset are (L to R): Saginaw President Arthur Clements, League President T. J. Halligan, Judge Landis, and Bay City owner W. I. Foss.

A destructive fire in March 1927 leveled the grandstand of Clarkson Park. A more modern stand soon replaced the old one, but it too fell victim to a blaze in 1929 and the park was never rebuilt.

Two contemporary views at the site of old Clarkson Park. On the left is shown the Village Market, looking southeast with the old playing field in the background. On the right, another view in the same direction shows the pedestrian pathway that replaced the abandoned railroad tracks adjacent to the parksite.

BELDING

PROFESSIONAL LEAGUE MEMBERSHIP

YEARS	LEAGUE	HOME FIELD
1914	Michigan State (transferred from Manistee)	Leonard Park (AKA Athletic Park) (west bank of Flat River)

The town of Belding, with a population of 5000, had a state-wide reputation of fielding tough independent teams to represent the community when they had their one brief fling at organized professional league baseball at the end of 1914. The Michigan State League, in its fifth and what would be its final season, was struggling at the gate in late summer as both Traverse City and neighboring Boyne City had already dropped out by Labor Day with losing records and poor attendance, reducing the circuit to only four cities—Muskegon, Ludington, Cadillac, and Manistee. Connie Lewis' Manistee club, nick-named Champions, had earned their sobriquet by winning consecutive league championships in the three previous seasons. Apparently spoiled by success, the 1914 "Champions" were anything but as they entered the season's final month far out of the race, barely over .500. Dismayed local fans stayed away in droves and the team was on the verge of financial collapse when the league transferred the franchise to Belding on September 8 with only two weeks left in the season. In an unusual move, Belding opted to field its existing independent team for league play rather than adopt the Manistee roster to finish out the season. New club owners overestimated the talent of the locals as they managed to win only once in 14 tries and finished a distant last in the final standings. In the end, it didn't matter as the Michigan State League closed up shop and did not resume play in 1915.

THE PLAYING SITE

> ## LEONARD PARK 1914
> ## (on west bank of Flat River, at Elm & Water Sts.)

In July of 1913, the City of Belding dedicated a new Athletic Park on the western edge of town between Kenwood Avenue and the State Road to Greenville. But a series of legal problems and court injunctions plagued the new facility from the start and within a year its use as a baseball park was in serious jeopardy. Responding to the crisis, local businessmen led by Henry J. Leonard secured a site for a new baseball field on the west side of the river at Elm Street. According to contemporary newspaper reports, home plate and the main grandstand were positioned in the northeast corner of the lot but it is not certain if the field was north or south of Elm Street. The

The 1914 Belding team that finished up the Michigan State League schedule for the Manistee club. The players are unidentified but the photo very likely includes many of the following names from the 1914 roster: Bailey, Barrand, Cherry, Gould, Green, Ireland, Maurer, Mooney, Oshinski, Patterson, Pfab, Sirrine, Smith, and Tesch.

fences and stands of the now defunct Athletic Park were dismantled and used in the construction of the new ballpark. It was to be called Leonard Park in honor of its principal benefactor. The first game was played on September 1, 1914 and 8 days later it would host league baseball for the balance of the summer when the failed Manistee MSL franchise was transferred to Belding. Leonard Park remained as the city's main baseball field in the years following. The date of its final demise is unknown but the site now contains a senior citizen housing facility.

Belding businessman Henry J. Leonard was responsible for the creation of the city's new baseball field in 1914. Accordingly, it was called Leonard Park.

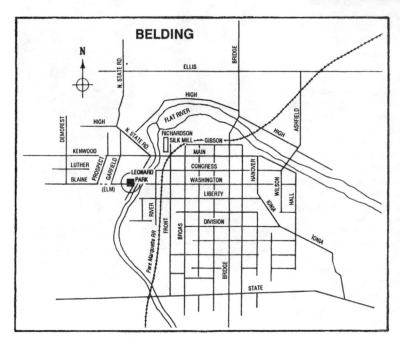

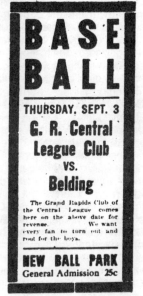

BASE BALL

THURSDAY, SEPT. 3

G. R. Central League Club

VS.

Belding

The Grand Rapids Club of the Central League comes here on the above date for revenue. We want every fan to turn out and root for the boys.

NEW BALL PARK
General Admission 25c

A newspaper ad promotes an exhibition game with the Central Leaguers from Grand Rapids only days after the park opened and just prior to the arrival of the State League club from Manistee in late 1914.

One of the only surviving photos of Belding's Leonard Park, taken around 1915

BERRIEN SPRINGS

PROFESSIONAL LEAGUE MEMBERSHIP

YEARS	LEAGUE	HOME FIELD
1910	Indiana-Michigan	(at City Park–SE on Lake Chapin)

The interurban railroad line that connected several communities in southwestern Michigan to towns in northern Indiana encouraged the formation of an Indiana-Michigan League in early 1910. The new circuit was to be a professional league fully recognized by the National Association but with a schedule limited to weekend and holiday games only. Original candidates included the eight cities of Benton Harbor, Berrien Springs, Elkhart (IN), Gary (IN), Goshen (IN), Niles, Dowagiac, and Ligonier (IN). Benton Harbor and Goshen defaulted before the season began and the schedule was finalized for the remaining six entries—three each from the two states. Because of the limited schedule and low rating (class D) of the league, the pay scale did not attract players with much potential but enthusiasm was high as the season got underway. G. O. McComber was chosen to manage the Berrien Springs club. Before the season was half completed, poor patronage forced two of the Indiana towns (Gary and Ligonier) to withdraw and when the schedule was completed in late August, the Berrien Springs Grays were the champions with a 15-4 WL record. Overall, the league venture proved to be a financial failure and 1910 was to be the only year that Berrien Springs would be a bona fide member of a professional baseball league.

The captain and second baseman for the 1910 Berrien Springs I-M League team, Robert Stillson

Harry Scribs (or Squibb?) played third base for the 1910 club.

THE PLAYING SITE

> **BERRIEN SPRINGS BALLPARK 1910 (at Grove City Park–at south end of Main St. on the shore of Lake Chapin)**

No photograph or detailed description has been found on this ballpark. We do know that it first opened in May 1909 and was referred to as the new interurban baseball park. The "Grove," a city park at the south end of Main Street, definitely included a ball field in later years and there seems no other likely site for a baseball field in Berrien Springs in 1910.

A 1910 newspaper ad for a Memorial Day game with visiting team Gary, Indiana of the Indiana-Michigan League

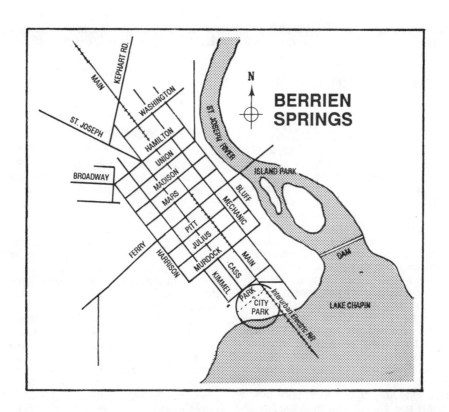

This group photo was taken during a local novelty contest between the "Fats" and "Leans" of Berrien Springs in 1909. Most certainly the picture was taken at the Berrien Springs Baseball Park.

BIG RAPIDS

PROFESSIONAL LEAGUE MEMBERSHIP

YEARS	LEAGUE	HOME FIELD
1887	Northern Michigan	Riverside Park

Baseball has been a popular pastime in Big Rapids since the Civil War but the city was represented in an organized professional league only on one occasion—that being the existence of the Northern Michigan League of 1887. The League was made up of nearby towns of Greenville, Evart, Reed City, and Ionia, along with Big Rapids. The teams played a limited schedule but the competition for "bragging rights" among these neighboring communities was fierce and spirited. The president of the Big Rapids entry was C. H. Olds, who also functioned as vice president of the league. Field managers for the local nine were E. H. Merritt and Charles Wiseman. As the season progressed, the partisanship of the fans as well as the town newspapers became ludicrous in their zealous support of the hometown boys and accusations of unfair play and inferior umpiring were abundant. In early August, Evart withdrew over a disputed forfeit and a week later both Big Rapids and Ionia folded their tent. With only two teams left, the league itself soon disbanded. Big Rapids was in fourth place in the standings at the time of its withdrawal. Among the Big Rapids players were William and Henry Pipp, father and uncle to Wally Pipp, who hailed from Grand Rapids. Young Wally had a fine major league career in later decades, mostly with the New York Yankees. According to final 1887 Northern Michigan League statistics published in The Detroit Free Press, H. Pipp was the club's top batter with .460 BA, followed by Miller with .407 and Mumby at .363.

THE PLAYING SITE

RIVERSIDE PARK 1887 (at Reunion Grounds along the Muskegon River)

William P. Nisbett published a Big Rapids city directory in 1882 in which he described the location of the local ball field as follows: "The land lay a little south of Mitchell Creek, between the Muskegon River and what is now known as Michigan Avenue—the same land now used as a baseball ground, and occasionally by a circus company." This information along with other clues found in later newspaper accounts seems to confirm the location as being on approximately the same site as the current Hemlock Park diamond. Newspaper ads and articles after the turn of the century identify the home field as Riverside Ball Park, New Reunion Grounds, Reunion Park, etc.—all of which very likely refer to the same general vicinity for the principal baseball field of Big Rapids. No details on the grandstand construction or the orientation of the diamond have thus far been located, and it follows that no photographs of the park are known to exist.

Today's Hemlock Park, the approximate site of 1887's ball park, also contains a ball diamond.

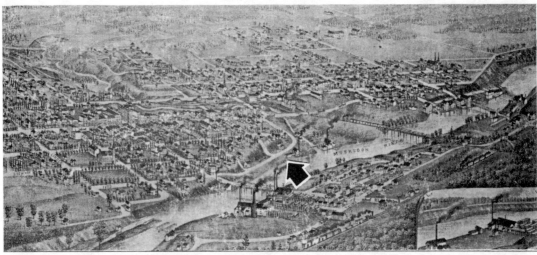

An 1880 bird's eye view drawing of Big Rapids looking northwest. The baseball park of 1887 was located along the Muskegon River in the area indicated by the arrow.

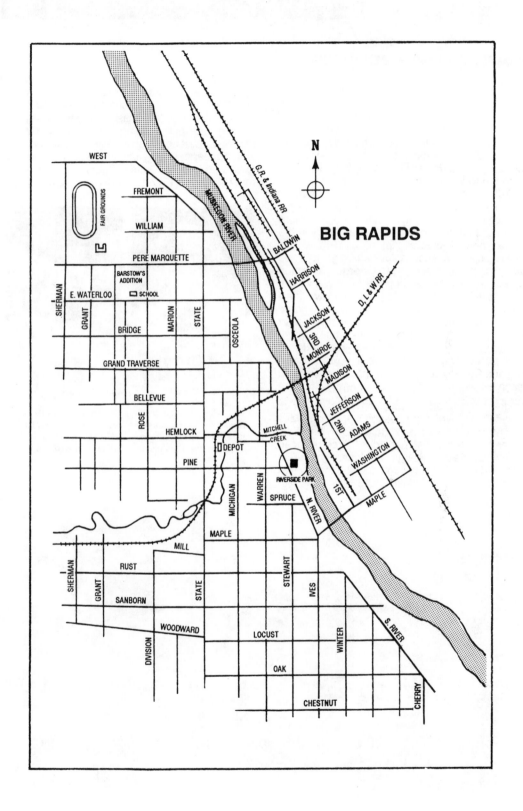

BIG RAPIDS

BOYNE CITY

PROFESSIONAL LEAGUE MEMBERSHIP

YEARS	LEAGUE	HOME FIELD
1911-14	Michigan State	Glenwood Beach ('11) Maple Park ('11-'14)

Boyne City, like many such communities in the state, had supported independent semi-professional teams for years when they made a losing bid to join the new Michigan State League in 1910. When the class D league managed to complete a successful maiden season with only four teams, Boyne City made another more determined bid to join nearby Traverse City in the league's new six-club alignment for 1911. Mayor McQuiston led a successful campaign to raise subscriptions in early 1911. George Houghton and E. C. Chase headed up the franchise which, along with Manistee, made up the two new members. At that time, the locals played home games at Glenwood Beach on the north shore of Pine Lake, but the league stipulated that a more centrally located ballpark was required for membership. New grounds were built at Maple Park and Sunday dates would use the Glenwood Beach facility.

Charles "Pete" Partlow was named manager of the local entry when the season opened on May 24. The new team got off to a poor start and former big league catcher Lou Criger replaced Partlow as field manager in June. The team continued its losing ways and finished the season firmly entrenched in last place with only 24

victories. The only bright spots in the dismal maiden season were third baseman Lynch, with a .357 BA, and outfielder Sharpe at .324. The Boyne Citys were also dead last in team batting and fielding and their pitching staff was equally horrendous. Catcher Archie Yelle, a Saginaw boy who appeared in 30 games for BC, was eventually signed by the Detroit Tigers and played for three seasons (1917-19) under Hughie Jennings.

Lou Criger, an Indiana native and a favorite battery mate of the great Cy Young, managed the Boosters in 1911.

A Michigan-born lad, Archie Yelle, caught for the 1911 BC club and later played for the Detroit Tigers.

The individual players in this 1912 group photo are unidentified, but very likely include some of the following names from the '12 roster: Mgr. Slear, Peckham, Tindall, Gillen, Pokorney, Broder, Myers, Kuhagen, Method, Kik, Minardo, Roberts, Stockdale, King, Foster, and Dworski.

Bo Slear, a veteran outfielder from the Southern Michigan League, was the new manager for 1912. The "Boosters" improved to fourth place with third baseman Milt Pokorney leading the offense with a .321 BA. First baseman Grover Gillen chipped in with a .291 average and Monte Method led the Booster pitchers with a 13-8 WL record. Manager Slear played in 104 games and hit .275. Grover Gillen took charge of the team for the 1913 and 1914 seasons and was unable to lift the Boosters any higher in the league standings. Gillen was the team's top batsman with a .327 average in 1913, followed by Kuhagen at .320. Utility infielder Pokorney hit a solid .292 while pitcher Hugh Roberts was the club's top winner with 18 decisions. After three quite successful seasons, the Michigan State League began to disintegrate in 1914. Attendance was down and losing seasons in Traverse City and its nearby rival Boyne City forced both clubs to withdraw at the beginning of September. Both teams were buried in the bottom of the standings and also deeply in debt. Manager Gillen had another good year at the plate with a .307 average and decent pitching by Myers and Roberts kept the Boosters out of the basement, but a 48-52 WL record made the situation hopeless. The State League managed to complete the season with the four remaining teams, but went out of business as a result of mounting debts throughout the circuit. Boyne City would never again participate as a member of a professional league.

Bo Slear, an experienced outfielder in several Michigan leagues, took over as field boss of the 1912 Boosters.

Veteran SML hurler Monte Method won 13 games for the Boosters in 1912.

A 1912 newspaper ad promotes the home opener against rival and neighbor Traverse City.

Grover Gillen's 1913 club started well but gradually faded into fourth place. TOP ROW (L to R): Purvis, Ginter, Myers, Pokorney, Kuhagen, Minardo, and Roberts. BOTTOM (L to R): Varley, Mgr. Gillen, Dworski, Tindall, and Krueger.

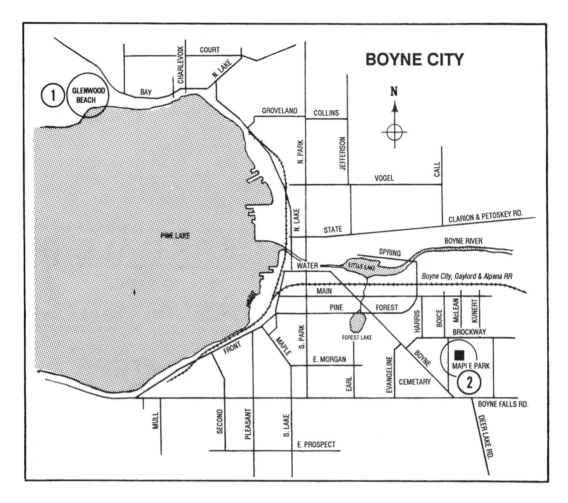

THE PLAYING SITES

GLENWOOD BEACH 1911
(north shore of Pine Lake—
Sundays & some holiday dates)

No photos or descriptive data available for this park. It was the city's main baseball facility up to the building of the new field at Maple Park in 1911. Boyne City fans would go to the games there by boat—a regular ferry cruised the lake to the popular Glenwood Beach park and picnic grounds. The 1911 club opened the season at Glenwood Beach, since the new Maple Park facility was not yet ready for play.

MAPLE PARK 1911-14
(southeast part of town,
between Boyne & Brockway)

The exact location of this diamond is uncertain. Period maps do not indicate a baseball park, but a later aerial photo suggests that it was on the site of the current high school football field. The Maple Park Association, formed in early 1911, purchased the 40 acre site and set about immediately to build a baseball facility to meet the State League requirements for professional league play. An amusement park was also planned for the Maple Park site.

The Maple Park site today still includes a ball diamond as well as a football field.

CADILLAC

PROFESSIONAL LEAGUE MEMBERSHIP

YEARS	LEAGUE	HOME FIELD
1910-14	Michigan State	Recreation Park (Fairgrounds)

The upswing of baseball's popularity at all levels in the latter years of the century's first decade encouraged Grand Rapids newspaperman and erstwhile league organizer Emerson Dickerson to call together interested West Michigan cities with a plan for a new Michigan State League in early 1910. After considering 6 or 7 potential member cities, the new class D circuit settled on the four communities of Holland, Muskegon, Traverse City, and Cadillac, with plans to expand in 1911. Salary limits and other safeguards were put in place to ensure the new organization's integrity and competitive balance. Dr. S. C. Moore headed up the Cadillac entry with F. Flynn named as secretary/treasurer. Home games would be played at Recreation Park, located on the fairgrounds site just north of the city proper. Cal Wenger, a veteran player with pennant winning teams in the Southern Michigan League and elsewhere, was picked to captain and manage the Cadillac team.

Dr. C. S. Moore was president of the Cadillac baseball club for most of their State League years.

Wenger, a Flint man, had strong baseball connections in Grand Rapids and quickly recruited a talented roster of experienced minor leaguers and young semi-pro prospects to represent Cadillac. Led by the lusty hitting of first baseman Martin Kubiak (.378 in 67 games) and steady pitching from Harry Gerloski (18-7), Peterson (10-5), and Collins (8-8), Wenger's charges took the 1910 championship in a close finish, with Traverse City finishing second. Shortstop Glenn Hale added a solid .312 plus steady performances from second sacker Francis Wittoski and outfielder/manager Wenger. With Wenger and many of the regulars returning, the City of Cadillac looked forward to a repeat pennant in the expanded State League of 1911. As the season progressed, it looked like the Cadillacs would indeed capture a second consecutive flag as they enjoyed the top spot virtually all summer and went into their final week needing only to win one game of the last five to clinch. But their closest pursuers, Muskegon and Manistee, swept all five contests and forced a most dramatic finish with all three clubs essentially deadlocked. Manistee finished 1/2 game ahead, but Muskegon protested an earlier loss to Traverse City that if reversed would have given the pennant to Muskegon. The protest was denied by Garry Herrmann of the National Commission and both Cadillac and Muskegon had to settle for a second-place tie. No cigar for Wenger's bunch, but it was an exciting finish. Cadillac had the best team BA with Wenger, Platte, Railing, Morrissey, and Moore all hitting well over .300. Pitchers Johnson (14-3), Gerloski (16-7), and Backus (19-14) made major contributions for the Cadillac contenders. Shortstop Glenn Hale probably cost the locals the 1911 pennant by abandoning the club in mid season. Partly due to the exciting windup of the season, league attendance was up and the same six clubs returned, hoping for another banner season in 1912.

Outfielder Cal Wenger led Cadillac to a pennant in 1910, the first year of the revived Michigan State League.

F. Flynn (on left) was secretary-treasurer of the Cadillac club. Shown here with team president Dr. Moore.

The 1913 Cadillac team which finished a lowly fifth. STANDING (L to R): Sharrock, Aronson, Eggleston, Pres. Moore, Warner (mgr.), Adams, Allison. BELOW (L to R): Young, Swick, Sherlock, Kleug, Baum. In center with hat is Secretary Harris.

The two challengers of 1911, Cadillac and Muskegon, both took a nosedive in 1912, finishing 5th and 6th respectively. Walt Reddick replaced Cal Wenger at the helm and only outfielder Al Platte was able to continue the lusty hitting of the previous summer, winning the batting title with a .367 average. Pitcher "Slab" Warner was the new manager for 1913 and the Cadillac team barely escaped the league basement on the final day of the season. Outfielder/first baseman Pete Allison had a sensational year at bat (.357) and Manager Warner won 16 games, but it was otherwise another dismal summer for Cadillac rooters. In 1914 the State League began to show signs of fatigue after four successful seasons. Both Traverse City and Boyne City quit at the beginning of September and shortly afterward the Manistee club transferred to Belding. The '14 Cadillacs under new manager Jay Parker rebounded to finish a strong third behind winner Muskegon and topped the league in team batting. Young, Baum, Swick, and new manager Parker all finished near the .300 mark. Slab Warner and Jay Sharrock provided consistent pitching to keep the club in contention. But the honeymoon was over for the once healthy Michigan State League as they did not regroup for 1915. For Cadillac, it was their first and last experience as a member of a bona fide professional baseball league, but it left behind a number of memories for local fans to cherish in the years following.

Some key players on the 1913 club:

Pete Allison

Jay Sharrock

*Williams
(finished season
with Ludington)*

O. Swick

THE PLAYING SITE

RECREATION PARK 1910-14 (at the Fairgrounds, on the north side of town)

With no microfilm available from the Cadillac newspaper of the period, descriptive details of this park are virtually non-existent. However, the fairgrounds location is a known fact and very likely the baseball diamond was positioned directly in front of the main grandstand of the race track.

The current fairgrounds grandstand, rebuilt after a fire in the 1950s, is on the same spot as the earlier stand.

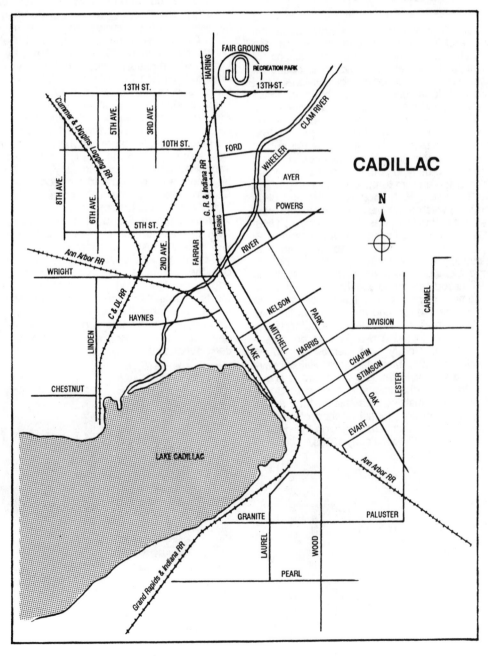

CALUMET

PROFESSIONAL LEAGUE MEMBERSHIP

YEARS	LEAGUE	HOME FIELD
1888-91	Upper Peninsula	Athletic Park Laurium Driving Park
1905	Copper Country-Soo	Athletic Park (Calumet & Hecla Park)
1906-07	Northern-Copper Country	Athletic Park

The general prosperity that accompanied the copper and iron mining booms of the late 19th and early 20th century gave the citizens of Michigan's Upper Peninsula money to spend on leisure activities, including professional and semi-professional baseball. For most of these years, either independent teams of professional league teams were recruited to represent the various small communities in the copper and iron districts and elsewhere. Calumet was the hub of the copper country and was always counted as a member of some type of competitive alliance that might provide a claim to the championship of the Upper Peninsula. With short summers and often unforgiving weather for baseball, schedules were limited but enthusiasm was not. As early as 1888, the Calumets finished second in a five-team U.P. League that included Champion, Hancock, Negaunee, and Marquette. By 1890, the UP League expanded its membership to six towns and increased its schedule to include some week day games. Hancock and Negaunee failed to complete the season and the Calumets finished last, nine games behind winner Houghton. The Calumet roster included two pairs of brothers— Joe & Frank Soddy and James & Robert Renwick. In 1891, Manager Jack Halpin gave Calumet a winner in the four-team circuit and a claim to the championship of the Upper Peninsula. Competitive baseball in the region continued to be an informal alliance of amateur and semi-professional teams through the decade of the nineties and into the early 1900s.

The popularity of the game as a spectator sport encouraged the towns of Calumet, Lake Linden, Hancock, and Sault Ste. Marie to form a fully recognized class D professional circuit to be called the Copper Country-Soo League in 1905. With money to spend, skilled players with solid minor league credentials were easily recruited to fill the rosters of the four league members. As a signatory to the National Association of Professional Leagues, the Copper Country-Soo League was covered in the two national baseball weeklies, The Sporting News and Sporting Life, as well as major newspapers in the midwest. John Cuddihy was the president of the Calumet "Aristocrats" and Dr. G. W. Orr of nearby Lake Linden was named president of the new league. Manager Charles Fichtel's 1905 Aristocrats won the championship by two games over runnerup Lake Linden. Despite the withdrawal of the Sault Ste. Marie club, interest in resuming the league for 1906 was high and attracted the attention of the neighboring Northern League. A merger of the two loops to include their more successful franchises was negotiated in early 1906. The new alignment was to be called the Northern-Copper Country League. The UP towns of Calumet, Houghton, Lake Linden, and Hancock joined Winnipeg, Duluth, Fargo (ND), and Grand Forks (ND) to make up the eight-team loop. Hancock and Grand Forks were forced to withdraw in mid-summer, but the remaining six clubs finished out the schedule with Calumet's Aristocrats edging out Houghton and Winnipeg to capture the flag. John Morrison's new champions were paced by pitcher Paul Grimes with 18 victories. Other notable contributors to the pennant winning campaign included Bobby Vorpagel, Nick Kaiser, Jack Bufka, and "Biddy" Dolan.

Dr. George W. Orr of Lake Linden was president of the Copper Country-Soo League.

Nick Kaiser was one of Calumet's best players around the turn of the century. He was also City Clerk and Secretary of the Water Board.

Biddy Dolan played for Calumet's winning club of 1906. He later surfaced with Indianapolis of the Federal League in 1914.

The 1907 Calumet team, which finished last in the Northern Copper Country League. (L to R): Corrigan, Ryan, Henderson, Rodgers, Schroeder, Mullane (mgr.), Dolan, Dunn, Newcombe, Burns, Orlet (or Crier?).

The Northern-Copper Country League's biggest problem was the travel distance between member cities in 1906, so the league was reduced to the four communities of Duluth, Winnipeg, Calumet, and Houghton when play resumed in 1907. For Calumet, Nick Kaiser and Biddy Dolan were back but the "salad days" were over as the Aristocrats finished in last place, 41-1/2 games behind a strong Winnipeg club. It was to be the final curtain for full-fledged professional league baseball in the Upper Peninsula, and the Calumets settled for their more accustomed brand of amateur or semi-pro teams in the following years. It was a brief but glorious run for local fans with pennant winners in two of the three years it lasted.

The current ball field at Laurium is probably the same diamond used occasionally for Copper Country League games.

A bird's eye view drawing of Calumet and Laurium from 1881, looking northwest. The open space in the center suggests a baseball diamond (arrow) which is the approximate location of Athletic Park, used later in league play.

CALUMET, LAURIUM & RED JACKET

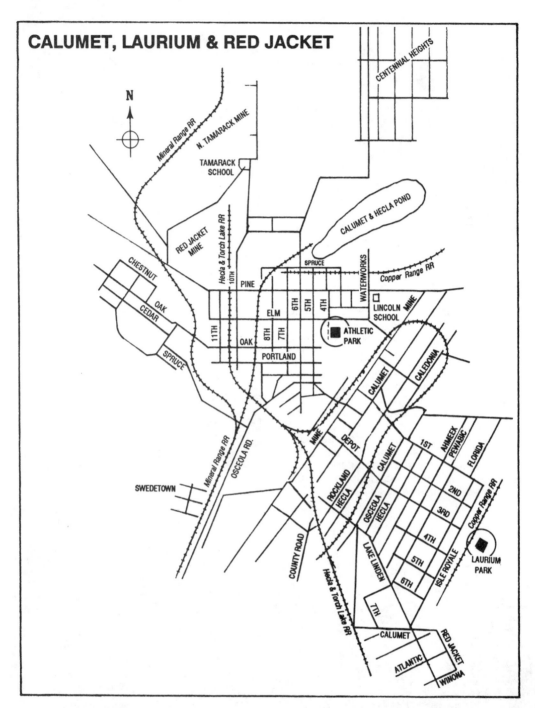

THE PLAYING SITE

> ### ATHLETIC PARK 1905-07
> ### (at 4th & Elm Streets)

The birth date of this baseball grounds is unknown, but it most certainly dates back to the 1880s or even earlier. During the years of league baseball after 1900, a small roofed grandstand occupied the southwest corner of the lot and a squared board fence completely encircled the field. From surviving photographs, it appears that "freeloaders" were able to view the games from atop the lumber piles that bordered the grounds. In later decades, the place was called Agassiz Park after one of the prominent founders of the Calumet & Hecla Mining Co., who owned the property. Some league games may also have been played at the Laurium Park across from the railroad tracks at 3rd Street in Laurium.

A remarkable photographic view of Calumet, from the turn of the century, looking in same direction (NW) as the 1881 artist's rendering. Athletic Park is clearly shown in the right center of the picture. The grandstand is in the southwest corner of the fenced-in field.

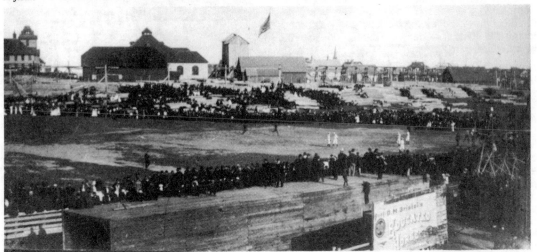

Another view from the same era, this time looking southeast. A big game is obviously in progress. This park area was later named Agassiz Park after one of the Copper barons of early Calumet days.

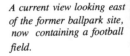

A current view looking east of the former ballpark site, now containing a football field.

CHARLOTTE

PROFESSIONAL LEAGUE MEMBERSHIP

YEARS	LEAGUE	HOME FIELD
1926	Michigan State (transferred from Flint)	Bennett Park

Much like tiny Belding had experienced in 1914, the small community of Charlotte's brief tenure as a member of a professional minor league in 1926 was not planned but fell in their collective laps after a franchise failure in mid-summer. The 1926 Michigan State League, a merged circuit of the struggling Central and Michigan-Ontario Leagues, consisted of eight of the larger Michigan towns outside of Detroit. By mid-July the restructured circuit was also having difficulties, especially in Flint where the franchise was hopelessly in debt. Prominent businessmen in Charlotte led by C. J. Marshall, got wind of Flint's predicament and made a pitch to take on the Flint operation for the balance of the season. Despite the smaller population base in Charlotte, the move was agreed upon by league officials in the hopes of completing the season schedule. The fans and the local newspaper were ecstatic and welcomed their new team (nicknamed Giants) on July 25 with a home game against the Muskegon Reds.

Unfortunately, the team they inherited was already hopelessly buried in last place and the change of scenery did little to reverse their losing ways. They finished out the season with a 14-37 WL record, 32-1/2 games behind first place Bay City. Undismayed, Charlotte felt confident that they had found their niche as a bona fide league baseball town, but the Michigan State League suffered losses throughout the circuit and opted not to resume operation in 1927. The Giants' horrendous pitching staff proved to be their undoing and the few bright spots were player/manager Ray Dunn (.265), infielder Herman Loepp (.320), and utility man Roy Keene (.285).

Infielder Ray Dunn was also manager of the Flint/Charlotte club.

Herman Loepp played infield and caught for the Giants. He was the team's leading hitter.

THE PLAYING SITE

> **BENNETT PARK baseball grounds 1926–adjacent to fairgrounds on South Cochrane (now Main) Street**

No detailed information or photos available at this writing.

The Bennett Park site now contains tennis courts and the local high school's football field.

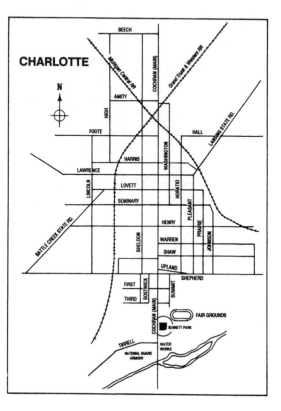

36

DETROIT

PROFESSIONAL LEAGUE MEMBERSHIP

YEARS	LEAGUE	HOME FIELD
1889-90	International	Recreation Park
1891	Northwestern	Riverside Park
1894-99	Western	Boulevard Park ('94-'95)
		Bennett Park ('96-'99) (Sundays—Ecorse Twp.)
1900	American	Bennett Park (Sundays—Burns Park)
1920-54	(Negro Leagues)	Mack Park (1920-29) Hamtramck Sta. (1930-) Dequindre Park (1937) Briggs Stadium (1940s)

Michigan's metropolis, home of the Detroit Tigers, enjoys a long history as a major league town but it was also a member of numerous minor leagues during the 19th century. Its first membership was in the National League from 1881 to 1888 where it claimed a world championship in 1887. Owner Frederick Stearns sold off most of the team after the 1888 season and the franchise was transferred to Cleveland. Determined to keep the city in Organized Baseball, owners Mills and George Chittenden entered Detroit in the International League in 1889-90. The league consisted of teams from Ontario and New York state plus Toledo, and the Detroits utilized the vacated home of the ex-National Leaguers, Recreation Park. Manager Bob Leadley led the club to a championship in '89, paced by Bobby Wheelock, Jake Wells, and Charles "Count" Campau, a descendant of one of the founding families of Detroit. The following year, Saginaw-Bay City joined the circuit and the Buffalo franchise transferred to Grand Rapids in early June, but the IL suffered from poor attendance and collapsed in early July. Contributing to the abrupt failure of the Detroit franchise was the "raiding" of star players by owner Chris VonDerAhe of the American Association St. Louis Browns.

Frank Knauss

Bob Leadley manager

George Shaffer

Jake Virtue

Bobby Wheelock

Jake Wells

George Rooks

Count Campau

Mike Goodfellow

Edgar Smith

Newspaper illustrations of the star players from the 1889 Detroit International League champions—arguably the best minor league club to represent Detroit. All of these men had major league experience before or after 1889.

An attempt to resurrect the old Northwestern League in 1891 included the Michigan cities of Grand Rapids, Bay City, and Detroit along with other comparable midwest towns. Detroit's entry was managed by outfielder William "Rasty" Wright, an outstanding minor league hitter with some big league credentials. Rasty, along with John Rainey, a teammate on the '91 Detroit club, had both played for Muskegon in the old Northwestern League of 1884. The Detroits opened the 1891 campaign at old Recreation Park, but soon moved into a new facility called Riverside Park on the Detroit River across from Belle Isle. Right from the start, this new league venture was doomed to failure as Detroit fans still seemed reluctant to embrace a minor league club after many seasons in the big show. The locals struggled with a 10-18 WL record before closing up shop on June 8. Bay City also withdrew at the same time and the league continued to limp along with two more drop-outs, Peoria and Dayton, in mid-July. With only four teams left, the NW League collapsed for good on July 30. Minor league baseball would not be attempted in the City of the Straits for three more summers.

An energetic and imaginative ex-baseball scribe named Byron Bancroft "Ban" Johnson organized another new circuit in 1894 to be called the Western League. The member cities were an impressive group of larger cities in the upper midwest, some of whom had claimed previous major league status, including Detroit. George A. VanderBeck, a wealthy former owner of successful minor league clubs on the West Coast, was the president of the Detroit entry and he quickly built a new facility to be called Boulevard Park on the city's east side. The Detroits, captained by second baseman Bob Glenalvin, finished next to the bottom at season's end, but this time managed to play out the full schedule with decent attendance that ensured a resumption- of league play in 1895. The new Western League proved to be a well-heeled and well-organized operation under President Johnson. Seven of the eight franchises from 1894 returned in 1895 with Sioux City being replaced by St. Paul. The new St. Paul club was headed by an ex-big league player named Charles Comiskey. Con Strouthers was the new manager of the '95 Detroits and led them to a fifth place finish. Count Campau had returned to Detroit from various minor league stops and had a big season, hitting .359.

Detroit owner VanderBeck, disenchanted with his "bandbox" at Boulevard Park, secured property at the corner of Michigan and Trumbull for a new home field for his 1896 WL franchise now called "Tigers" because of their stocking stripe colors. 28-year-old outfielder George Stallings was selected to captain and manage the '96 "Tigers" in their new lair. The name chosen for the new field was Bennett Park, in honor of Charley Bennett, a former star catcher for the 1887 Detroit NL champions. Bennett, by this time out of baseball as a result of a tragic train accident which cost him both lower legs, took part in the official opening on April 28, 1896. The Detroits were victorious over the Columbus Senators 17-2. The Stallings-led Tigers improved to a third place finish in their third WL season with a record of 80 wins, 60 losses. Bob Allen took over as manager in 1897 and the Tigers slipped to a distant fifth followed by a sixth place finish in '98 under Tony Mullane. Noteworthy players during this period were hard-hitting outfielder Sam Dungan, catcher Fritz Buelow, and third baseman Harry Steinfeldt, all of whom went on to major league careers. Even the great eccentric lefty Rube Waddell had a "cup of coffee" with the Tigers in 1898. The Western League was on solid footing as one of the healthier minor leagues by this time and Detroit fans, in spite of a run of disappointing finishes, had rallied behind their hometown club.

Charles "Count" Campau, a descendant of one of Detroit's founding families, had a colorful major and minor league career with stops in Detroit, Grand Rapids, and elsewhere.

Frank Bowerman, from nearby Romeo, played for Detroit in '94. He later enjoyed a long big league career and was Christy Mathewson's favorite catcher.

Con Strouthers managed the 1895 Western League club.

George VanderBeck brought Detroit into the Western League in 1894 and built Bennett Park at Michigan & Trumbull in 1896.

A newspaper illustration depicts the opening of Detroit's new ballpark in 1896 with the park's namesake, Charley Bennett, participating.

Hard-hitting outfielder Sam Dungan starred for the Detroits in the late 1890s. He also had some good years in the majors before and after his Detroit years.

'97 Detroit infielder Harry Steinfeldt went on to a 14-year career in the NL. He was the third baseman for the legendary Tinker-to-Evers-to-Chance Cubs infield.

George Stallings played, managed, and later owned the Detroit WL club.

Bob Allen was Tiger manager in 1897.

Ex-big league star pitcher Tony Mullane managed the Detroit WL club of 1898.

Catcher Fred Buelow of the '98-'99 Detroits also played for the first AL Tiger teams of 1901-04.

In 1899, VanderBeck rehired the feisty George Stallings to manage the Detroits and he brought them back to a more respectable third place finish. The '99 Tiger lineup was sprinkled with several outstanding new players that would eventually become the nucleus of the Detroit major league club of 1901—namely Norman "Kid" Elberfield, Jimmy Barrett, Dick Harley, and Jack Cronin. When the 12-team National League pared itself down to eight teams, a surplus of quality players was turned loose and Ban Johnson's league corralled a number of them to upgrade the quality of play. With an eye to the future, Johnson renamed his circuit the American League and transferred two of the members to major league territories in Chicago and Cleveland. Meanwhile, VanderBeck sold the franchise to James Burns and George Stallings. Stallings' club was reinforced with quality players like Jimmy Casey, Ducky Holmes, Dick Cooley, and Lew McAllister, and finished fourth in the beefed up American League of 1900. The following year, the AL gave up all minor league pretensions and declared themselves in direct competition with the established National League. Thus ended a 13-year absence from the big leagues for the City of Detroit, and a storied tradition of Tiger baseball at the major league level was underway.

Since this treatise deals with minor league operations only, Detroit's role in the story was essentially over in 1901. But at the risk of stretching the definition of "minor league," another brand of professional league baseball entertained Detroit fans from 1920 to the mid-1950s and deserves mention here. Kept out of Organized Baseball by the "Jim Crow" mentality of the times, the Negro Leagues developed a following of their own and even flourished financially from time to time during this period. With a sizable black population mostly recruited from southern states by the auto industry, Detroit was well represented in the long history of the Negro Leagues. Even though the Motor City was unable to produce a Negro League dynasty such as the Kansas City Monarchs or the Homestead Grays, the Detroit Stars of several eras were the best remembered franchise. Over the 3-1/2 decades of Negro League baseball in Detroit, they played most of their games at Mack Park on the east side until it was consumed by fire in 1929. In the remaining years they played at Hamtramck Stadium, Dequindre Park, and even a few dates at Briggs (Tiger) Stadium in the early forties.

The Negro League Detroit Stars of 1920. TOP ROW (L to R): Holland, Wesley, Petway, Harper, Gatewood, (unknown), (unknown). MIDDLE ROW: Hewitt, Hill, owner Blount, Lyons, Cooper. BOTTOM ROW: (unknown), Force, Riggins, (unknown).

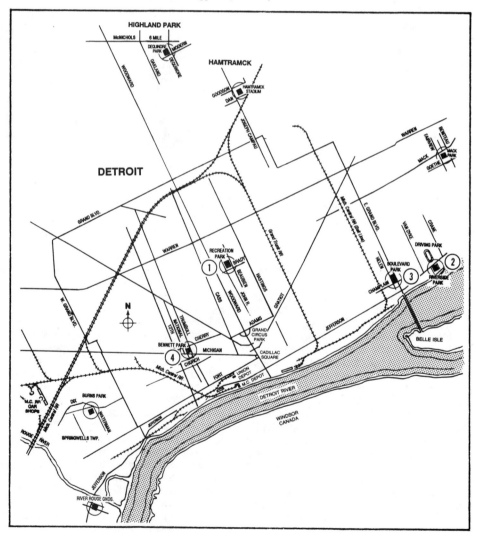

THE PLAYING SITES

① RECREATION PARK 1889-1890 (at Brush & Brady, adjacent to Harper Hospital)

Recreation Park was formally opened on May 12, 1879 with much fanfare, speeches, band music, etc. The long-awaited facility was designed for a variety of events including horse races, croquet, cricket, skating, and of course the national pastime of baseball. On that opening occasion, the home team was trounced by the visiting Troys, 7-1. The park project was created by a group called the Park Company, headed by Joseph Taylor and F. O. Davenport. The spacious field was surrounded by a high fence and included a grandstand structure at the south end. The entrance and reception building sat on the Brady Street southeast corner. Eventually, a chain of additional bleachers was added to form a horseshoe seating arrangement. The park's ample acreage provided plenty of room for standees and carriage parking. Major league professional baseball made its Detroit debut at the park in 1881 with the arrival of the National League, which survived for eight seasons here. After the big league team left Detroit for Cleveland in 1888, the International League played their home games at Recreation Park for the next two seasons. The ill-fated Northwestern League club of 1891 opened the season at Recreation Park but soon thereafter moved to their new Riverside Park grounds. Recreation Park had seen the last of professional league baseball. Photos of the old grounds have survived among the very rare photographic images of any 19th century baseball park in Michigan.

The park entrance and reception building at Recreation Park, on Brady Street

An overflow crowd fills Recreation Park for a big game when Detroit was in the National League during the 1880s.

Another view of game action at Recreation Park in the 1880s

② RIVERSIDE PARK 1891 (between Jefferson and the Detroit River, across from Belle Isle)

The least known of Detroit's 19th century league baseball parks, Riverside Park was the home field for the city's Northwestern League club of 1891. It was located on the property of today's Owens Park, then beyond the city limits and part of what was then Hamtramck Township. Its life as a minor league facility was a brief one as the team folded in early June. One of the many problems that plagued the franchise was the state's ban on Sunday baseball. Threatened and harassed by township authorities whenever they attempted to play a scheduled date on the Sabbath, they even attempted to evade arrest by playing at one of the old driving parks which lay directly across Jefferson Avenue from the Riverside grounds. But enthusiasm for the NW League was lacking throughout the circuit and the league itself did not survive past July.

③ BOULEVARD PARK 1894-1895 (on Champlain between E. Grand Blvd. and Helen)

Opened in May 1894 as the new home of the Western League's Detroit entry, this property was a poor choice for a baseball park. On the city's far eastern boundary, its narrow width forced some unusual ground rules. The distances down the foul lines were so short that a double set of white foul poles were erected along the right and left field fences—any ball hit over the fence between

the primary pole and the second pole was declared a ground rule double. In its first year there was no grass, only a hard clay surface over the entire field. Total seating capacity was 3400, which included an 1800-seat main grandstand with 100 box seats. Open bleachers were placed on either side of the grandstand. Its close proximity to neighboring houses on Helen Avenue invited many "freeloaders" to view the games without contributing to the gate receipts. Even though the franchise attracted a good following, two seasons in this horrendous "bandbox" were enough for owner VanderBeck and he was determined to find a more suitable location for the 1896 season.

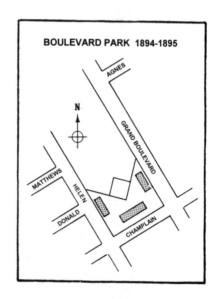

The only surviving image of Boulevard Park is this newspaper sketch from early 1894.

④ BENNETT PARK 1896-1900 (corner Michigan & Trumbull Aves.)

ultimate enlargement of Navin Field and its 100 consecutive years of Detroit baseball at the same location represents the longest such tenure in Organized Baseball.

An old haymarket site at the intersection of Michigan and Trumbull Avenues was purchased for the new home field for the 1896 Detroits. An L-shaped grandstand with a full pitched roof was hastily erected in the southeast corner of the lot. Home plate was located in this corner with an open bleacher along Trumbull and the first base line. The ticket office and main entrance were at the Michigan/Trumbull corner, where streetcar lines made convenient stops to drop off and pick up park patrons. A flagpole stood in the left field corner and a small clubhouse was eventually placed in deep centerfield. A huge lumberyard occupied the property immediately north of the right field fence and although it was a considerable distance, many game balls found their way into the stacks of lumber over the years. An alleyway ran along the left field fence and homeowners were quick to erect rickety homemade bleachers overlooking the fence for "bootleg" patrons. These so-called "wildcat" stands became an ongoing nuisance for team owners for most of the life of Bennett Park.

Charley Bennett, by now a much revered Detroit resident and one-time star catcher for the Detroit NL team of the 1880s, was the park's namesake and honored guest at the 1896 grand opening. When Detroit re-entered the major leagues in 1901, they continued to use the Bennett Park facility and continually made enlargements and improvements to the park up to its razing in the fall of 1911. The new concrete and steel Navin Field of 1912 was built on the same property but the diamond was repositioned into the southwest corner of the lot. Today's Tiger Stadium is the

Charley Bennett, the great backstop of Detroit's 1887 World Champions, remained a big local hero after a train accident ended his career and cost him both lower legs. He became a Detroit resident and the city honored him by naming the new '96 ballpark Bennett Park. He participated in opening game ceremonies in Detroit every year until his death in 1927.

A newspaper artist depicts the grand opening of Bennett Park in 1896.

A photo of the crowd gathering at the Michigan & Trumbull entrance of Bennett Park for the first major league game played there on April 26, 1901.

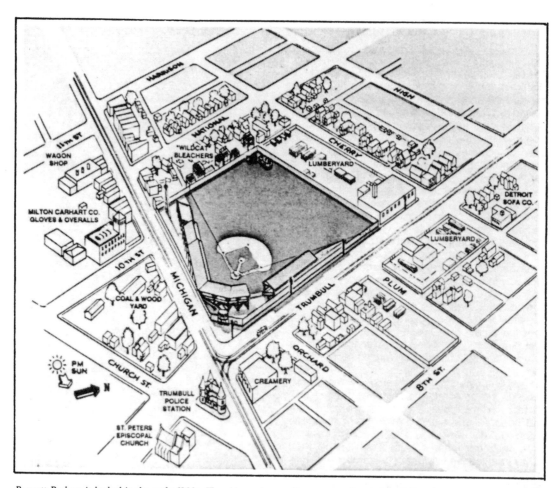

Bennett Park as it looked in the early 1900s. The old wooden stands were torn down in the fall of 1911, replaced by a modern concrete and steel structure to be renamed Navin Field (later Briggs/Tiger Stadium). The Navin Field diamond was repositioned with home plate moved to the southwest corner. The houses along National and the lumberyard along Cherry were cleared to make room for the larger Navin Field facility. The location is the oldest continuous site for major league baseball in the USA.

PROFESSIONAL LEAGUE MEMBERSHIP

YEARS	LEAGUE	HOME FIELD
1910	Indiana-Michigan	Pokagon Park

Most recorded memories associated with ball teams in Dowagiac in the early decades of the 20th century center around independent nines like the "Doe-Wah-Jacks" or the Round Oaks clubs sponsored by the famous local stove manufacturer. But in 1910 Dowagiac enjoyed its only season as a member of a professional circuit called the Indiana-Michigan League. It consisted of the northern Indiana towns of Gary, Elkhart, and Ligonier, along with the southwestern Michigan communities of Niles, Berrien Springs, and Dowagiac. Convenient travel connections encouraged the formation of this league since all the towns were connected by an interurban railway. It was a modest class D loop with a limited weekend schedule. The players hired were a mixture of talented locals and outsiders with little potential to advance up the professional ladder. But enthusiasm was high and competition spirited when the Dowagiac team opened the home season on May 15 with a 7-1 victory over nearby Niles. Despite its lowly standing in the hierarchy of the minor leagues, coverage of the league was published regularly in the Chicago newspapers. L. L. Lavenberg was picked to manage the locals. As the season progressed,

patronage waned in the Indiana towns of Gary and Ligonier and both cities dropped out, making it a four-team circuit. The season ended on August 25 with Dowagiac in last place with a record of 7 wins and 12 losses. The disappointing gate receipts spelled the demise of the league and thus ended Dowagiac's lone venture in Organized Baseball.

THE PLAYING SITE

> **POKAGON PARK 1910 (west side of town, on the highway to Niles, just across Dowagiac Creek)**

Pokagon Park opened for baseball in May 1906. Five acres of the Tuthill farm were subleased from one Henry Jones, who held a lease on the property. A 7-foot-high fence was erected around the grounds, followed by a modest grandstand seating 300. Unfortunately, no photographs or diagrams of the park are known to exist, so the exact location and orientation of the diamond are unknown. A True Value hardware store and other smaller businesses presently occupy the property that is believed to be the original site of Pokagon Park.

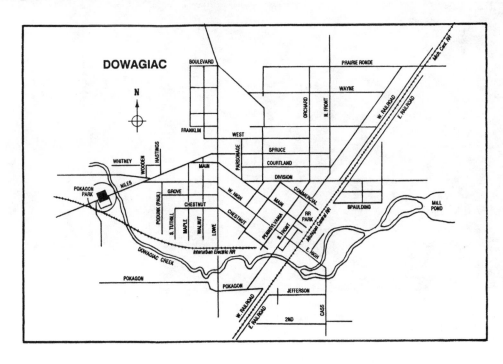

EVART

PROFESSIONAL LEAGUE MEMBERSHIP

YEARS	LEAGUE	HOME FIELD
1887	Northern Michigan	(no name)

Tiny Evart had the distinction of claiming membership in one of the earliest professional baseball leagues in Michigan, the Northern Michigan League of 1887. It was one of the most compact circuits in the country, consisting of the neighboring communities of Reed City, Big Rapids, Greenville, Ionia, and Evart. The Evart franchise was put together by local businessmen Frank Postal and David Woolf. Postal's brother Fred, who operated the Evart House Hotel, was also involved and in later years became a major league club president. R. A. Bennett was named manager and the team captain was catcher John Whalen. Although the talent level was several notches below other professional leagues at that time, competition between the rival towns was fierce and games were hotly contested. Arguments accompanied every loss and complaints about inferior and biased umpiring were prevalent. The Evart team was leading the league when they refused to take the field in a game vs. Reed City in late July because of their dissatisfaction with the umpire assigned to the game. Reed City's owner, W. A. Higbe, was also president of the league, and he upheld the choice of umpire and further annoyed the Evart fans by backing the umpire's decision to forfeit the game to Reed City. An ugly incident ensued when the Reed City players and umpire Punches were bombarded with rotten eggs as they boarded their train. Not long afterward Evart withdrew from the league. Big Rapids and Ionia also withdrew a week later and the league itself was forced to fold with only Reed City and Greenville remaining. E. Schnur was Evart's leading batter with a .419 average, followed by Conklin at .375.

Evart House owner Fred Postal was a baseball enthusiast. He later became a successful hotelier in Detroit and from there he bought stock in the 1901 Washington AL team to become its president for three years.

Evart-born Aloysius "Wish" Egan played briefly in the major leagues and later became a legendary talent scout for the Detroit Tigers. He made Wyandotte his hometown for most of his life.

The 1887 Northern Michigan League club. STANDING (L to R): Ed Phelan, E. B. Farrar, C. F. Stout, John Whalen (captain), P. J. Sullivan. MIDDLE: Truey Andrus, F. W. Lyons, R. A. Bennett (mgr.), Nick Schnur, A. Dickey. BOTTOM: John O'Donnell, E. J. Egan, S. Conklin

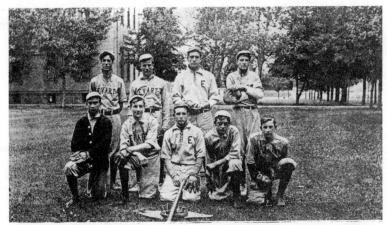

The Evart High School team of 1908 poses on the field next to the school. This is very likely where the 1887 NM League club played its home games.

THE PLAYING SITE

EVART BASEBALL GROUNDS 1887 (Pine & 5th Sts., adjacent to the High School)

Descriptive features or photographs of the site have not been found so we know next to nothing about the field itself. Even the location is unconfirmed, but since the local school and adjacent playfield were in existence in 1887 and there is no indication that the team played their games at the fairgrounds or Riverside Park, very likely this is the correct location of the grounds.

A current view of the same high school field as it looks today, with the high school on the left.

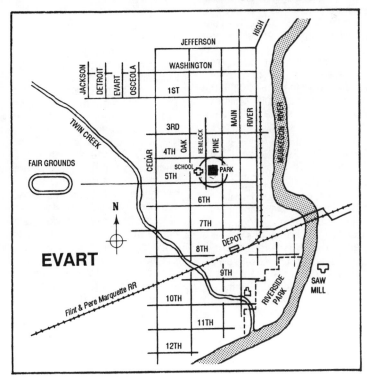

FLINT

PROFESSIONAL LEAGUE MEMBERSHIP

YEARS	LEAGUE	HOME FIELD
1889-90	Michigan State	9th St. Grounds
1897	Michigan State (transferred from Bay City)	Fairgrounds
1902	Michigan State	Fairgrounds
1906	Interstate Assn.	Fairgrounds Athletic Park (Sundays–Burton Township)
1907-15	Southern Michigan	Athletic Park
1919-26	Michigan-Ontario (MINT)	Athletic Park
1926	Michigan State	Athletic Park
1940-41	Michigan State	Atwood Stadium
1948-51	Central	Atwood Stadium

The City of Flint's history as a minor league baseball town ranks with Grand Rapids, Bay City, and Saginaw among Michigan communities. Their first professional league team arrived in 1889, when the troubled Kalamazoo franchise of the Michigan State League was transferred to Flint in early September. They finished that season as a last place club but immediately made plans to enter the league as a bona fide member in 1890. First baseman James A. Lombard was the captain and field manager of the Flint entry. The 1890 season was barely underway when the league began to flounder. It was a disruptive year for all of professional baseball marked by the revolt of the majority of big league players, who left their established teams to form their own league called the Players League, or Brotherhood. Grand Rapids delivered the final, fatal blow to the State League when they abruptly bolted to join the higher class International League in early June. The 1890 Michigan State League dissolved on June 10 with Flint in third place. It would be seven more seasons before the city would try professional league baseball again.

Flint's second attempt to support a league team occurred in 1897 under a scenario quite similar to its original try in 1889. The Bay City franchise of the struggling Michigan State League was transferred to Flint on July 2 in hopes of salvaging the season. But Lansing and Jackson, the first and second place teams, called it quits on July 26 and within a week the league itself went under. Flint settled for the independent variety of baseball until 1902 when they were enticed to make yet another entry in the latest version of the Michigan State League. Col. Frank Clark headed the franchise and William Whitton was named field manager. This 1902 edition of the MSL

seemed in the beginning to be better organized and better supported than in previous years and managed to survive intact into mid-July before Saginaw and Grand Rapids withdrew. By this time the circuit was beset with a host of troubles, including dissatisfaction with umpires, player revolts, and disruptive political bickering among club owners. The league finally suspended operations on August 20 with Flint in third place among the five remaining clubs. Eddie Zinram had replaced Whitton as field manager for the Flints. Notable players on the Flint roster included former major league pitcher Fred Clausen and catcher Monte Beville, who was signed by the New York Americans the following year.

Henry "Monte" Beville caught for the '02 Flint club, then moved up to the big leagues for two years (1903-04).

Fred Clausen pitched in the majors in the mid-1890s and wound up on the 1902 Flints of the Michigan State League.

Flint's next adventure in league baseball took place in 1906. Grand Rapids newspaperman and baseball organizer Emerson Dickerson assembled an eight-team class C circuit consisting of four Indiana towns, one from Ohio, and the three Michigan cities of Saginaw, Bay City, and Flint. The new league was named the Interstate Association (not to be confused with the class D Interstate League in Pennsylvania) and its Michigan entries directly competed with the fledgling Southern Michigan League territories. Early problems plagued the Interstate right from the start as Muncie (IN) and Bay City withdrew barely two weeks into the season. The remaining two Michigan cities of Saginaw and Flint were in default of payment to visiting outstate clubs and were forced to drop out in late June-early July. Once again the league venture was abandoned for good in July with the Flints in contention with a creditable 34-23 W-L record. Also courted by the Southern Michigan League early in the year, Flint chose the wrong organization as the SML managed to survive a full season intact. Determined to establish themselves as a minor league town, when the SML expanded to eight clubs for 1907 Flint was awarded a franchise.

A record crowd of 2,307 turned out to inaugurate Flint's hometown team in the 1907 Southern Michigan League home opener at their new Athletic Park. Although the Flints finished in the cellar, they finally managed to survive a full season and made plans to resume SML play the following year. The 1908 club did not improve much, finishing next-to-last with a 56-70 W-L record. One of the bright spots in the 1908 lineup was slugging outfielder Jim Bowser, who led the circuit with 11 home runs. After so many aborted attempts at league baseball, Flint had finally found a home in the SML and they regrouped for the 1909 season with a new stable of talented players who could seriously contend for the championship. In addition to the steady play of Bowser, Manager Joe Wright added the talents of Cogswell and Alperman to give the Vehics (their new nickname) arguably the circuit's best outfield. The pitching staff also ranked with the league's finest, paced by 23-game winner Eugene "Rubber" Krapp and including "Stub" O'Connell, "Dad" Roach, and "Jud" Weeder. Manager Wright played most of the year at first base. As the 1909 season drew to a close in early September, the Vehics were in a close three-way struggle with Saginaw and Jackson for the top spot. Flint was tied for first going into their final weekend series in Jackson and could have won the pennant outright with only one victory. But the best the Vehics could manage was two losses and two ties, which left them 1/2 game behind Saginaw in the final count. But Flint was claiming the championship based on the argument that four of Saginaw's victories should be thrown out since they used a "suspended" player. But in the end, League Secretary Percy Glass ruled in favor of Saginaw, thereby upholding their claim to the championship. A bitter disappointment for Flint fans and the closest they would come to a pennant in their nine seasons in the SML.

Joe Wright led the 1909 Flint Vehics to a near-miss for the Southern Michigan League pennant.

Outfielder Red Cogswell was a key player in Flint's 1909 pennant chase.

Three important members of the 1909 pitching staff

"Rubber" Krapp   *"Stub" O'Connell*   *Jud Weeder*

The much-traveled Bobby Vorpagel started the 1909 season with Flint.

The 1909 Flint team that lost the Southern Michigan League flag by 1/2 game following an unfavorable league ruling at season's end. STANDING (L to R): O'Connell, Kuhagen, Alperman, Main, Brown, Cogswell, Bowser, Hildebrand, Lawler, Wright. SITTING (L to R): Nichols, Roth, Krapp, Hadley, Weeder, Harlow.

Jim Bowser returned in 1910 with a sensational performance, leading the circuit with 14 home runs and a .342 batting average, but the Vehics finished a distant fifth, 18-1/2 games behind the leaders. Manager Dan Collins' 1911 club improved to a third place finish, paced by first baseman Clarence Kraft's 19 home runs. The 1912 Vehics made another strong run but once again finished third under new pilot Jack Burke. The new hometown hero was second baseman Fred "Rabbit" Ochs, who led the league in runs scored and was Flint's version of Ty Cobb on the basepaths. The Vehics' fortunes in the Southern Michigan loop went steadily downhill after 1912, the club finishing no higher than fifth in '13 and '14 and dead last in the league's final aborted season of 1915. That 1915 club featured an unusual dual role in the person of Bob Wells, who was not only president of the club but also the team's backstop. Manager Ed Wheeler was in fact the "boss's boss" when Wells was in the lineup. The World War I period spelled the demise of the SML as it did with much of professional baseball, and not until the armistice was signed did league baseball re-energize itself.

Detroit baseball writer Joe Jackson, who founded the Southern Michigan League back in 1906, assembled a new baseball circuit in 1919 to be called the Michigan-Ontario (MINT) League. Flint, Bay City, Battle Creek, and Saginaw represented Michigan along with four cities in Ontario. The Flint entry was a disaster under Manager "Hump" Pierce, finishing dead last with a 35-74 W-L record. Catcher Andy Lotshaw, who split the season between Flint and Brantford (ONT), tied for the league's home run leadership with 13. Lotshaw later gained fame as the beloved trainer of the Chicago Cubs. Back for another try in 1920, Flint improved to a fifth place finish sparked by a spectacular "triple crown" season by Frank Wetzel (.387 BA, 72 RBIs, 12 HRs). A Flint man, Thomas J. Halligan, took the helm of the MINT League in 1922.

Lanky Miles Main from nearby Montrose MI pitched for Flint in 1909-10 and for Detroit in 1914.

Well-known Chicago Cubs trainer Andy Lotshaw played for Flint in the 1919 MINT League.

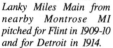
Jack Burke led the Vehics in 1912.

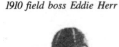
1910 field boss Eddie Herr

Billy Hunter starred in the Flint outfield in 1912.

Bobby Wells was team president and catcher for the 1915 club.

After two more dismal seasons at or near the league basement, Flint rebounded under new Manager Dan O'Leary with a 70-63 record in 1923, good enough for 4th place in the MINT standings. Frank Luce led the upsurge with a league-leading .382 BA. Art Jahn chipped in with 18 homers, also tops in the circuit. Luce came back in '24 and his 23 home runs led the Vehics to a lofty runner-up spot behind pennant winner Bay City, Flint's best season in their six years in the MINT League. In a split-season format, Flint won the first half-season easily, but faltered in the second season and then lost the post-season playoffs to second-half champion Bay City four games to three. The following year, the Flint club tumbled to 5th place. In the MINT League's final year of 1926, Flint was wallowing in last place among the four Michigan teams which made up the failing MINT League in early June. The class C Central League was also struggling with only four Michigan towns and the two circuits attempted to salvage the season by regrouping as the Michigan State League on June 15. The new alignment managed to finish out the summer schedule, but the last place Flints were transferred to Charlotte in late July to complete the season there. It was the last of professional league baseball in the Vehicle City for 14 more years.

Tom Halligan of Flint was the architect of the 1940-41 State League and the 1948-51 Central League.

Gene Woodling hit .394 for the 1941 Flint Indians. He later had a fine career in the American League with Cleveland, New York, and Baltimore.

foiled by the powerful Indians' winning of both races, thereby negating the need for a championship series. The final combined standings gave Flint the flag by a 9-game margin over runner-up St. Joseph. Indian bats, paced by outfielder Gene Woodling's remarkable .394 season, provided the Flint club with a league-leading .307 team batting average. Steve Gromek paced the pitching staff with a 14-2 record and a fine 2.90 ERA. Schultz and Presser chipped in with 17 and 15 victories. The Flint dynasty was short-lived however, as World War II put the State League out of business, never to return.

With a resurgence of interest in minor league baseball as the Great Depression finally wound down in the late 1930s, T. J. Halligan and others revived the Michigan State League as a class C circuit in 1940. By this time, the so-called "farm systems" of major league clubs had taken hold and the Cleveland Indians were sponsors of the Flint entry. It was to be a stroke of good fortune for the Vehicle City as the parent club supplied enough talent for Flint to virtually dominate the league in its brief two-year existence. The Flint Gems ran away with the 1940 State League pennant. Unfortunately, they were upset in the semifinals of post-season play by St. Joseph, but in the end it didn't matter as inclement weather forced eventual postponement of the finals. Several players on Manager Jack Knight's 1940 Flint roster later surfaced in the big leagues— namely Cliff Mapes, Steve Gromek, and Red Embree. The team nickname "Gems" was replaced by "Indians" in 1941 to identify more closely with the parent big league club. The '41 State League opted for a split-season format with first and second half winners to meet in a post-season playoff. The playoff scheme was

The ace of the 1941 Flint pitching staff, Steve Gromek, went on to a 17-year ML career with Cleveland and Detroit. Gromek was a Hamtramck, MI native.

The 1940 regular season State League champions. BACK ROW (L to R): McMeans, Lange, Kohler, Mapes, Sidlo. MIDDLE ROW: Thompson, Hooks, Gromek, Sabota, O'Dea, Dwyer, batboy. FRONT ROW: Duitsman, Stoeber, Shoff, Mgr. Jack Knight.

Baseball's popularity at all levels reached an all-time high in the post-WWII years and T. J. Halligan soon orchestrated a revival of the Central League in 1948. Flint joined Muskegon, Saginaw, and Grand Rapids as the Michigan entries in the class A six-team loop. The Detroit Tigers agreed to sponsor the new "Arrows" and hired the popular Jack Tighe as field manager. Tighe's charges picked up where the State League Indians left off and captured another regular season championship for the Flint fans—120,000 of whom flocked to Atwood Stadium to root for the Tiger farmhands. A successful maiden season was, however, tainted by an early exit in the playoffs at the hands of the Fort Wayne Generals. Pitcher Alex Nedelco paced the league hurlers with a 16-7 record and outfielder George Lerchen led the offense with a .337 season. In 1949, the Arrows slipped to 2nd place and once again were quickly eliminated in the playoffs by Grand Rapids. Ernie Funk was the circuit's top hurler with a fine 2.13 ERA and a 12-10 W-L record. Young backstop Frank House, the Detroit Tigers' celebrated bonus baby, was a big gate attraction in Flint and around the league in 1949. Gene Desautels replaced Tighe as Arrows' pilot in 1950 and once again gave Flint the league championship. This time the Flints did not falter in post-season play and made short work of Grand Rapids and Muskegon in capturing the Central League's final prize in the playoffs. Ernie Funk had returned to anchor the pitching staff with 22 victories. Diminutive shortstop "Scooter" Koshorek was back for his third season to spark the infield. Another future big league performer, outfielder John "Bubba" Phillips, was a key contributor for the Arrows' success in 1950.

The popular Jack Tighe was picked by the parent Detroit club to manage the 1948 Flint Arrows of the new Central League. Tighe's long managerial career began with Muskegon in 1940 and included a short stint as Detroit's field boss in 1957-58.

The Detroit Tigers' celebrated bonus baby, catcher Frank House, was Flint's most publicized player in 1949.

Outfielder George Lerchen was the Arrows' best hitter in '48, hitting .337. But he lasted only two years in the majors with Detroit and Cincinnati.

Tiger prospect Al Federoff was Flint's second baseman in 1948. He played in 74 games for Detroit in 1952, but never quite made the grade in the big show.

Pitcher Alex Nedelco led the Arrows to a regular season championship in 1948 with 16 wins.

Ernie Funk was the CL's top pitcher in 1950, winning 22 games for the Flint champions.

Arguably the finest team in the four years of the 1948-51 Central League, the 1950 Flint Arrows won the season championship by eight games and breezed through the post-season playoffs. The players are unidentified, but Manager Gene Desautels is in the center of the front row.

By 1951 the Central League, like most minor league operations in the country, was in a life or death struggle to survive. The parent Tigers had withdrawn their support and attendance plummeted, not just in Flint but in most of the other Central League cities. By the time the long summer season came to an end, the league was so desperately in debt that the playoffs were abandoned and the Central League was out of business. A pitiful season total of 25,900 fans trickled through the Atwood Stadium turnstiles to watch the last place Arrows play out the 1951 schedule. It was the end of a long journey for professional league baseball in Flint, but at least the city enjoyed a winning or contending team in five of its last six years in organized baseball. With the recent resurrection of minor league baseball in Michigan, rumors persist that the Vehicle City may soon be once again a member of a professional league.

Infielder/outfielder John "Bubba" Phillips went on to a solid 10-year career in the American League.

Little Clem "Scooter" Koshorek was Flint's shortstop for three of the four years in the CL. He later played with the Pittsburgh Pirates.

Flint product Steve Boros played in the majors for seven seasons from 1957 to 1965. He also managed at Oakland and San Diego in the 1980s.

53

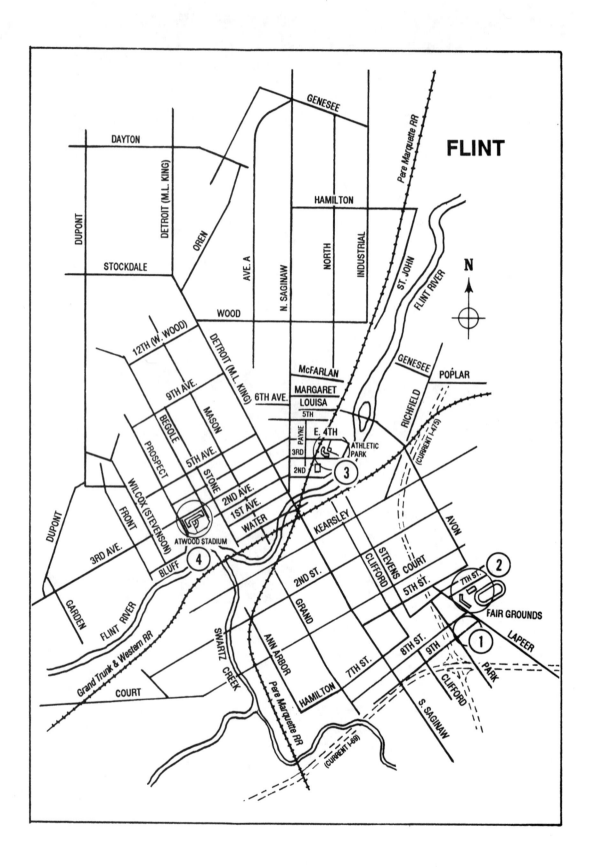

FLINT

THE PLAYING SITES

(1)

NINTH ST. GROUNDS 1889-90 (southeast section on 9th Street near Park & Lapeer Streets)

The only clues thus far uncovered regarding the precise location of this park indicate that it was on 9th Street in the city's Second Ward and donated by owner H. A. Thayer. The park was erected in early 1889 and included a grandstand seating 500 people. The grounds were officially dedicated in early June of that year.

(2)

FAIRGROUNDS 1897-1902-1906 (Genesee County Fairgrounds race track at 7th & Lapeer Streets)

As was common practice in many Michigan towns needing a suitable site for staging professional baseball games, Flint utilized the existing grandstand and race track infield of the Genesee County fairgrounds facility. According to newspaper reports in 1902, the grandstand was commodious and was supplemented by open bleachers on one side of the diamond to accommodate 400 to 500 additional spectators. Home plate was positioned directly in front of the main grandstand and the race track judges stand was reserved for reporters.

(3)

ATHLETIC PARK 1907-26 (downtown on the Flint River between 3rd & 4th Streets)

Flint inaugurated its new downtown baseball facility on May 14, 1907 as the city's new Southern Michigan League team lost to defending champion Mt. Clemens 6-3. A good crowd of over 2000 witnessed the historic event. Home plate and the horseshoe grandstand lie in the southwest corner of the property. Railroad tracks ran along the western edge of the park and the distant right field fence bordered the Flint River on the eastern end. The left field fence was less than 300 feet away along the foul line, but in every other direction the distances were enormous and well beyond the home run distance of even the mightiest of sluggers. Athletic Park served Flint league teams through 1926 and was the city's principal baseball park into the 1930s.

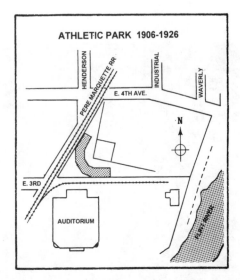

This photo purports to be at Athletic Park in 1908, but the configuration of the grandstand suggests it may actually be the earlier fairgrounds site.

BASE BALL

Base Ball
At Athletic Park
Tomorrow
Last year's Pennant Winners, SAGINAW
vs
FLINT
Game called at 3:00 P. M.
Admission 25 cents.

Above, a newspaper ad from 1909. At right, another ad urges Flint fans to attend the 1914 opener at Athletic Park.

OPENING DAY

Southern Michigan League

ADRIAN
VS.
FLINT
Athletic Park
Tomorrow, Tuesday, May 5th
Game Called 3:00 p. m.

Everybody will be at the game
Tomorrow—Come with the
Crowd and see Flint

WIN

Mayor J. R. MacDonald
Will Pitch
The First Ball

F. A. Allen, President
of the Board of Commerce
Will Catch
The First Ball

General Admission, 25 Cents
BOX AND RESERVED SEATS AT MAC'S CIGAR STORE.

An aerial view of downtown Flint looking northeast clearly shows Athletic Park in the top center of the photo.

ATWOOD STADIUM 1940-41, 1948-51 (on 3rd Avenue between Prospect and Begole, immediately north of the Flint River)

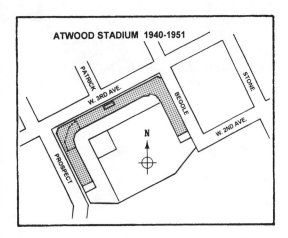

The multi-purpose, all concrete rectangular horseshoe stand was built in the 1930s to host baseball and home games for local high school football. For baseball, home plate was positioned in the northwest corner. In contrast to Athletic Park, the right field fence was a fairly short distance but it required a more gargantuan effort to deposit a baseball into the distant left field stands or over the fence in center field. Although seldom used for baseball in recent decades, Atwood Stadium is still in use for home football games of Flint Central, Flint Northern, and others.

Atwood Stadium, an all-purpose facility built during the 1930s, served as home for Flint baseball in the State League and Central League in the forties and fifties. It is still the city's principal home for football and is one of the state's oldest survivors of the professional league baseball years.

GRAND RAPIDS

PROFESSIONAL LEAGUE MEMBERSHIP

YEARS	LEAGUE	HOME FIELD
1883-84	Northwestern	Jefferson & Franklin Sts.
1889-90	Michigan State	Fountain St. Park (Sundays–Alger Park)
1890	International	Fountain St./Alger
1891	Northwestern	Fountain St./Alger
1894-97	Western	Recreation Park (Sundays–Alger Park)
1898-99	Interstate	Recreation Park (Sundays–Alger–'98)
1899	Western	Recreation Park
1900	International	Reeds Lake Park
1901	Western Assn.	Reeds Lake Park
1902	Michigan State	Reeds Lake Park
1903-17	Central	Reeds Lake ('03) Loyalty Park ('04-'09) Ramona Park (Sundays '04-'09, '12-'17) (weekdays '10-'11) Island Park ('12-'17)
1920-22	Central	Ramona Park
1923-24	Michigan-Ontario (MINT)	Ramona Park
1926	Central/Mich. State	Ramona Park
1934	Central	Ramona Park
1940-41	Michigan State	Bigelow Field
1945-54	AAGBL (Girls)	South Field ('45-'51) Bigelow Field ('52) South Field ('52-'54)
1948-51	Central	Bigelow Field
1994-	Midwest	Old Kent Park

Michigan's second city is the undisputed king of minor league baseball in the state. Dating back to the 1883 Northwestern League club on up to the currently successful West Michigan Whitecaps franchise, the Furniture City has always been represented whenever minor league baseball flourished in Michigan and very often at a higher class level than other traditional minor league towns in the state. Many players who wore the Grand Rapids uniform found their way to the majors and some even made it to baseball's Hall of Fame. The story of professional baseball in Grand Rapids is a book of its own and this summary of its historic role may not do it justice.

The first recognized professional minor league with Michigan representation was the Northwestern League of 1883-84. Grand Rapids, Bay City, and Saginaw were members of the eight-team loop that included cities in Ohio, Indiana, and Illinois. Elias Matter and I. M. Weston assembled a strong club which included future

big league stars Bob Caruthers and famed "Pretzel Battery" of pitcher Charles Getzein and catcher Ed Gastfield. Charles Eden and Henry Jones were the field leaders of the team which finished in 4th place with a 47-36 record. The following year the circuit over-extended itself to 12 teams and was unable to complete the season. When Grand Rapids withdrew on August 5, they were in the top spot with a 46-15 WL record. But with the league in shambles, it was a dubious claim for the championship and the city abstained from league baseball for the next four summers.

Charles Getzein was GR's star pitcher in 1883-84. He went on to a fine career in the NL, winning 29 for the Detroit champions of 1887.

Bob Caruthers had stops in GR at the beginning and end of his years in the majors— 1883 and 1894.

Their next venture in Organized Baseball came in 1889 when Frank Hine and George Leonard entered the city in the six-team Michigan State League. The league managed to complete the schedule and Grand Rapids finished a creditable third, eight games behind the leaders. The circuit re-grouped in 1890 and Grand Rapids was on top with a 17-8 record when they abruptly pulled out to join the higher class International League on June 10. Their departure spelled the end of the MSL and their new surroundings proved no panacea as the International League also collapsed a month later. Manager John Murphy's transplanted Buffalo franchise was one game out of the IL cellar when the floundering circuit went under. Determined to find its destiny in league baseball, the City of Grand Rapids in 1891 joined Detroit (two years removed from major league status) and Bay City in a revival of the old Northwestern League. The league secretary for the new edition of the eight-team circuit was one of the GR principals, Louis Heilbroner, who would later manage the local club in the 1904 Central League and would eventually preside over the same league in the latter years of its existence. John Murphy returned to manage the '91 NW team and led them directly into the cellar when the diminished circuit finally caved in on July 30. Despite the disappointing ending, GR's first baseman Breckenridge tore up league pitching with a .424 BA. The star hurler for the locals, Ted Breitenstein, went directly from Grand Rapids in 1891 to a solid 11-year career in the majors.

Frank Killen, twice a 30-game winner for Pittsburgh, pitched for Grand Rapids in 1890.

Ted Breitenstein went on from GR in 1891 to become one of the NL's best pitchers of the 1890s.

The Furniture City deferred further attempts at league baseball until 1894 when George E. "Deacon" Ellis joined Ban Johnson's new Western League along with Detroit. The GR "Rustlers," as they were first nicknamed, found a home in a fairly solid league for the next four years. Unfortunately, Ellis was unable to assemble a competitive team in his three seasons at the helm as the Grand Rapids entry plummeted to the league basement in 1895 and 1896 with pitiful gate receipts the result. The 1894 team managed to play .500 ball with a stable of talented players like Harley Parker, Bob Caruthers, Rasty Wright, Bumpus Jones, Bobby Wheelock, and Billy Rhines but it was all downhill after that. The Deacon, who later became the city's mayor, finally had to sell out to Bob Leadley and Bob Glenalvin in 1897. The Leadley/Glenalvin combine fared no better as once again the "Bobolinks" (a name derived from the new owners' given names) finished in the WL cellar, 63 games out of

first place. The '97 Bobs did showcase some popular stars, including Jimmy Slagle, Count Campau, and John Ganzell. Slagle became an outfielder on the great Chicago Cub dynasty ten years later. Big "Jawn" Ganzell also followed with a noteworthy professional career as a player and manager in Grand Rapids and elsewhere.

Charles "Lady" Baldwin, a 42-game winner for Detroit in 1886, was on the 1894 GR Western League club.

The colorful and talented "Count" Campau hit .303 for Grand Rapids in 1897.

One of several brothers in pro baseball, Michigan native John Ganzell played with, managed, and owned teams in GR beginning in the 1890s. He was easily the most revered baseball figure of his time in the Furniture City. He also had some fine years in the big leagues.

Deacon Ellis' 1894 Western League team finished fifth, their best showing in their four years in the WL. STANDING (L to R): Spies, Wright, Carroll, Jones. SEATED: Egan, Parker, Mgr. Ellis, Rhines, George, Wheelock, Callopy. BOTTOM: Capt. Caruthers.

Greenville's Charles Hemphill played on Grand Rapids' 1898-99 Interstate League clubs.

George "Deacon" Ellis sponsored Grand Rapids' entry into the new Western League in 1894. Unfortunately, the Deacon's teams were cellar-dwellers and he finally gave it up in 1897. Ellis did not win many ball games but he did win many friends in Grand Rapids and he became the city's mayor a few years later.

Pitcher Nick Altrock, later a star of the '06 White Sox "hitless wonders" and one of baseball's noted clowns, made a "pit stop" in GR in 1898.

The great Rube Waddell was a member of Loftus' 1899 WL club that transferred to Grand Rapids.

Four years of frustration forced Grand Rapids out of the Western League after 1897, but Clifford A. Mitts and Frank Torreyson kept baseball of the league variety alive by entering the Furniture City in the Interstate League of 1898. New manager Torreyson signed future big leaguers Nick Altrock, Charles Hemphill (from nearby Greenville), Topsy Hartsel, and Jiggs Donahue and finished a respectable fifth place in the new league. The "Cabinet Makers" under Torreyson resumed Interstate League play in 1899, but a disastrous start soon turned GR fans against Torreyson and he took his franchise to Columbus, Ohio on July 19. In an odd turn of events, the current Columbus club of the Western League under Tom Loftus simultaneously transferred operations to Grand Rapids. In effect, the two cities swapped leagues and franchises without skipping a beat. The peculiar exchange was fortuitous for Grand Rapids as they were suddenly reinstated in the higher class Western League with a bumper crop of outstanding player personnel. Loftus' "Prodigals" finished fourth, but gave Grand Rapids fans a "blue-ribbon" roster of future big league stars to root for. Heading the list were pitcher Rube Waddell and outfielder "Wahoo Sam" Crawford, both destined for baseball immortality in Cooperstown's Hall of Fame. Other future stars on that club included Captain George Tebeau, Louis Bierbauer, Ollie Pickering, Frank Eustice, "Bumpus" Jones, "Frenchy" Genins, and Billy Sullivan. Local baseball fans would relish recollections of this galaxy of baseball names for years afterward.

Tom Loftus brought a galaxy of star players to GR in 1899 when he relocated his Columbus WL club here.

19-year-old "Wahoo Sam" Crawford was just beginning his Hall of Fame career when he entertained GR fans in 1899 with Loftus' WL team.

By 1900 Ban Johnson's Western League changed its name to the American League and made grandiose plans to invade the abandoned markets of the scaled-down National League. This strategy forced Grand Rapids, with its limited fan base, out of the AL landscape and once again former Interstate mogul Clifford Mitts came forward with a GR franchise in the Class B International League of 1900. It was another

Louis Bierbauer of the '99 WL team had just completed a fine 13-year career in the majors.

Shortstop Ed Holly was a fan favorite on GR's 1900 International League team. Holly later played for the St. Louis Cardinals and the Pittsburgh Federals.

One-time big league mound star Jouett Meekin helped GR capture the Western Assn. flag in 1901.

Gus Hoff was one of Dickerson's prize hurlers on the ill-fated State League team of 1902.

Emerson Dickerson was a player and manager on GR baseball teams at the turn of the century. He was also a sportswriter and a patriarch of many baseball leagues in Michigan for several decades.

six-team circuit with a mix of Michigan and Ontario towns. Mr. Mitts' "Boers" played their games on a new site at Reeds Lake but were unable to generate much fan interest in a lower class of league baseball. The Boers were in 2nd place when they finally ceased operations on June 25. The league itself was history by July 4.

Deacon Ellis and W. C. Chinnick were determined to keep the city in Organized Baseball and assembled yet another minor league franchise for the Western Association of 1901. The "Colts" lineup included one of the famed Delahanty brothers as well as veteran hurler Billy Rhines, the ex-big leaguer who had been a GR favorite with the 1894 WL club. In another peculiar "switch" reminiscent of 1899, the Colts abandoned Grand Rapids for Wheeling, WV but within a month the city was right back in the Western Association when Walter Wilmot's first-place Louisville club transferred operations to the Furniture City. Once again, after a month without league baseball, Wilmot brought winning baseball back to Grand Rapids as the new franchise captured the league championship by a narrow margin over runner-up Dayton (OH). The new roster featured former New York Giants' pitching ace Jouett Meekin, local West Michigan favorite "Kid" Luther, and future big league umpire Billy Evans. The pennant claim was hotly disputed by Dayton and Toledo over a controversial win by GR late in the season, but at least the city could savor a winning combination after a decade of mostly losing teams.

The Western Association did not return in 1902, but local newspaperman and baseball enthusiast Emerson Dickerson collaborated with G. E. Morrison to set up a revived version of the Michigan State League. Morrison was picked as president of the league and partner Dickerson would play, manage, and captain the Grand Rapids team. The six-team circuit included Battle Creek, Saginaw (later Jackson), Flint, Muskegon, and Lansing. The new league was cursed from the start by unfavorable weather plus numerous other problems including shady management, resistance to Sunday baseball, mediocre umpiring, unstable player rosters, etc. Dickerson, one of the architects of the league, was eventually the catalyst in the loop's demise as he abruptly withdrew his forlorn Colts on July 20. Saginaw transferred its franchise to Jackson and the State League limped along into late August until it finally folded. "Dick" did not endear himself to other member cities as he reacted childishly to all negative developments involving his last place club. His antics left a bad taste everywhere, but in later years he mellowed and matured to become the patriarch of baseball programs in West Michigan.

No more league ventures were planned for Grand Rapids in 1903, but the city was too good a baseball town to be left neglected by the professional leagues. The class B Central League came courting in late May of that year when their Anderson, IN franchise was threatening to fold. President and Manager McVey Lindsay agreed to relocate his last place team to Grand Rapids and once again the city was on the minor league map. It was a dreadful team to inherit but after a shake-up in ownership, Grand Rapids was in line to become a full-fledged Central League member for the 1904 season. The real highlight of the 1903 season came on Sunday May 24 when the Detroit Tigers defeated the Washington Senators 5-4 at Reeds Lake Park. This was not an exhibition game but an official game that counted in the standings—the only time a major league contest was played in Michigan outside the Detroit area. The Tigers had planned on more Sunday dates in Grand Rapids that summer (Sunday games were still forbidden in the City of Detroit) but the sudden arrival of the Central League team required the use of Reeds Lake by the local club.

A. H. Collins was the new owner of the GR Central League franchise for 1904, and an old familiar name, Louis Heilbroner, was the new field manager. Heilbroner's crew fared poorly and when the season closed, the locals were in last place (actually 7th, but 8th place Evansville withdrew before the season ended). Another Grand Rapids favorite, John Ganzell, took the reins in 1905 and guided the locals to a third-place finish. Ganzell held down first base on the team while pitcher Walter Miller contributed 24 victories. Brother Joe Ganzell, Lansing's John Morrissey, and John "Lefty" Geyer were other standouts on the '05 club. The following year (1906), Ganzell's charges ran away with the Central League flag, winning 99 games and finishing eight full games ahead of runnerup Springfield. Big "Jawn" Ganzell had another fine season with the bat, hitting .323 with 13 home runs. Ganzell's boys were the toast of the town, giving Grand Rapids their first undisputed championship in many years.

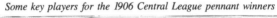

Some key players for the 1906 Central League pennant winners

GR's Burt Farrell threw a no-hitter vs. Wheeling in 1904.

| outfielder Lefty Geyer (.292) | pitcher Ed Van Anda (23-13) | pitcher Ed Summers (21-10) | pitcher Elmer Bliss (19 wins) |

Owner/manager/first baseman John Ganzell's 1906 Central League champions. TOP ROW (L to R): Backof, Bliss, Miller, Summers, Geyer, Curtis, Van Anda. MIDDLE ROW: Warner, Howley, part owner Phil Arnold, Manager Ganzell, Groeschow, Graham. BOTTOM: Hawkins, Francis, Smith.

Phil Arnold was the new owner for 1907, as John Ganzell returned to the major leagues with Cincinnati. New manager Elmer Bliss fared no better than 7th place and was succeeded in 1908 by veteran major leaguer Bobby Lowe. Lowe's club also finished in the second division. The local hero during these years was the speedy Bert Noblett. Arnold finally sold the franchise to Charles F. Brotherton and the 1909 club under Manager Joe Raidy moved up to a 4th place finish. The most memorable moment in 1909 at Ramona Park occurred on July 7 when Zanesville and Grand Rapids played an exhibition game at night under an experimental lighting system. The contest was a qualified success as over 4500 fans, including Mayor Deacon Ellis and other notables, watched the locals pull out an 11-10 victory. It was a truly historic occasion as scheduled night baseball was still over 20 years into the future.

The 1910 Central Leaguers once again changed hands as Bert Annis became the new owner. Joe Raidy returned as pilot and the team returned to the second division. Dr. Harley Parker, an old GR favorite from the 1894 Western League club, was also part owner and field manager of the 1911 "Graduates." For the third time, Grand Rapids engineered another weird exchange of franchises during the 1911 CL season. Parker's team relocated to Newark on June 27 and on July 14 the South Bend club in turn transferred to the Furniture City. The first franchise was in 6th place when it left town and the 2nd franchise finished 4th. Some local favorites during this odd season were outfielder Donald "Lefty" Core and pitcher "Vinegar Bill" Essick. Bert Annis was back as owner in 1912 and his first priority was to relocate to a new ballpark closer in to the central city for weekday games. Island Park became the new primary home for 1912 under pitcher/part owner/manager Ed Smith. Smith's "Black Sox" finished deep in the second division but featured some outstanding stars, namely slugging outfielder Larry LeJeune with 25 HRs and a .361 BA and future big league pitcher Jeff Pfeffer. Over the following winter the team was purchased outright by Ed Smith and pitcher Bill Essick.

Bert Noblett was a fan favorite in GR from 1907-09.

Famed major leaguer Bobby Lowe (on left) became GR manager in 1908. His team could do no better than sixth place. STANDING (L to R): Mgr. Lowe, Holmquist, Warner, Noblett, Francis, Backof, Gill, Geyer. KNEELING: Dickson, Sterzer, Kipp, Hausen. BOTTOM: Betts, Hagerman, Breen, Kelly.

Ed Smith was a pitcher, manager, and part owner of the GR Black Sox in the teens.

One-time Cincinnati Red hurler Bill Essick pitched for the 1911 team and became team owner in 1913.

New owners Smith and Essick assembled the finest Grand Rapids ball team in many years for the 1913 season. Back were Core, LeJeune, and Pfeffer as they sparked the '13 club to a 92-48 record, finishing a full 15 games up on second place Fort Wayne. With a pennant-winning club to represent it, Grand Rapids was the pride of the Central League and its position as a solid minor league town seemed secure indeed. "Vinegar Bill" Essick became sole owner and manager by 1914 and gave Grand Rapids fans quality baseball for the next four summers. The Black Sox slipped to 5th place in 1914 but surged back into contention with a runner-up finish in 1915. On June 25, Ty Cobb and his Detroit Tigers treated Island Park fans to an exhibition of big league baseball, defeating the Black Sox 6-4.

Grand Rapids' 15-year run in the Central League came to a grand climax in 1917. Because of the great war, the league suspended operations for 1918, but Essick's boys had another grand summer as they took the 1917 regular season flag by six games over Springfield. To add icing to the cake, they defeated South Bend in the playoffs in dramatic fashion. After losing the first three games and facing elimination, they stormed back with four straight victories to assert their league supremacy. Eddington and DeVormer were back from the '16 club with productive seasons but the fine pitching of Faeth (20-8) and Jess Carpenter (23-10) were the key contributors. The thrills of that final season stayed with local fans for the next two years as they awaited a revival of the Central League in 1920.

Grand Rapids' own Emerson Dickerson became president of the Central League in 1916 and was instrumental in bringing nearby Muskegon into the circuit as Michigan's second representative CL town. The league opted for a split season format to determine post-season playoff opponents in 1916 and this formula deprived the Grand Rapids club of a pennant. The Black Sox, or "Billberts" as they were sometimes called, actually compiled the best overall won-loss record but finished second in both halves. Key players during this period were outfielder Frank Eddington, pitcher "Dixie" McArthur, and catcher Al DeVormer, a Grand Rapids lad. DeVormer later had a brief journeyman's career in the big leagues.

GR Catholic Central graduate Wally Pipp came from a baseball family and was arguably the city's finest ball player. He played for Kalamazoo in 1912 and from there became one of the premier first basemen in the big leagues from 1913 to 1928.

Grand Rapids native Al DeVormer caught for the 1916-17 CL teams and advanced to a journeyman's career in the big leagues. He later resurfaced as an umpire in the Michigan State League of 1940.

During the winter of 1919-20, Emerson Dickerson was unable to convince former Central League clubs to abandon their new league affiliations of 1918-19 to resurrect the old Ohio-Indiana-Michigan flavor of the reborn Central League. Undaunted, "Dick" nevertheless convinced Kalamazoo, Ludington, and Muskegon to form an all-Michigan four-team edition of the CL along with Grand Rapids. Hopefully, the out-of-state towns would be persuaded to come back into the fold in subsequent years, but it never happened.

William T. "Bill" Morrissey was the president of the 1920 GR entry and one of John McGraw's ex-New York Giant stars, Josh DeVore, was named manager. DeVore, still in his early 30s, was also an active outfielder and hit .344 in leading Grand Rapids to the 1920 CL pennant. The "Joshers" presented an impressive array of talent, led by a solid pitching rotation of Ross, Gyer, and Charmichael. Infielder Lance Richbourg was the leading hitter in all professional baseball that summer with a spectacular .416 average in 87 games. Leo "Doc" Payne and Mgr. DeVore's brother Harry (playing under the name Carey) also contributed to the team's 76-50 WL record. The four-team circuit was a financial success and Dickerson was eager to add more cities for 1921. Still unable to recruit out-of-state towns into the Central League, Jackson and Lansing were added to make it a six-team race for 1921. Manager DeVore returned and had another good year with the bat, hitting .355 in 57 games. But the 1921 team sagged to 5th place and Josh was replaced by Louis Wolf before the season ended.

For 1922, owner Bill Morrissey hired veteran minor league catcher Bob Wells as the new field manager and from this combination the new team nickname "Billbobs" was selected. The Billbobs and the Ludington Mariners emerged as the class of the league, each winning a half of the split-season. The best-of-9 post season playoff went to Grand Rapids 5 games to 3. The key to the Billbobs' success was the signing of Ludington's 1921 ace hurler Bill Shoup, who gave Grand Rapids a 20-15 season. The ace of the Billbobs' staff was 20-game winner Wilcy Moore, the Central League's top pitcher of 1922. Moore later starred on the mighty New York Yankee teams of the late twenties. The new batting hero was outfielder Leo "Doc" Payne, who was the circuit's top hitter with a lofty .370 average. Catcher/manager Wells chipped in with a .361 season at the bat.

Outfielder Doc Payne was Grand Rapids' top slugger from 1920 to 1924.

W. T. Morrissey was president of the new GR franchise in the 1920 Central League.

Former NY Giant outfielder Josh DeVore led GR to a 1920 pennant.

Lance Richbourg was all of the minor league's top hitter in 1920 with a .416 average.

Josh's brother Harry also played for GR teams in the early '20s under the name Harry Carey.

Grand Rapids foiled Ludington's bid to repeat as CL champs in '22 by signing their best '21 pitcher, Bill Shoup, who won 20 for GR.

Righthander Wilcy Moore was a big winner for GR in 1922. He later starred for some great New York Yankee teams in the late '20s and early '30s.

Over the winter of 1922-23, Flint's T. J. Halligan took over the rival class B Michigan-Ontario (MINT) League and persuaded Grand Rapids, Kalamazoo, and Muskegon to abandon the Central League and enter the MINT circuit. GR owner Morrissey retained Bobby Wells as manager and also re-signed most of the key position players from the '22 CL champs. Returning were Jimmy "Speeds" Walker, Howard Pennington, and popular slugger Doc Payne, who appeared in only 41 games but ripped up MINT League pitching with a .442 percentage. But 1922 pitching aces Shoup and Moore were gone and the 1923 Billbobs were unable to finish higher than 7th in the MINT standings. Grand Rapids favorite Josh DeVore returned to pilot the 1924 GR MINT Leaguers, now called "Homoners." Once again, Doc Payne feasted on MINT pitchers with a league-leading .397 average but the Homoners could do no better than 6th place in the final league standings. The two-year run of MINT baseball was top-notch and furnished many outstanding players to the majors and higher minors, but overall the circuit was a losing proposition. Grand Rapids, Muskegon, and Kalamazoo were too far distant to make travel costs manageable and all three dropped out after the 1924 season. Grand Rapids sat out the 1925 season, but in 1926 Emerson Dickerson recruited

Ludington, Muskegon, and Kalamazoo to join GR in a restoration of the four-team Central League of 1920. With a lower class C rating, the new loop had more modest ambitions, but public response was poor in all four towns. Meanwhile, Halligan's MINT League was also hurting with only four Michigan cities left, so both leagues decided to merge and make a fresh start as the Michigan State League. The new alignment managed to finish out the schedule, but poor patronage spelled curtains for the latest version of the State League. Manager Pat Devereaux' GR club finished fourth with outfielder Joe Shields hitting .352 and future big league hurler Milt Shoffner winning 10 games. The area's appetite for minor league ball had faded badly by this time and it would be well into the next decade before the waters would be tested again.

Despite the woes of the Great Depression, Emerson Dickerson made yet another attempt to get Grand Rapids back into Organized Baseball in 1934 with a new edition of the Central League. Wally Wolgamot was the choice as manager and the team was 11-13 when the league collapsed on June 10. This ill-fated league adventure produced only one GR player of note, that being pitcher Claude Passeau, who had an outstanding career in the National League. The 1934 Central Leaguers would be the last GR pro team to play at aging Ramona Park. One of the city's biggest boosters of the national game, Clarence E. Bigelow, was at work arranging for a more up-to-date baseball facility on South Division. The new park opened in 1937 and was aptly named Bigelow Field.

Bert Grimm was 16-10 for the 1923 GR MINT Leaguers.

George Quellich   Joe Heving

Two of GR's key players in 1924. Both advanced to the big leagues.

Grand Rapids participated in Emerson Dickerson's short-lived attempt to revive the Central League in 1934. Wally Wolgamot (on left) was manager. Other team members included (L to R): Dick Hosinski, Albert Morse, Jim Stevenson, Jim Minogue, and Claude Passeau. Only Passeau advanced to the majors as a top-flight pitcher for three NL clubs.

With the economy finally rebounding from its lengthy doldrums in the late thirties, serious talks were underway in 1939 regarding the formation of a class C version of the Michigan State League. With the backing of major league clubs, the new league began play in 1940 with six Michigan towns as members. Former GR owner Bill Morrissey lined up the Brooklyn Dodgers as a parent club and former pitching great Burleigh Grimes was assigned by Brooklyn to pilot the cast of young Dodger prospects. One of Morrissey's partners in the venture was H. W. MacPhail, a Michigan banker who happened to be a brother of Dodger executive Larry MacPhail. Grimes' tenure in Grand Rapids was short-lived as he was expelled in July for spitting in an umpire's face. Interim Manager Ducky Holmes led the Colts to a 4th place finish and a quick elimination in the post-season playoffs. Red Lucas was the new pilot for 1941 and took the team to third place. The standouts on the '41 club were pitcher Tom Hamill (15-9, 188 K's) and infielders Ed Moore (.350 BA), and Clarence Etchison (.325). The advent of World War II put the new State League out of business for the duration.

The Grand Rapids "Dodger Colts" infield of 1940 (L to R): Jim "Doc" McLoud 1B, Jimmy Cooney SS, Joe WoJey 2B, Bob Ogle 3B.

The war years gave Grand Rapids an entirely different brand of professional baseball—the All-American Girls Professional Baseball League (AAGPBL). Started by Cubs owner P. K. Wrigley in 1943 as a wartime substitute for men's minor league baseball, the AAGPBL transferred its Milwaukee Chicks franchise to the Furniture City for the 1945 season. The operation was a big success, especially in the early years, and lasted 10 seasons here. The Chicks were always competitive and gave the city three playoff championships during its stay in Grand Rapids. The girls team played mostly at South Field but moved into Bigelow Field when the men's team left. Outstanding stars for the GR Chicks over the years were Connie Wisniewski, Thelma Eisen, Merle Keagle, Ruth Lessing, Mildred Earp, Alice Haylett, and Alma "Gabby" Zeigler.

Connie Wisniewski was one of the AAGBL's superstars. She spent her entire career with the Milwaukee/Grand Rapids Chicks.

In 1948, minor league baseball of the men's variety returned to Grand Rapids with the formation of the class A Central League. Oscar Salenger was the president of the new CL "Jets," who had a working agreement with Sacramento of the AAA Pacific Coast League. Vice-president Milt Galatzer began the season as field manager, but gave way to former State League pilot Jack Knight. The Sacramento connection proved to be disappointing as the needed talent to contend was not forthcoming. The Jets finished dead last in team batting as well as in the final standings. The most memorable player from the hapless '48 Jets was outfielder Dave Hoskins, who hit .393 in 46 games. Hoskins eventually made it to the Cleveland Indians as a pitcher in 1953-54. The 1949 Jets, again managed by Jack Knight, found some decent talent and made the post-season playoffs with a third-place finish. They "ambushed" a strong Flint club in the semi-finals then disposed of Charleston to claim the 1949 league championship. Slugging first-sacker Ev Robinson's contribution was a big factor in the Jets' improved status in 1949 and he became a mainstay in Grand Rapids for two more seasons. The pitching staff of Larry King, Gene Costello, Sanford Lambert, Lou Prempas, and Mel Waters was also a big improvement over 1948. Knight's 1950 club dropped a notch to 4th and then succumbed to league champion Flint in the first round of the playoffs. The final season of 1951 was a total disaster for Grand Rapids and for

First baseman Everett Robinson was a Jet favorite from 1949-51.

1950 opening game action—the Grand Rapids Jets vs. Dayton Indians at Bigelow Field.

most of the Michigan-based member cities. Knight's entourage barely escaped the league basement and a pitiful total of 21,230 paid their way into Bigelow Field during the entire summer of 1951. But all minor leagues were suffering catastrophic gate receipts mainly caused by the advent of television and the Central League was only one of many who were forced to cease operations. It would be another 40 years before any minor league would dare consider Michigan as a viable place to locate a franchise. The lasting stigma of the 1948-51 Central League experience was finally broken in 1994 when professional baseball made a triumphant return to Grand Rapids.

During the long interlude without a professional league team, some very good amateur and semi-pro teams entertained Grand Rapids baseball fans. The most memorable were Ted Rasberry's black teams and the Sullivans, organized by local businessman and baseball enthusiast Bob Sullivan. The Sullivans were the cream of the semi-pro United Baseball League and also claimed several national semi-pro championships. The primary home fields in this era were Valley Field on the west side and Wyoming's Kimball Field. Sullivan owned a furniture store but also played and managed his own team and was a scout for the Detroit Tigers. Among the many GR area players who found their way to the big show were Jimmy Command, Phil Regan, Mickey Stanley, Dave Rozema, Rick Miller, and John Vanderwall.

Even after minor league baseball experienced a steady resurgence in popularity throughout the USA in the 1970s and 80s, Michigan was shunned as a likely territory for new franchises. New stadiums, new marketing techniques, and stronger support by an expanding number of major league clubs made the prospects for success more likely. Even so, Michigan was a hard sell even for a rare survivor of the lean years of the minors like the Midwest League. But two local entrepreneurs with a passionate dream, Lew Chamberlain and Denny Baxter, were determined to somehow bring professional baseball back to Grand Rapids. At great personal risk, the two men

waged a long struggle to organize financial support and solicit a commitment to build a brand new ballpark in the Grand Rapids area. The Midwest League was their logical target and the two partners got a foothold in the league by purchasing franchise rights to the defunct Wausau (WI) Timbers in 1989. The franchise was eventually relocated to Kane County, Illinois where it was a tremendous financial success, leading all class A clubs in attendance in its first year.

But Chamberlain and Baxter were still fixed on the Grand Rapids goal and eventually gathered enough financial backing to persuade Old Kent Bank to underwrite a new state-of-the-art park on the Grand River just north of the city. The next step was to purchase the troubled Madison (WI) Muskies franchise and relocate the team to Grand Rapids to become the West Michigan Whitecaps. In 1994 the dream finally became reality as the Whitecaps began play as the first minor league team in the state since 1951. Still considered a huge financial gamble, the Whitecaps exceeded the hopes of even their more optimistic supporters by drawing almost a half-million fans into Old Kent Park in their first year. Now in their third season of operation, the phenomenal attendance continues to grow and solidify the state as a prime location for the rebirth of minor league baseball in other cities like Battle Creek, Lansing, and Kalamazoo.

The Whitecaps logo was designed to attract a West Michigan following.

Managing partner Lew Chamberlin helped bring minor league baseball back to the state of Michigan after an absence of over 40 years.

Former big league pitcher Jim Colborn was chosen as the first manager of the Whitecaps, a class A farm club of the Oakland A's.

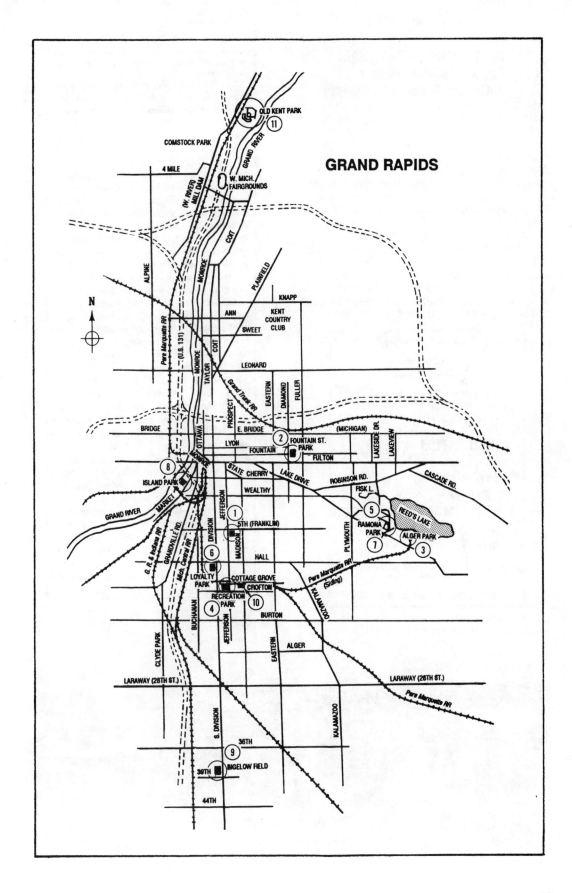

GRAND RAPIDS

OLD KENT PARK

COMSTOCK PARK

(11)

GRAND RIVER

4 MILE

W. MICH. FAIRGROUNDS

W. RIVER MILL DAM

ALPINE

MONROE

COIT

PLAINFIELD

KNAPP

ANN

SWEET

KENT COUNTRY CLUB

Pere Marquette RR

(U.S. 131)

MONROE

TAYLOR

COIT

LEONARD

PROSPECT

Grand Trunk RR

EASTERN

DIAMOND

FULLER

BRIDGE

OTTAWA

E. BRIDGE

LYON

FOUNTAIN

(2) FOUNTAIN ST. PARK

(MICHIGAN)

LAKESIDE DR.

LAKEVIEW

FULTON

STATE

CHERRY

LAKE DRIVE

ROBINSON RD.

CASCADE RD.

(8)

MONROE

ISLAND PARK

MARKET

WEALTHY

JEFFERSON

FISK L.

REED'S LAKE

GRAND RIVER

GRANDVILLE RD.

DIVISION

(1)

5TH (FRANKLIN)

(5)

RAMONA PARK

ALGER PARK

(3)

G. R. & Indiana RR

Mich. Central RR

MADISON

HALL

PLYMOUTH

(7)

(6)

LOYALTY PARK

COTTAGE GROVE

CROFTON

Pere Marquette RR (Siding)

RECREATION PARK

(10)

BUCHANAN

(4)

JEFFERSON

BURTON

KALAMAZOO

EASTERN

ALGER

CLYDE PARK

LARAWAY (28TH ST.)

LARAWAY (28TH ST.)

Pere Marquette RR

S. DIVISION

36TH

(9)

39TH

BIGELOW FIELD

KALAMAZOO

44TH

N

THE PLAYING SITES

① **GRAND RAPIDS BASE BALL PARK 1883-84 (corner Jefferson & Franklin Streets)**

The "Base Ball Park" was formally opened in September 1882 with an exhibition game between the GR independent team and the Detroit Wolverines of the National League. Originally called Recreation Park, the name was soon changed to a more generic Base Ball Park. The site of this ballpark was on the southeast corner of Jefferson and Franklin (then 5th Street). Newspaper accounts indicate a grandstand and bleachers holding roughly 1000 spectators plus, with a "freeloaders" view occupying a woody bluff east of the park near Madison Street. A high board fence surrounded the field. The main grandstand occupied the northwest corner of the lot and a long open bleacher extended along the third base side parallel to 5th (Franklin) Street.

An 1883 newspaper ad promotes Northwestern League baseball at the new ballpark.

BASE BALL.

The Opening of the New Recreation Park
—The Finest Game Ever Seen Here—Miscellaneous.

The long-expected and much-talked-of event, the opening of the new base ball grounds or Recreation Park, at the southeast corner of Fifth and Jefferson avenues occurred yesterday afternoon, and proved a brilliant success. The new grounds are not yet fully completed, but were sufficiently finished to admit of the playing of the most brilliant and exciting game of base ball ever seen in this city. The new grounds are ample in extent, even though an occasional foul ball or foul tip may find its way over the fences and outside the grounds. They are well laid out for the public to see the games that may be played on them, and though an afternoon sun will sometimes—as was the case once in the left field yesterday—interfere with the fielders, the grounds on the whole, are well located. The grand stand is exceedingly cosy and admirably located to give spectators a full view of the entire play. The left or north side of the stand is to be reserved for the use of ladies and their escorts. The grounds have been leveled, very nicely, but have not yet been sodded or seeded. The infield is to be sodded as soon as possible and the outfield will be either sodded or seeded. The grounds will be connected with the city by telephone, and the South Division Street Railway Company will run a branch track through Fifth avenue directly to the entrances, a double track branch, making the grounds particularly convenient for spectators to reach. No city in the country will have grounds better located or more convenient and admirable, next season, than will Grand Rapids.

The Grand Rapids Eagle of Sept. 12, 1882, provided a vivid description of the city's new Baseball Park.

A rare photograph of the baseball park at Jefferson & Franklin shows a game in progress between Grand Rapids and Saginaw—probably 1883.

<table>
<tr><td>

②

</td><td>

FOUNTAIN ST. PARK 1889-91 (on Diamond St. NE where Fountain intersects)

</td></tr>
</table>

No known photos or diagrams of this park are known to exist. The Baxter Laundry occupied the site after the ballpark was dismantled.

③

ALGER PARK (Sundays 1889-99) (on south shore of Reeds Lake—east of Ramona Park)

No detailed information has been found on Alger Park. It was never a primary home field for professional teams—used for Sunday dates only. It was believed to be near the end of the old Pere Marquette railroad spur which angled toward the southern shore of Reeds Lake. When Reeds Lake Park was built in 1900, Alger Park had already been abandoned as a Sunday site for league baseball.

BASE BALL
INTERNATIONAL LEAGUE.
ALGER PARK.
SAGINAW-BAY CITY VS. GR'ND RAPIDS
SUNDAY, JUNE 6, 4 P. M.
Admission, 25 cents.   Grand stand 15 cents.

An 1890 newspaper ad for a Sunday game at Alger Park

④

RECREATION PARK 1894-99 (on north side of Cottage Grove SE—between Jefferson and S. Division)

Recreation Park was the home field for GR Western & Interstate League teams from 1894 up to 1900. The grounds lie basically east and west with home plate and the main grandstand on the west and dead center field to the east. The playing field was wedged in on the north by railroad tracks and on the south by Cottage Grove Street. Distances down the foul lines were short, resulting in numerous "cheap" home runs, while the centerfield fence was an enormous distance from home plate. The afternoon sun had to be treacherous for outfielders, especially in left and center field since they faced west. The grandstand was dismantled and re-assembled for the new Reeds Lake Park in 1900. The Macey factory later occupied the site immediately west, on Division Street.

⑤

REEDS LAKE PARK 1900-03 (on west shore of Reeds Lake immediately south of the Amusement Park)

One of the most intriguing and least documented of Grand Rapids' baseball parks, Reeds Lake Park was built by team owner Clifford A. Mitts after unsatisfactory terms were offered for use of Recreation Park, particularly its unavailability for Sunday baseball. Vague newspaper clues suggest that the grandstand was positioned in the southeast corner of the property used by its immediate successor Ramona Park—in the area of what would be the left field corner of Ramona. Or possibly it may have been located slightly to the west of the Ramona location. In any case, we know it contained the usual grandstand and bleacher combination with a seating capacity of roughly 2000. An unusual feature of the park when it opened was the "backward" combination of a grass infield and dirt outfield. The park's most glorious day as a baseball facility occurred on May 24, 1903 when the Detroit Tigers played an official American League game vs. the Washington Senators. The park's brief existence came to an end in 1904 when the new Ramona Park ballgrounds were built on the same property.

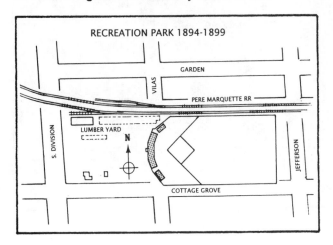

A 1901 newspaper ad for a Western Assn. game at Reeds Lake Park

LOYALTY PARK 1904-1911 (corner of Hall & Ionia Sts. SW)

With distant Ramona Park available in 1904 for Sunday dates, GR owner A. H. Collins found a more central location for weekday games at the corner of Hall and South Ionia Streets. The main grandstand and home plate were placed in the northwest corner of the lot. An ample parking lot for buggies and automobiles was located on the northeast corner of the property. Bleachers were provided along both foul lines and a press box was built on the grandstand roof. Unlike its predecessor, Recreation Park, distances from home plate to the steel fence around the outfield were ample enough to prevent an over-abundance of "cheap" home run drives. Enough seating for 2000 people was furnished by the grandstand and two bleacher sections. Owner Collins' indebtedness almost forced the franchise into bankruptcy early into the 1904 season, but investors from Terre Haute and Fort Wayne rescued the operation and made further improvements to the grounds. The first base bleachers were expanded and bathrooms and dressing rooms added under the main grandstand. The playing field was brought up to league standards with a sprinkler system added. In 1905 flags to represent the member cities of the Central League were erected on the grandstand roof.

RAMONA PARK 1904-34 (on west shore of Reeds Lake)

The need for a suitable location for Sunday games, frowned upon in the City of Grand Rapids, encouraged the City of East Grand Rapids to erect a modern baseball facility to replace the inadequate Reeds Lake Park in the summer of 1904. Professional baseball games attracted good crowds and complemented the resort-amusement park atmosphere at Reeds Lake. Because of its distance from the central city, Ramona Park was utilized only for Sunday dates (except in 1910-11) by the Central League teams in the early years. But it was always well maintained as a first-class baseball facility and eventually became the everyday home park for Grand Rapids league teams by the 1920s. The proliferation of automobiles and improved streets offset the earlier inconvenience of distance for local fans and the growing popularity of the Reeds Lake recreational complex made Ramona Park a desirable permanent home for local baseball after the demise of Island Park. By the 1930s, when the aging facility was home for the ill-fated Central League club, the old ballpark and its resort surroundings had begun to lose its appeal and its days were numbered. If league baseball were to return to Grand Rapids, a new ballpark in a different location was needed.

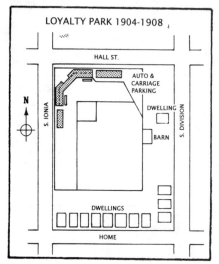

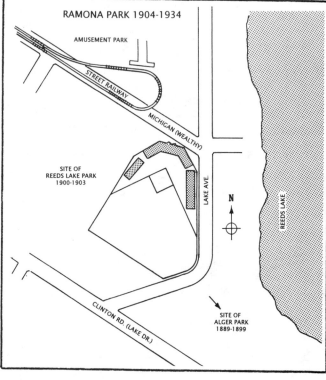

72

A fine aerial photo of Ramona Park on the shore of Reeds Lake. The adjacent amusement park can be seen on the left.

The new grandstand as it looked in 1904

The magnificent main entrance to the grandstand

The historic night game experiment at Ramona Park on July 7, 1909—Grand Rapids vs. Zanesville

ISLAND PARK 1912-17 (on the Grand River, off Market St. at the Williams St. intersection)

With the dismantling of Loyalty Park, another downtown location was needed for weekday games of the 1912 Central League team. Ramona Park was an ideal site for Sunday games, but too remote to attract a following from local fandom on weekday afternoons. Owner Bert Annis made arrangements with the city to rent the new ballgrounds located on the river within walking distance of downtown. The property was adjacent to the old city market site which was originally on an island, hence the name Island Park. The grandstand was on the north end of the field and a lengthy bleacher section extended down the third base line. The park officially opened on May 2, 1912 with Mayor Deacon Ellis, an early pioneer of league baseball in the city, tossing out the first ceremonial pitch. The new park provided seating for 3500 fans and witnessed some of the best ballclubs to represent Grand Rapids in the late teens under "Vinegar Bill" Essick. When the Central League went into hibernation after their pennant-winning season of 1917, the City of Grand Rapids failed to maintain the Island Park field and it was abandoned in favor of Ramona Park when the league resumed play in 1920.

Team owner Bert Annis was behind the creation of Island Park in 1912.

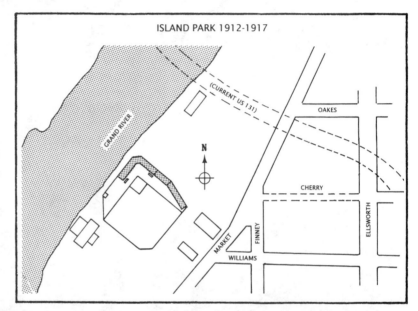

A view of the new Island Park grandstand in early 1912

BIGELOW FIELD 1940-1951 (on South Division at 39th Street)

Local baseball booster Clarence Bigelow led a movement to replace Ramona Park with an up-to-date baseball grounds in the south part of the City in the late thirties. The new park was built on an open field on South Division Street at 39th Street, outside the city limits with plenty of space for parking. Bigelow Field was ready and waiting when Grand Rapids entered the Michigan State League in 1940. In an age before freeways, Division Street and 36th Street provided adequate access and egress for automobile traffic. With the new popularity of night baseball and other events like midget auto racing at Bigelow, light towers were installed in July 1940. Even during its years without league baseball, Bigelow Field fans were entertained by Jess Elster's talented negro teams as well as numerous visits by major league clubs including the Detroit Tigers. When the Central League Jets went out of existence in 1951, the Chicks of the AAGPBL girl's league moved their home quarters from South Field to Bigelow. The park came to a sudden and inglorious end on July 15, 1952 when fire totally destroyed the grandstand. With no prospects of profitable baseball in the immediate future, Bigelow Field was never rebuilt.

Local baseball booster Clarence Bigelow spearheaded the construction of the new field in the 1930s.

An aerial view of Bigelow Field looking southwest. The main street through the center of the photo is South Division.

The end of Bigelow Field came on the night of July 15, 1952 when a spectacular fire consumed the entire grandstand.

An AAGBL game in progress at South Field

 ## SOUTH FIELD 1945-1954
(on Madison SE at Dickinson)

When the Milwaukee Chicks of the new professional girls' league transferred to Grand Rapids in 1945, they made an arrangement with the Board of Education and South High School to use the school's football field for their home games. It worked out well, since the field dimensions were suitable for the girls game and it was centrally located. With the field unused during the summer months, the Chicks were able to provide field improvements plus some needed revenue for the city's recreation department and were spared the expense of either building a new ballpark or paying steep rates for the restricted use of Bigelow Field. When the Central League Jets vacated Bigelow Field after 1951, the Chicks relocated there until fire consumed the park in July 1952. They returned to South Field after the fire and played there until the league went out of business in 1954. South Field and Grand Rapids South High School no longer exist in Grand Rapids today.

 ## OLD KENT PARK 1994-
(north of the city, between the Grand River and US-131—in suburban Comstock Park)

Once the intended transfer of the Midwest League Madison Muskies to Grand Rapids became a fact in early 1993, construction of a new ballpark north of the city was the team owners' top priority. Initial excavation began in May of that year and continued at a steady pace throughout the summer, fall, and winter months. The architects were M. C. Smith & Associates and the general contractor was Wolverine Building, Inc. Total cost was close to six million dollars. Seating capacity of 5,700 included 1,600 box seats and 3,760 reserved seats. Twenty corporate suites plus generous areas of lawn seating swelled the park's capacity to over 8,000. Additional seats plus permanent bleacher construction around the outfield fence in 1995-96 have increased the total park capacity to 10,000. Old Kent Bank & Trust Co. purchased naming rights for the new stadium in August 1993, hence the name Old Kent Park. Field dimensions are 327 feet down both foul lines and 402 feet to dead center. Since the park officially opened on May 12, 1994, attendance has been a baseball phenomenon with close to 500,000 that first year, which placed the franchise sixth in all levels of minor league baseball. Fears of the novelty wearing off have thus far been unfounded as attendance has continued to increase and shows no signs of abating. It appears that minor league professional baseball is here to stay in the Grand Rapids area and other Michigan communities as well.

Old Kent Park under construction in early 1994

Laying down sod for the outfield grass

The modern grandstand includes 24 luxury suites with a splendid view of the field.

The new UFP deck was added behind the RF fence in 1995.

A view from behind home plate of game action in April 1994

GREENVILLE

PROFESSIONAL LEAGUE MEMBERSHIP

YEARS	LEAGUE	HOME FIELD
1887	Northern Michigan	(Baseball grounds)
1889	Michigan State	(Baseball grounds)

The small community of Greenville, just northeast of Grand Rapids, hosted professional league baseball on two occasions in the late 1880s. In the summer of 1887, Greenville joined the nearby villages of Evart, Reed City, Big Rapids, and Ionia in a compact little circuit called the Northern Michigan League. The teams played a spartan schedule of weekend dates with teams made up of a mixture of hired professionals and local players. Expectations for profitable revenue were modest but interest was high, and neighborly rivalries for "bragging rights" were intense as the season got underway. C. L. Hecox was behind the Greenville entry and also served as secretary/treasurer of the league. C. H. Gibson took over as field manager. The team included some players with good professional baseball reputations like James Lombard and Al Manassau. Lombard later was a successful manager in various leagues in Michigan, and Manassau had a long career as player and umpire in numerous pro leagues, including the majors. The Northern Michigan League had a stormy, aborted life as the league was forced to fold up in early August with only Greenville and

Reed City left after other towns withdrew over a myriad of protests. The team finished either in first or third place, depending on how the often reconstructed standings were interpreted each time a member city withdrew.

League baseball returned to Greenville in 1889 when they joined the new Michigan State League, which included the much larger cities of Grand Rapids, Jackson, Saginaw, Lansing, and Kalamazoo. This time they were able to complete the 100-game schedule intact, but finished a distant fourth in the race for league honors. Bud Fowler, the team's second baseman, hit .302 in 92 games for the Greenvilles. Fowler's main claim to fame was his African heritage. A gifted player in his own right, he was one of the rare blacks to cross the color line that persisted in professional baseball even in the 19th century. Although Greenville almost replaced Grand Rapids in the troubled 1902 Michigan State League, they settled for crack independent teams after 1889 and enjoyed a reputation as one of Michigan's better baseball towns. The community also provided an occasional gifted player that made it to the higher leagues. The most notable big leaguer to hail from Greenville was Charles Hemphill. He had a fine 12-year career as a major league outfielder with several major league teams from 1899 through 1911. Charlie's brother Frank also had a brief stay in the big show with Chicago's "hitless wonders" of 1906.

Greenville's Charles Hemphill had a productive career as a major league outfielder from 1899 to 1911. He also played minor league baseball for Grand Rapids and other Michigan towns.

Frank Hemphill, younger brother to Charles, was also a fine player, appearing with numerous Michigan teams. He was also a member of the 1906 World Champion Chicago White Sox club.

Bud Fowler, one of the rare blacks to participate in professional league baseball in the 19th century, was a star player on the 1889 Greenville club.

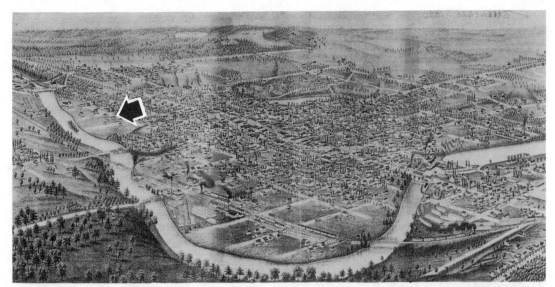

An 1880 bird's eye view drawing of Greenville, looking southwest. The arrow indicates the location of the baseball grounds used by the locals in the late 1880s.

THE PLAYING SITE

> **BASEBALL GROUNDS 1880s (NO NAME KNOWN) (along Flat River between Benton & Oak)**

No map information or descriptive details have been found to verify this location. But an 1889 newspaper item mentions a grandstand and fences around the field. It is possible that the league teams might have played at the fairgrounds site at the west end of Washington.

A current view of the old ballpark site—now occupied by the Greenville Housing Commission

BASE BALL !

JACKSON

—vs.—

GREENVILLE,

AT GREENVILLE,

May 13 and 14.

Admission 25c, Ladies 15c.

MAY 16 and 17,

LANSING VS. GREENVILLE.

An 1889 newspaper advertisement

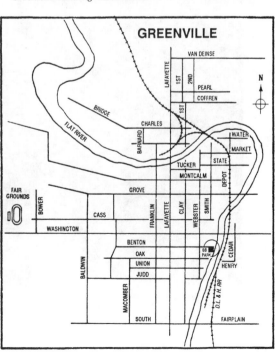

HANCOCK

PROFESSIONAL LEAGUE MEMBERSHIP

YEARS	LEAGUE	HOME FIELD
1888, 1890	Upper Peninsula	Sack's Park (Driving Park)
1904	Upper Peninsula (joint franchise with Houghton)	Sack's Park
1905	Copper Country-Soo	Sack's Park
1906	Northern-Copper Country	Sack's Park

Despite less than ideal summer weather for the game, Michigan's Upper Peninsula caught the baseball bug along with the rest of the country in the 19th century. Communities like Hancock, in the heart of the Copper Country, were quick to assemble a home town team to compete against rival towns in the region. The teams were a mixture of the best home town talent with a few hired professionals recruited from outside the area. In 1888, the towns of Hancock, Calumet, Champion, Negaunee, and Marquette agreed to form a semi-professional alliance called the Upper Peninsula League (UPABBL) and drew up a modest weekend schedule of "official" league games in combination with numerous "unofficial" games. Hancock finished third behind the Champion club, and the following year (1889) they finished first in a purely amateur version of the UP League. In 1890, a more serious attempt was made to organize a near-professional Upper

Peninsula baseball circuit with a longer schedule and more outside professionals brought in to stock the teams. M. R. Redmond was the president of the Hancock entry and Thomas Ryan was named manager. Unfortunately, Hancock withdrew before the season was completed, as neighbor Houghton ended up with the league championship. For the next 15 summers, Hancock was content with strictly amateur independent teams to represent the community.

In 1904, Hancock and Houghton joined forces and fielded a "Portage Lakes" club in the semi-pro version of the Upper Peninsula loop. Baseball was riding a wave of renewed popularity at this time and over the winter of 1904-05 the four towns of Calumet, Lake Linden, Hancock, and Sault Ste. Marie established a full-fledged class D professional circuit to be called the Copper Country-Soo League. Dr. George W. Orr of Lake Linden was named league president and F. C. Mayworm headed up the Hancock franchise. John Condon was Hancock's field manager. With a 100-game schedule and full recognition by the National Association of Professional Leagues, the league was able to attract a host of promising professional players from all over to fill team rosters. The Hancock "Infants" under Manager Condon (later replaced by Charles Rogers) finished a distant third, 22-1/2 games behind champion Calumet but the league itself was solvent enough to negotiate a merger with the nearby Northern League for the 1906 season. The new alignment would be eight teams, with the four UP teams joining Winnipeg, Duluth, Fargo

One of the earliest uniformed baseball teams in Michigan, the 1869 First National Club of Hancock. TOP ROW (L to R): J. Bittenbender, A. Brockway, Billy Harry, J. Johnson. SEATED: James Trembath, Archie Scott, Thomas Meads, J. V. Trembath, O. Kukath.

Outfielder Ed Kippert of the '05 Hancocks had a "cup of coffee" with Cincinnati in 1914.

(ND), and Grand Forks (ND) to make up the new 1906 Northern-Copper Country League. Michigan's Percy Glass was named league president. The new league got underway with much optimism and enthusiasm and new manager P. B. Wreath's Infants played winning baseball, but gate receipts were inadequate to compensate the full-salaried hired professionals and Hancock, along with Grand Forks, was forced to withdraw on July 23. The league survived one more year with four teams but it was the finale for fully professional league baseball in the Upper Peninsula. Despite the disappointing ending, little Hancock had the distinction of witnessing a caliber of play not often seen in communities its size for a couple of years. Many of the players on the Hancock roster went on to decent professional careers, including outfielder Ed Kippert and shortstop Clyde "Buzzy" Wares. Both had a "cup of coffee" in the big leagues and Wares eventually became a familiar face as a coach and minor league manager in the St. Louis Cardinals organization.

"Sis" Hopkins, a pitcher for Hancock in '06, had a brief trial with the Cardinals in '07 as an outfielder.

An infielder for Hancock in 1906, Clyde "Buzzy" Wares played two years in the majors and later became a coach and minor league manager in the Cardinals' organization.

THE PLAYING SITE

SACK'S PARK 1888-1906 (AKA Driving Park–at west end of Ingot)

No photos, map details, or other descriptive information have been found on this park. It was also a race track and fairgrounds facility and was sometimes referred to as the Driving Park.

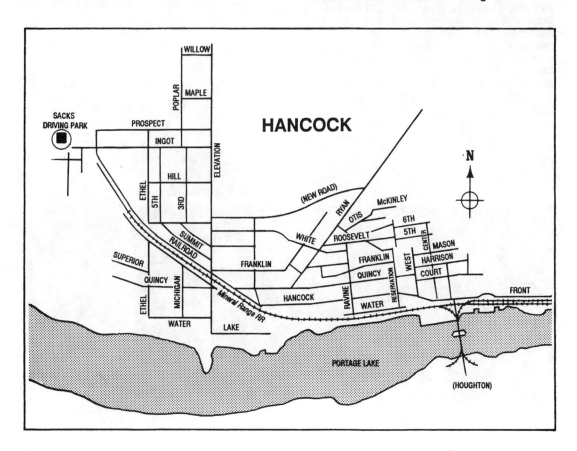

HOLLAND

PROFESSIONAL LEAGUE MEMBERSHIP

YEARS	LEAGUE	HOME FIELD
1910-11	Michigan State	Athletic Park (19th St.) (Sundays–'11 Ramona Park–Grand Rapids)

With new minor leagues springing up all over the country in 1910, the West Michigan coastal communities of Traverse City, Muskegon, and Holland joined Cadillac to form a reborn version of the Michigan State League. Local businessmen Con DePree and Benjamin Van Raable were among the financial backers of the Holland entry. Oscar Paterson and John Vandersuis were president & vice-president of the franchise. Business Manager Forest Dickerson, brother of League President Emerson Dickerson, ran the day-to-day operation of the team. The league was carefully organized with pooled gate receipts, limited rosters, and a salary limit enforced to ensure competitive balance and guarantee completion of a full season. For Holland, it was their first venture in organized baseball and they were cursed with a horrendous start, losing 14 of their first 15 games under Manager Fred Doyle. Dickerson eventually took charge and the team became more competitive, but their poor beginning prevented them from finishing better than last place with a 40-56 WL record. Outfielder Clyde McNutt was their top hitter with a .292 BA and pitcher Ralph Woldring's 16-10 WL record was among the league's best. A West Michigan product, Johnny Lavan, was a good field/no-hit standout at shortstop. Woldring had a brief tryout with the Chicago White Sox and Lavan later enjoyed a 12-year stay in the majors with several clubs.

After a successful 1910 season, the State League expanded to six members in 1911, adding Manistee and Boyne City. Forest Dickerson returned as business manager of the Holland club and turned over managerial duties to first baseman Ted Penfold. The "Wooden Shoes" got off to a better start than the previous year, but soon fell out of contention and only the pitiful performance of newcomer Boyne City prevented Holland from winding up in last place when the season ended. Once again, Clyde McNutt had a fine season with the bat, hitting .350, and Woldring led the pitchers with a 14-6 record. But another losing season and the resulting loss of support by Holland fans forced the franchise to withdraw. The ban on Sunday baseball in the strongly religious Holland community also contributed to the team's financial woes and discouraged any future designs for league baseball. The game remained popular, though, and Holland continued to support its local programs and independent teams in the years following. Numerous players with local connections had productive careers in professional baseball, including Frank Doesburgh, Neal Ball, Johnny Lavan, George Zuverink, and Jim Kaat.

A brother of State League President Emerson Dickerson, Forrest Dickerson was business manager and eventually field manager of the 1910-11 Holland club.

The 1910 edition of the "Wooden Shoes." TOP ROW (L to R): Wickler, Stratton, Wilson, Lavan, McNutt, Shaffer. SEATED: Batema, Shaw, Spriggs, Stauffer, McCarthy, Hines, Woldring.

Allegan's Clyde McNutt was Holland's star player during their two years in the Michigan State League.

The 1911 Holland team. TOP ROW (L to R): McNutt, Shaffer, Boonstra, Smith, Dillon. BOTTOM ROW: Spriggs, Currie, Hine, Mgr. Dickerson, Kubiak, Jewell, Woldring.

A West Michigan boy, Neal Ball, played in Holland for independent teams. He went on to the big leagues and made baseball history in 1909 with an unassisted triple play.

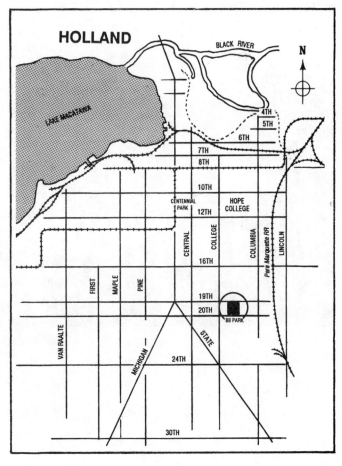

Johnny Lavan played 12 years in the majors from 1913 to 1924 and later became a prominent physician in Grand Rapids. He began his pro career with Holland and Muskegon in the 1910-11 State League. He also attended Hope College.

THE PLAYING SITE

ATHLETIC PARK 1910-11 (19th Street between College and Columbia)

On property owned by the City of Holland, the park opened in 1901 and became the city's principal baseball diamond. When Holland was admitted to the new Michigan State League in 1910, considerable improvements, including a new grandstand, were made to bring the facility up to league standards. Home plate and the main grandstand were in the northeast corner of the lot along 19th Street. A high board fence surrounded the field and extended into 19th and 20th Streets. Its location in the heart of a residential area made the park a nuisance to some residents and its poor upkeep after the State League years led to its eventual abandonment. By 1920 the new Riverview Park replaced the 19th Street grounds as the city's main baseball facility.

With the ban on Sunday baseball strictly abided by in the Holland community, the 1910 State League schedule forced the Holland club to play home Sunday games in their opponents' parks. In 1911, the Wooden Shoes arranged to have their scheduled Sunday games in Grand Rapids' Ramona Park whenever the Central League club was on the road. But the distance was too great to attract a profitable following from Holland faithful, especially since the team was seldom competitive in the State League pennant race.

A game in progress at Holland's Athletic Park

HOUGHTON

PROFESSIONAL LEAGUE MEMBERSHIP

YEARS	LEAGUE	HOME FIELD
1890-91	Upper Peninsula	E. Houghton Grounds
1904	Upper Peninsula (joint franchise with Hancock)	Ripley Sands Park
1906-07	Northern-Copper Country	Ripley Sands Park

Houghton, in Upper Michigan's Copper Country district, was usually represented by its own baseball team in the late 19th century, either as an independent club or as a member of periodic semi-pro or amateur alliances among neighboring communities. Among the better organized semi-pro alignments of this period was the Upper Peninsula League of 1890-91. J. P. Mason was league president of the six-team league consisting of major towns in the Copper and Iron mining region of the Upper Peninsula. Houghton, Hancock, and Calumet represented the Copper Country versus the iron mining towns of Marquette, Ishpeming, and Negaunee. Hancock and Negaunee failed to complete the season, but the four remaining cities finished the race with Houghton claiming the 1890 championship with a 23-12 record. The players were mostly locals with a few professional "hired guns" added to beef up the lineups. Houghton's catcher Charles Ingraham had a professional background, including a brief trial with Baltimore of the American Association in 1883. In 1891, the Houghtons plummeted to last place in the four-team UP League.

In 1904 Houghton and Hancock joined forces and fielded a combined entry in the semi-pro Houghton County Baseball League. They were identified as the "Portage Lakes" and good patronage encouraged the formation of a recognized class D Copper Country-Soo League in 1905. Hancock was the representative entry that first year with Houghton left out, but the following year (1906) both cities were included when the league merged with the Northern League to become the Northern-Copper Country circuit. Houghton, Hancock, Calumet, and Lake Linden were the Michigan members of the new amalgamation. William Miller was the president of the Houghton club and Howard Cassiboine the field manager. The traditional nickname of "Giants" was temporarily replaced by "Bridegrooms." The salary limit of $1,000 was high for a class D organization and before the season was barely underway, the National Association elevated their status to class C. The season started well but soon Hancock and Grand Forks (ND) had trouble making ends meet and

dropped out in late July. The schedule continued with the remaining six clubs and ended up as a three-way dogfight between Winnipeg, Calumet, and Houghton. Calumet held down the top spot for most of the summer, but Houghton overtook them in late August. The Aristocrats (Calumet) then rallied to win four of their last five games to capture the championship. Houghton's pitching duo of Roy Beecher and Rube Barry led the charge with 18 victories apiece. Other members of the runner-up Bridegrooms included Clyde "Buzzy" Wares (picked up from the defunct Hancock roster) and Jerry Utley (star pitcher at the University of Michigan). Despite the loss of the Hancock and Grand Forks clubs, the N-CC survived 1906 in pretty good condition and made plans for an encore season in 1907.

When league moguls convened in early 1907 to line up the franchises for the new N-CC season, it was decided to reduce membership to the four financially soundest cities—two in Michigan (Calumet, Houghton) plus Winnipeg (Canada), and Duluth (MN). Houghton's John Mann was named league vice president and the Giants' (the "Bridegrooms" name never caught on) new field manager was M. O. "Kid" Taylor. Unfortunately Winnipeg, with a full stable of star players, made a mockery of the pennant race as they ran away with the championship. The remaining three clubs all finished under .500 with Houghton finishing third, a full 30 games behind the Winnipegs. Local fans soon lost interest in the hopeless scenario and the league went out of existence for good.

University of Michigan ace Jerry Utley pitched for the Houghtons in the Northern-Copper Country League of 1906-07.

A Copper Country native, George Brunet embarked on a remarkable 32-year career as a pitcher in pro baseball, including 16 years in the majors. He began his odyssey with Shelby NC in 1953 and ended it with Monterrey (Mexico) in 1984.

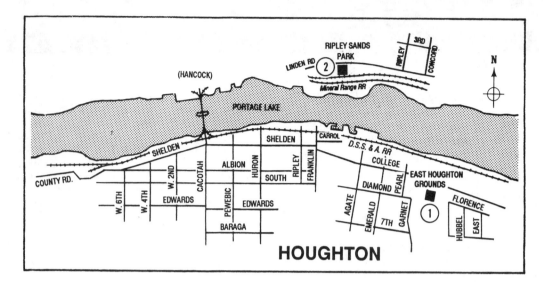

HOUGHTON

THE PLAYING SITES

① **EAST HOUGHTON GROUNDS 1890-91 (on Jay Hubbel property along Portage Lake)**

This baseball ground was very likely put together in the 1880s. The property was owned by Michigan Tech founder Jay Hubbell and was leased for use as a playing field. It was situated directly south of Hubbell Hall, the original landmark structure of the mining college.

Michigan Tech's Hubbell Hall in the 1890s. The East Houghton Grounds were on a vacant lot just south of the building.

A game in progress at the East Houghton Grounds c. 1890s. Note Hubbell Hall on the extreme righthand edge of the photo.

② **RIPLEY SANDS PARK 1904-07 (on Hancock side of the Portage Lake channel—near the Quincy Smelter)**

This ballpark was actually in Hancock, across the Portage Lake channel. Both Houghton and Hancock rooters traveled to the park by water, using one of the numerous passenger steamers that served both communities. The park was believed to have been constructed in 1904 or earlier. No photos or map diagrams are known to exist.

IONIA

PROFESSIONAL LEAGUE MEMBERSHIP

YEARS	LEAGUE	HOME FIELD
1887	Northern Michigan	Fairgrounds
1921-22	Central	Fairgrounds (Riverside Park)

Among the smaller towns of Michigan, Ionia had the distinction of membership in one of the earliest professional minor leagues in the midwest—the Northern Michigan League of 1887. This compact little alliance included the nearby communities of Greenville, Big Rapids, Reed City, and Evart. Ionia's Thomas G. Malone was one of the league's founders and was its first president. Malone also was the Ionia team's president, business manager, and field manager. The already spirited rivalries between member towns added enthusiasm to the venture but also led to its undoing as good sportsmanship gave way to complaints, accusations, and constant bickering over biased umpiring and other matters. In early August Evart dropped out, followed by Big Rapids a week later. Ionia, in last place, followed suit and with only Greenville and Reed City left, the Northern Michigan League was history. The leading Ionia batters in the final statistics were Lund (.534 in 11 games), Shaughnessy (.457), and O'Connor (.403). League baseball was not tried in Ionia for decades afterward but the town fielded independent semi-pro teams that established the town as the home of top flight baseball among the many tough independents representing Michigan communities. On many occasions the Ionias claimed the title "state champions" of independent teams, a title perhaps well deserved but always subject to heated debate among unaffiliated clubs. In 1903 Joe Ganzell's Ionias, stocked with legitimate professionals like Bobby Vorpagel, won with regularity and even managed to embarrass the Detroit Tigers by handing the big leaguers a 3-2 defeat in an exhibition game at Ionia's fairgrounds on Aug. 10. The Tigers returned at season's end to assert their superiority with a 14-3 drubbing behind the pitching of Allegan's Frank Kitson. The following year Ganzell took his entourage of professionals intact to Lake Linden in the Upper Peninsula to represent that community in the newly formed Copper Country circuit.

With Ionia's long-standing reputation for quality baseball in mind, an unexpected opportunity to join the tough class B Central League suddenly surfaced in the summer of 1921. League President Emerson Dickerson of nearby Grand Rapids was desparately searching for a new location for the struggling Jackson franchise and made overtures to interested parties in Ionia like

Mayor Fred Green and businessmen Charles C. Skelley and Fred Chapman. It was a huge jump for little Ionia, but the argument was made that Central League member Ludington was not much bigger and was holding its own in such faster company. The townspeople of Ionia rallied to offer support for the idea and with much pomp and ceremony the transplanted Jacksons opened in their new home city on July 30 with a 4-3 victory over league-leading Ludington before a huge gathering. Business manager for the "Mayors" was Arthur Pipp, brother of GR big-leaguer Wally Pipp. Bill Hartwell was retained as field manager, as was the entire Jackson roster. Unfortunately, one of the reasons for Jackson's predicament was its woeful won-loss record and the team ended up a distant last. Outfielder Harry Purcell was the lone standout on the cellar-dwellers, leading the league with a robust .380 average. But Ionia was determined to make its mark in the ranks of organized baseball and made plans to return as a full-fledged member of the Central League for 1922.

BASE BALL!

CENTRAL LEAGUE

LUDINGTON VS. IONIA

SATURDAY, 3 P. M.

RIVERSIDE PARK

This Invitation Is Extended to Everyone

A 1921 newspaper ad for a Central League contest vs. Ludington at Riverside Park

In an effort to field a more competitive team in 1922, wholesale changes were in order and few of the 1921 Mayors were re-signed. Carrington Sweeney was the new field manager. Sweeney's new player roster proved not much different from the '21 club as the Ionias once again brought up the rear of the Central League. Former Pittsburgh Pirate John Meador provided some decent pitching but wound up in Muskegon before the season was over—as did Manager Sweeney. Outfielders H. Brooks and Blenkiron provided some batting punch, but the Mayors were unable to field a competitive team all summer and fan interest went decidedly downhill. The league itself was in bad straits by this time and over the following winter it was disbanded with its more successful franchises entering the Michigan-Ontario League for 1923. Ionia was not invited (nor was champion Ludington) and thus ended the final era of professional league baseball for Ionia fandom.

Outfield candidates for the 1922 club. TOP (L to R): Brooks, Barry, Blake. BELOW: Puhrman, Dunn.

Arthur Pipp, brother of Grand Rapids' big leaguer Wally, was business mgr. for Ionia in 1922.

Carrington Sweeney played first and managed the 1922 Ionia club. He finished the season with Muskegon.

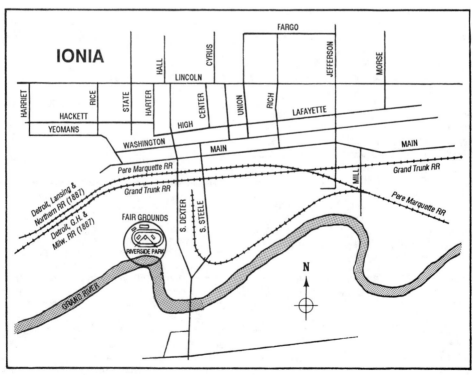

THE PLAYING SITE

RIVERSIDE PARK 1887, 1921-22 (Fairgrounds race track site—on Grand River west of S. Dexter)

When Ionia entered the Northern Michigan League in the spring of 1887, team owner Thomas Malone used the existing fair grounds property for the location of new baseball grounds. A new grandstand was erected at the southeast corner to seat about 400 with additional accommodations to bring the park's capacity to 1,200. A substantial board fence surrounded the field. Newspaper accounts make it unclear as to what part, if any, of the existing race track was used as part of the diamond itself. Existing grass was removed to create a dirt infield, so we assume that this grass area was part of the race track infield. Apparently, just before the Central League team commenced play in 1921, the baseball diamond was repositioned squarely in front of the newest addition to the main racing grandstand on the north side of the track. The inner fence for the racing track would be made portable so it could be temporarily removed for baseball games. A new canvas fence was built to enclose the baseball grounds. Since the league assumed ownership of the franchise from Jackson, most of the cost of park improvements were borne by the league. William Silvers, a noted groundskeeper from Grand Rapids, was recruited to supervise the work on the new diamond. When work was completed, home plate was placed just inside the race track infield and the outer fence in center field was about 450 feet from the plate, directly south of the main grandstand. When Central League play was inaugurated on July 30, 1921, then-Mayor Fred Green tossed the ceremonial first pitch to League President Emerson Dickerson. The ball used was a revered souvenir—the same ball with which "Happy" Harris drove in the run that defeated the Detroit Tigers in a 1903 exhibition game. It was loaned for the occasion by long-time Ionia baseball booster Bert Lampkin. In 1922, the first base bleacher was relocated to the third base side and a brand new bleacher replaced the old one on the first base side. Unfortunately, at this writing no photograph of baseball action at Riverside Park has surfaced and much of the above description of the facility is speculative.

An aerial view of the Ionia fairgrounds, which was adapted for use by the local baseball teams

ISHPEMING-NEGAUNEE

PROFESSIONAL LEAGUE MEMBERSHIP

YEARS	LEAGUE	HOME FIELD
1890	Upper Peninsula	Ishpeming: S. Main St. Negaunee: Union Park
1891	Upper Peninsula	Ishpeming: Union Park
1892	Wisconsin-Michigan (joint franchise)	Union Park

The neighboring towns of Ishpeming and Negaunee in the Upper Peninsula's iron district were often represented individually or jointly in various editions of an amateur or semi-pro alliance of UP communities in the late 1880s and 1890s. None of these leagues were fully professional in the strictest sense, but competition was spirited and claims to a "championship" of the Upper Peninsula were taken seriously by member cities. The first such league with a full summer's schedule of games was in 1890 and both Ishpeming and Negaunee had representative clubs. Bert Cook's Negaunee club dropped out in mid-season but the Ishpeming team managed by James Tray proved to be a serious contender and finished a close second behind the champion Houghtons. The following year only Ishpeming participated and Manager Tray's hopefuls were in third place in mid-August when they were forced to disband.

In 1892 the two cities shared a franchise in a legitimate professional league called the Wisconsin-Michigan League. Marquette and Menominee were the other Michigan clubs in the six-team circuit. The Ishpeming/Negaunee team assumed the nickname "Unions" because of their combined franchise and also since their home field was Union Park, which was halfway between the two towns. Former major leaguer Joe Quest managed the Unions to a 21-20 WL record up to early August, when they once again failed to complete the season. After Marquette disbanded on August 5, travel expenses to only one member club in the iron district by other league members also forced the Unions out of the circuit. It was the last time either Ishpeming or Negaunee attempted to participate in a professional baseball league.

William D. "Dolly" Gray was born in Ishpeming in 1878. He pitched three years (from 1909 to 1911) with the Washington American League club, winning 15 and losing 20.

Joe Quest had a lengthy career in the early years of the National League with Chicago, Detroit, and several American Association clubs. His big league career ended in 1886 and he was signed to manage the 1892 Ishpeming-Negaunee club of the Wisconsin/-Michigan League.

A bird's eye illustration of Ishpeming looking southeast c. 1881

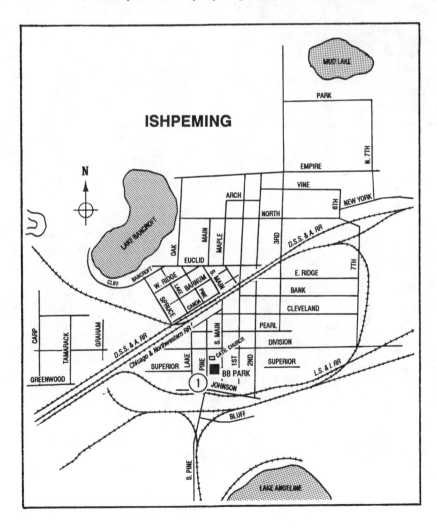

THE PLAYING SITES

① **ISHPEMING GROUNDS 1890 (at south end of Main St. near St. John's Catholic Church)**

② **UNION PARK 1891-92 (at Fairgrounds Driving Park–midway between Ishpeming and Negaunee)**

Very little is recorded about the details of this park. It was built by the local baseball association in 1890 on property leased from the Cleveland Iron Mining Company. According to newspaper reports, the field was enclosed by a 10-foot fence and the grandstand would comfortably seat 600 people.

A modern view looking south of Ishpeming's South Main Street and St. John's Church, still standing from the 1890s. The current auto dealer just behind the church occupies the site of what was once the baseball park.

As was the common practice in many rural American towns, the local driving park, AKA Association Grounds, was adapted for use as a baseball diamond. In 1892 the diamond was moved a short distance to the east and directly in front of the main grandstand, with the catchers box on the track itself. The judges tower was placed on rollers and moved away from the diamond area to improve visibility. A sizable bluff adjacent to the property provided a free view of games up to 1890, when park management closed this area off for spectators. An interurban electric car line passed right along the park site and connected the two communities of Ishpeming and Negaunee, giving patrons convenient access in either direction.

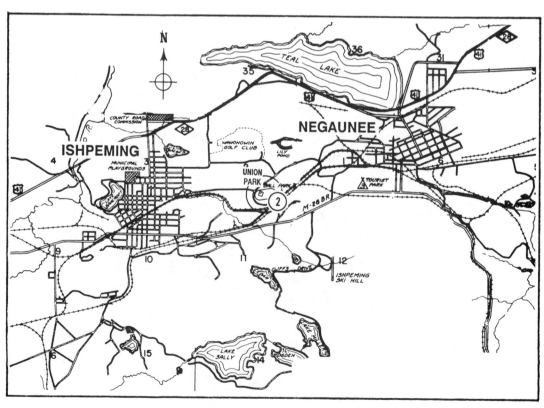

JACKSON

PROFESSIONAL LEAGUE MEMBERSHIP

YEARS	LEAGUE	HOME FIELD
1888	Tri-State	Recreation Park (Franklin & 4th Sts.)
1889	Michigan State	Recreation Park
1895	Michigan State (transferred from Battle Creek)	Fairgrounds (Keeley Park)
1896	Interstate	Fairgrounds (Keeley)
1897	Michigan State	Fairgrounds (Keeley)
1902	Michigan State (transferred from Saginaw)	Fairgrounds (Keeley)
1906-15	Southern Michigan	Fairgrounds (Keeley)
1921	Central	Fairgrounds (Keeley)

Famed as the home of Michigan's State Prison, Jackson was also home for numerous minor league baseball teams in the 19th and early 20th century. Their earliest venture in organized baseball occurred in 1888 when the Ohio-based Tri-State League invited Jackson and Toledo to become the 9th & 10th member cities of the circuit. Kalamazoo was the only other Michigan town in the Tri-State. George Burbridge was business manager of the "Jaxons" and M. J. Moore was field manager. Jackson managed to play out the full schedule, but was hopelessly mired in last place when the season ended. In 1889, the Jaxons elected to stay closer to home by entering the newly formed Michigan State League. Bob Hart, George S. Wilson, and W. S. Cobb headed up the Jackson franchise with James Tray chosen as field manager. The '89 season proved to be much more gratifying for Jackson fans as the locals finished out the season in first place. Their claim to the championship was, however, tainted by controversy as runnerup Saginaw protested several late season Jackson wins. In an effort to overtake Saginaw, Jackson arranged on its own to reschedule some make up games with other league opponents to give them enough additional victories to claim the pennant. League Secretary D. Z. Curtis cried foul, but his ruling was ignored and Jackson declared itself the champion. Among the key contributors to the Jacksons' winning season was outfielder George Stallings, who would gain later fame as a major league manager.

NEWTON H. SEARS.

The accompanying portrait will be recognized by most of The Citizen's readers as an excellent likeness of Newton H. Sears, of Horton. Mr. Sears is a native of Jackson county in the strictest sense of the term, as he was born 32 years ago in Spring Arbor and has passed most of his life in Horton, near which village he owns a fine farm conducting also a general store in town. His first base ball experience was in 1870 at Ann Arbor, during his attendance at the state university, when he played with telling effect with the university team. For the past fifteen years he has been one of the foremost players with the Horton Reds, a strong amateur team for whom he won eighteen successive games, while in the box, last season, against Hillsdale, Jonesville, and other towns in the vicinity. He is five feet, eleven-and-one-half inches in hight, weighs 190 pounds and is of powerful built. Although Sears is said to be a most successful pitcher, his favorite position is on a base or in left field for which work he was signed with Jaxon. Last season he played with Petosky part of the season and received many compliments on his efficient work.

An 1888 Jackson Citizen article on a local member of the Tri-State Jaxons, Newt Sears

The 1889 Jackson club that claimed the championship of the Michigan State League. The players are unidentified, but among this group are very likely Manager James Tray and outfielder George Stallings.

George Stallings was an out-fielder on the 1889 Jaxons. He had a long career as player and manager in the minors and majors, notably with Detroit and the 1914 "Miracle" Braves of Boston.

After 1889, Jackson fielded independent teams to represent the city for the next six years. But once again the Michigan State League came calling in August 1895 when the struggling Battle Creek club was relocated to Jackson. The transplanted Jaxons under Leigh Lynch salvaged the balance of the season with a respectable 20-12 record. The Jackson Daily Citizen, using its own self-serving accounting of the restructured four-team schedule, declared Jackson league champions. But since the league was forced to rely on so many confusing and contradictory formulas to explain the league standings after Battle Creek and Owosso defaulted, several member teams could lay claim to the top spot, depending upon which scenario suited their cause. Jackson's leading hitter with a .404 average was a deaf-mute named George "Dummy" Kihm. Another member of the 1895 Jackson team worth noting was an outfielder playing under the name of Pearl Zane. His real name was Pearl Zane Grey and in later years he became one of America's most famous novelists. His brother "Reddy" Gray was also a member of that team.

Famed author Zane Grey played baseball for Jackson in the 1895 Michigan State League under the alias of Pearl Zane (his first two given names).

With a renewed interest in league baseball, the City of Jackson entered the interstate League in 1896. Leigh Lynch returned as manager, as did the hard-hitting Dummy Kihm. The team finished a distant sixth in the final standings, so Jackson decided to return to the Michigan State League in 1897. Once again, the State League began to flounder by July as Kalamazoo dropped out, Bay City's franchise moved to Flint, and the defunct Kalamazoos filled the void in Bay City. Even though Jackson was in first place by a comfortable margin, they contributed to the league's disintegration by withdrawing (along with

Lansing) on July 26. With only four cities remaining, the State League lasted another week and subsequently went out of business. Five years later (1902) another edition of the Michigan State League was attempted and was again beset by beleaguered franchises a month or so into the schedule. Jackson became an unexpected member when the Saginaw team relocated there on July 17. "Doggie" Miller's club was in second place when the league called it quits on August 20. After so many disappointments in league play, Jackson settled for independent style baseball teams for the next few seasons.

Renewed nationwide interest in minor league baseball encouraged the formation of the Southern Michigan League in 1906. The league's founder was Detroit sportswriter Joe Jackson and member cities were Mt. Clemens, Kalamazoo, Tecumseh, Battle Creek, Saginaw, and Jackson. The SML's chances of success were much better than the State League, especially since five of the six member towns were connected by an interurban rail service which kept travel costs to a minimum. A pair of Detroit men took charge of the Jacksons—namely, President A. S. Burkart and Manager Morris "Mo" Myers. The best the Myers men could do in the 1906 campaign was 4th place and an even 52-52 WL record. In 1907 owner Burkart switched his allegiance to take over the Saginaw club and Jackson withdrew from the circuit in July. It proved to be only a temporary absence and they were right back in the thick of the 1908 race as Bo Slear's men finished a strong third, 4-1/2 games behind winning Saginaw. The 1909 race proved to be a thriller right down to the final day as Jackson, Flint, and Saginaw finished only a game apart. Saginaw was acclaimed SML champ after a joint protest by Jackson and Flint over several Saginaw games won was rejected by League Secretary Percy Glass. Even had the protest succeeded, Flint would have edged Jackson out. Pitchers Elmer Criger (22-7) and Alex Norcabbage were the main contributors to Jackson's fine 1909 season.

Lefty Heinie Steiger won 32 games for the 4th place Jacksons in 1906.

Mo Myers began the '06 season as Jackson manager. He returned later to pilot the '13 club.

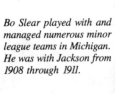

Bo Slear played with and managed numerous minor league teams in Michigan. He was with Jackson from 1908 through 1911.

Famed Brooklyn Dodger coach in the '40s & '50s, Jake Pitler played for Jackson in 1913.

W. S. McLaren headed up the Jackson Central League club of 1921.

By 1910 the Southern Michigan League had proved to be one of the more stable minor leagues in the country and Jackson had seemingly found a permanent home in organized baseball. The popular Bo Slear's 4th and 5th years at the helm (1910-11) proved disappointing as Jackson took a nosedive in the standings, finishing 7th and 8th (last). John Connors' lusty hitting gave local fans something to cheer about during those dreary seasons, winning the league batting title in 1911 with a .377 average. By 1912 Slear was gone but Connors had another good year at the place to help elevate the Jacksons to a 4th place finish. "Mo" Myers returned as manager in 1913 and they rose another notch to third, but slipped to sixth in the 10-team expanded SML of 1914 (Toledo and South Bend were the new entries). Some notable players who wore the Jackson uniform during the 1910-14 period were Laverne "Bunny" Fabrique, a Clinton MI native who later played for Brooklyn in 1916-17, and Jake Pitler, who played for Pittsburgh in 1917-18 and was a Brooklyn Dodger coach in the '40s and '50s. Danny Collins was the new field boss for the final, fateful 1915 season of Southern Michigan League baseball. Minor league baseball was in one of its downward cycles by this time and the SML was unable to continue past July 5. Jackson was in third place when the circuit suspended operations, never to resurface. Much of baseball went into hibernation until long after the great World War finally came to a halt.

Laverne "Bunny" Fabrique from nearby Clinton played for Jackson in 1909-11. He later played in the big leagues for Brooklyn.

The old Central League was resurrected in 1920 with only four members, all in Michigan. After a financially successful maiden season, Emerson Dickerson's circuit expanded to six for 1921, adding Lansing and Jackson. W. S. McLaren was the president/owner of the Jackson entry and Danny Jenkins, long-time minor league player and manager in Michigan circles, was chosen to manage. Difficulties with fairground management over suitable modifications to the grounds plus a losing team resulted in poor patronage right from the start and by mid-season the team transferred to Ionia. Fine seasons by outfielder Harry Purcell (a league-leading .380 average) and Hartwell (.308) could not elevate the Jacksons out of the league cellar and it was the "last hurrah" for minor league baseball in the Prison City.

Bennie Frey, who pitched for Cincinnati in the '30s, had Jackson roots. He committed suicide in 1937.

THE PLAYING SITES

RECREATION PARK—1880s (at Franklin & 4th Streets, southwest of downtown)

This park was built in early 1888 to provide home grounds for the Tri-State League club. The Jackson Citizen of April 3, 1888 reported "the Jackson Baseball Association... will begin at once the erection of fences, grandstand, etc., and work on the grounds—leveling, rolling and layout out of (the) diamond—will begin as soon as the frost is out of the ground." No photos or map diagrams have been located regarding this baseball park.

② FAIRGROUNDS–KEELEY PARK 1895-1921 (downtown— directly west across the Grand River from the old State Prison)

The downtown convenience and the ready-made grandstand for fairgrounds activities was enough reason to utilize this property for baseball through the decades. One negative feature which possibly hurt attendance in Jackson was the absence of a roof on the grandstand, according to one newspaper report. Minor modifications and temporary adaptations of the race track field kept the facility compatible with fair events when Keeley Park was an active fairgrounds site. The property was owned by the Fair Association and occasional battles were fought over proposed modifications for baseball use. In 1921 the grandstand was extensively rebuilt with a reported seating capacity for 7000 persons. The park is still used for harness racing for much of the year.

The Jackson fairgrounds as it looks today, still in use for harness racing.

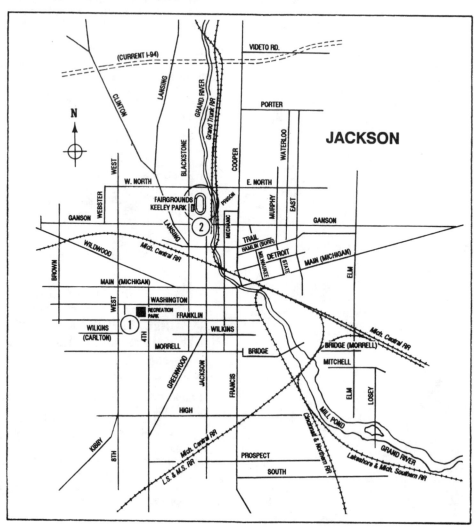

KALAMAZOO

PROFESSIONAL LEAGUE MEMBERSHIP

YEARS	LEAGUE	HOME FIELD
1887	Ohio State	Athletic Park
1888	Tri-State	Athletic Park
1889	Michigan State	North St. Park
1895	Michigan State	North St. Park
1897	Michigan State	North St. Park
1906-14	Southern Michigan	Riverview Park (County Fairgrounds)
1920-22	Central	Stationery Park (Harrison St.)
1923-24	Michigan-Ontario (MINT)	Stationery Park
1926	Central/Mich. State	Stationery Park
1950-54	AAGBL (Girls)	Lindstrom Field CAA Field Summer Home Park (Long Lake)
1996-	Frontier	Sutherland Park

Al Buckenberger was player/mgr. for the 1887 Ohio State League champs. He later managed for three different NL clubs from 1892 to 1904.

Clarence "Cupid" Childs played for Kalamazoo in 1888. He went on to a magnificent 12-year career in the National League, hitting .313 lifetime.

Kalamazoo's first venture in professional league baseball took place way back in 1887 when they were admitted into the distant Ohio State League. Robert W. Smith was president of the local club and also named a league director. The field manager was second baseman Al Buckenberger, who years later became a manager and executive at the major league level. The admission of a Michigan-based team in the Ohio League met with some resistance in the Buckeye State and the Kalamazoos further aggravated their questionable membership status among Ohio's member cities by running away with the championship by a full 11 games over runnerup Zanesville. The talented Kalamazoos punctuated their winning season with a victory over the NL Indianapolis team in a post-season exhibition game. In 1888, the Ohio League was renamed the Tri-State League and added another Michigan city (Jackson) to the 10-team circuit. Buckenberger moved on to the Wheeling WV club (which featured future great Ed Delehanty) and O'Neill took over as manager of the Kalamazoo "Blues." The Blues had another winning season but failing attendance forced the club to withdraw in early September. Lima OH was the new champion, with the Kazoos in third place when they folded. In 1889 Kalamazoo chose to enter the Michigan State League with veteran player James Lombard named as new field manager. The Kazoos were in last place with a 32-44 record when the franchise was moved to Flint in early September. After two straight incomplete seasons of professional league ball, the city opted for independent baseball through the next five summers.

In 1895 Kalamazoo rejoined the Michigan State League with E. F. Mayo as business manager and Ollie Hungerford as field manager. By early August the league was struggling to survive the full season as Battle Creek transferred to Jackson and both Owosso and Jackson withdrew a month later, leaving only four teams to complete the schedule. The "Zooloos" were never in contention, but they showcased the circuit's premier battery in pitcher Van Giesen (19-11) and catcher Lou Criger. Criger later enjoyed a long big league career for several clubs. Blanford was the team's most consistent batsman with a .353 BA. Kalamazoo did not resume league play in 1896 but returned to the State League fold for the 1897 season. Fred Popkay was the new pilot for '97 until July 2, when Kalamazoo relocated its team to Bay City to fill the void after the previous Bay City franchise had moved to Flint. Jackson and Lansing dropped out on July 26 and a week later the entire league collapsed. Enough was enough, and Kalamazoo chose to avoid organized baseball for another eight seasons.

Catcher Lou Criger started his pro career with Kalamazoo in 1895. From there he went on to play 17 years in the big leagues with five clubs.

Professional baseball's popularity at the minor league level slipped badly during the AL-NL wars in the first years of the new century, but once peace was attained and the newly organized National Association took control of the minor leagues in 1902, the number of new leagues had almost tripled by 1906. The Southern Michigan League, founded by Detroit baseball writer Joe Jackson, was one of the new circuits to surface in 1906 and Kalamazoo became a charter member. After so many aborted tries at league ball, the Kazoos found a home in the SML and gave the city a steady diet of professional baseball for the next nine summers. The 1906 "White Sox," under C. W. Pickell, finished a strong second, paced by Captain Wade "Red" Killefer from nearby Bloomingdale. New Manager "Mo" Myers led his White Sox to runnerup spots in 1907 and 1908 and Kalamazoo fans rallied behind their contending teams. Monte Method was the team's top hurler during these years, leading the league with 24 victories in 1908. The 1909 club, paced by Harry Martin (.330) slipped to fourth place but the Kazoos were on the verge of their finest seasons in the Southern Michigan League.

The years 1910 and 1911 were the glory years of the minor league experience for Kalamazoo fandom. J. W. Ryder succeeded James Frank as team president and Charley Wagner became field manager for the last five seasons in the SML. Wagner's troops wound up the 1910 season in a dead heat with Lansing for the league championship with identical records of 87-52. But Kalamazoo prevailed as league champions by winning the post-season playoffs. Pitcher Jacobson was the hero for Kalamazoo, winning four playoff games. The Kalamazoos boasted the best pitching tandem in the SML in 1910 with B. Valliere (23-6) and Berne Hughey (193 K's). Other key performers were outfielders Fred Streeter and Leonard Cote plus Manager Wagner, who played a solid second base. In 1911 the Kazoos won the flag all to themselves, finishing 6-1/2 games up on runnerup Lansing. Former big league pitcher Al "Beany" Jacobson was the key to their successful season, winning 26 games for the new champions. Denny Mannix and Hughey gave the pennant winner two more 20-game winners with 21 and 22 respectively. Streeter led the hitters at .320, followed by Cote at .303 and Grover Gillen at .287. Another successful season for the 1911 SML under new President Judge Bowen encouraged the National Association to elevate their status from class D to C.

C. W. Pickell piloted Kalamazoo's first SML club in 1906.

Mo Myers was "White Sox" manager in 1907 & '08.

Harry Martin managed and hit .330 for the '09 team.

Second baseman Charles Wagner managed the Kalamazoos to flags in 1910 and 1911.

Wade Killefer starred for Kalamazoo College and the 1906 SML club. The Detroit Tigers brought him up in '07.

Brother Bill Killefer also went on to a fine major league career as a catcher with several clubs.

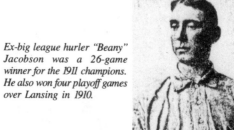

Ex-big league hurler "Beany" Jacobson was a 26-game winner for the 1911 champions. He also won four playoff games over Lansing in 1910.

A team photo from around 1910: STANDING (L to R): Mgr. Wagner, Gillen, Ryan, McLafferty, Keener, Hughey, Doty. SEATED: Streeter, Ragan, Pokorney, Danaher, Graham, Martin.

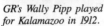

GR's Wally Pipp played for Kalamazoo in 1912.

Ernie Koob, a local product, pitched for Western Normal (WMU) on his way to the majors.

Wagner's 1912 club plummeted to a fifth place tie with Lansing. A newcomer who attracted some attention around the league was Grand Rapids native Wally Pipp, Kalamazoo's first sacker, who advanced to a long career in the majors the following year. For the SML, 1912 was a troubled season as both Bay City and Saginaw were temporarily disbanded by the league in July, and the league itself was demoted back to class D status. The 1913 season saw the return of Bay City and Saginaw to the fold, but for Kalamazoo it was a dreary sixth place finish. Fred Bramble was the only bright spot with a .349 league-leading BA. Kalamazoo's James Frank succeeded Judge Bowen as league president in 1913. Under new President Frank, the SML expanded to 10 teams for 1914, adding out-of-state towns South Bend and Toledo. The National Association also restored the new enlarged circuit to class C status. But for the Kazoos, 1914 was a dreadful finale for their long run in the Southern Michigan League as they finished at the bottom, losing 96 games. Accordingly, attendance also plummeted and Kalamazoo did not rejoin the circuit in 1915. The prospect of league baseball in the Celery City was shelved for the duration of the World War period.

The war effort also resulted in suspended operations of other minor leagues in the midwest, including the 15-year-old Central League after 1917. Emerson Dickerson of Grand Rapids was determined to revive the Central loop for 1920 but was unable to re-enlist the former Ohio-Indiana-Illinois cities from 1917. In the end, he settled for a four-team version with all Michigan towns, which included former CL members Grand Rapids and Muskegon plus Ludington and Kalamazoo. Expansion to six or eight teams was planned for 1921. Heading the local ownership group for the 1920 Kalamazoo franchise were E. M. Sargeant, Calvin Mahoney, Harrison Merrill, D. R. Curtenius, and former major league pitcher Harry "Rube" Vickers, a native of Pittsford MI and manager of the new "Reubens." A new, modern ballpark was soon under construction just north of the downtown area at Harrison Street. The facility would be called Stationery Park. Grand Rapids won the 1920 championship rather handily but the Reubens finished second, 11 games behind the leaders. Fenner and Schaufel were the leading pitchers for the Reubens with 13 and 15 victories apiece. In 1921 George Tomer replaced Vickers as manager and once again Kalamazoo finished a distant second behind a powerful Ludington club. The now six-team Central League (Lansing and Ionia were the 5th and 6th additions) decided upon a split-season format for 1922 to decide the playoff teams, but Tomer's "Celery Pickers" finished out of contention in both halves. First baseman/-manager Tomer had a productive '22 season with the bat, hitting .325 but mediocre pitching kept the team under .500. Over the winter of 1922-23, Central League member cities Kalamazoo, Grand Rapids, and Muskegon were persuaded to abandon their circuit and enter the rival class B Michigan-Ontario League for the 1923 season.

E.M. Sergeant was president of the new Central League club of 1920.

Former big league hurler Rube Vickers was manager of the 1920 "Reubens."

A group of Kalamazoo pitchers from the 1920-21 period. L to R: Lahaie, Saffran, Harvey, Collins, Schaufel, Wright.

First baseman George Tomer replaced Vickers in '21 and hit .325 for the CL runnerups.

Bill Hallahan went 8-5 for the '24 MINT Leaguers. He became a starting pitcher for the St. Louis "gashouse gang" of the 1930s.

Old Detroit Tiger favorite Charlie Schmidt managed the Central League club of early 1926.

Kalamazoo Central High's Neil Berry played infield for the Detroit Tigers in the late '40s, early '50s.

Kalamazoo fared little better in their new MINT League surroundings of 1923-24. They at least produced a winning record in 1923 (69-64) and the season highlight was a no-hit game by pitcher Brown on August 14. The following year Manager Marty Becker's charges charged directly into the MINT League cellar with a 45-88 record, a full 11 games behind 7th place Muskegon. Center fielder Parry O'Brien was one of the few standouts of 1924 with a fine .361 season. A young pitcher on the Kalamazoo staff who attracted some attention that year was Bill Hallahan, who later starred with the St. Louis Cardinals. At season's end the bottom three clubs—Grand Rapids, Muskegon, and Kalamazoo—withdrew from the MINT League after suffering financial losses. Minor league baseball was in another downward cycle at this time, but Emerson Dickerson of Grand Rapids was determined to make another attempt to revive the old Central League in 1926 with the same four Michigan teams of 1920 (Kalamazoo, Ludington, Muskegon, and Grand Rapids). The MINT League was also pared down to four

Michigan entries and both leagues found the going rough early in the season. The two circuits agreed to merge and start the season anew on June 15 as the Michigan State League. They managed to struggle through the balance of the schedule, but it was a lost cause as mounting debts forced the league to close up shop at season's end. Kalamazoo, led by one-time Detroit Tiger catching great Charley Schmidt, was in first place in the Central League phase but finished a distant sixth in the final standings of the State League under Fred Hutton. With the decline of interest in minor league baseball combined with the arrival of the Great Depression, Kalamazoo's baseball fans settled for the amateur or semi-pro brand of independent teams during the ensuing decades. Some excellent teams such as the Sutherland Paper Co. club and some outstanding players like Neil Berry, Ron Jackson, and nearby Paw Paw's Charley Maxwell entertained local fans during the long draught of no professional baseball in the Celery City.

100

In the early 1950s, another brand of professional baseball arrived in Kalamazoo to fill the long void for local fans. The Muskegon Lassies of the All American Girls Baseball League transferred to Kalamazoo in early 1950 and gave the city an entertaining and unique variety of the national pastime for the next five summers. Unfortunately, the Lassies were never able to field a contending club during their tenure here but they survived down to the last days of the league's existence in 1954. Their brightest star was pitcher/outfielder Doris Sams, who ranks as one of the AAGBL's greatest players. Their only winning season was in 1953 when they finished third with a 56-50 record. Dwindling attendance throughout the circuit forced the AAGBL into extinction after the 1954 season, but nostalgic interest remains to this day—fueled by the recent film "A League of Their Own."

After 70 years (discounting the AAGBL years) without league baseball, a renaissance of interest surfaced in Michigan in the early 1990s with the establishment of Midwest League franchises in Grand Rapids and Battle Creek. Kalamazoo Mayor Edward J. Annen Jr. recognized the prospects of his city joining the new wave of minor league interest and spearheaded a movement to renovate the city's decaying baseball facility, Sutherland Park. With Battle Creek staking claim on the territory for the Midwest League, an effort was launched to secure a franchise in the independent Frontier League. In 1995, Michiganians Doug James and Steve Hill purchased the Newark OH franchise and announced plans to relocate the club to Kalamazoo's Sutherland Park for the 1996 season. Veteran minor league coach and manager Glenn Gulliver from Allen Park MI was named to pilot the new "Kodiaks" in their inaugural season. With Kalamazoo thus far the only Michigan representative in the circuit, it is rumored that other state communities may soon join the Frontier League and hopefully another new and long tradition of minor league baseball will be launched in the state of Michigan.

Lassies' pitcher/outfielder Doris "Sammy" Sams was a superstar in her playing days with Muskegon and Kalamazoo.

Kalamazoo Kodiak owners Doug James (left) and Steve Hill

Dottie Schroeder played shortstop for the Lassies in their final seasons of 1953-54.

Glenn Gulliver was picked to pilot the new '96 Kodiaks franchise.

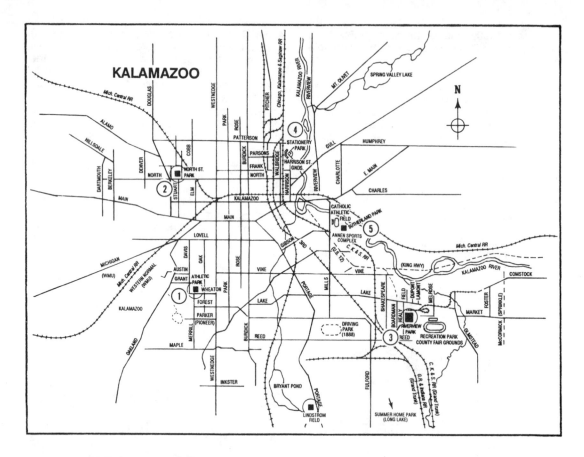

KALAMAZOO

THE PLAYING SITES

(1)
ATHLETIC PARK 1887-88
(southwest of downtown at
Wheaton & David Streets)

(3)
RIVERVIEW PARK 1906-14
(AKA RECREATION PARK) (on
Healy St. south of Lake St.
near the current fairgrounds)

No descriptive details or historical data have been found on this park. Newspaper accounts mention that it was located on the northwest corner of Wheaton and Oak Streets, which would place it just east of David Street. Its date of origin is unknown, but a newspaper item from September 1888 reports its dismantling and apparent extinction as a baseball facility.

The name Riverview Park for this field causes much confusion over its actual location. Previous to 1906, the name Riverview referred to another earlier ballpark located on the approximate site of today's Sutherland Park. When this new park was erected near the current fairgrounds site in 1906, much of the grandstand and fence lumber from the original Riverview site was reused for the new site, and even the Riverview name was transferred. In any case, the name Riverview Park was used in all newspaper accounts of the Southern Michigan League team games from 1906 through 1914 and games were definitely played at the fairgrounds location.

(2)
NORTH ST. PARK 1889-97
(intersection of North & Stuart
Sts.—on west side)

(no details available on this park)

The streetcar line which carried patrons directly to the fairgrounds race track grandstand ran east and west along the north edge of the baseball park. According to period maps, home plate and the main grandstand were on the north end of the grounds. A second grandstand down the first base line was added in 1908. By 1914 the old park was showing its age and club President J. W. Ryder hired an expert groundskeeper, Michael Ryan, to restore the field to tip-top condition. Despite the good intentions, it was an exercise in futility as it was the last year for league baseball in Kalamazoo until the great World War was over.

RIVERVIEW PARK

BASEBALL OPENING

NEW PARK. NEW TEAM, NEW LEAGUE.

Kalamazoo vs. Tecumseh

Southern Michigan League Teams.

THURSDAY, MAY 17th

Parade Starts at 2 O'clock; Game called at 3:30

SOUVENIR TICKETS for Opening Game, including grand stand, $1.00; on sale at the following places: Kools' Cigar Store, S. P. Fitzgerald's Cigar Store; B. Cleenewerck & Son's Cigar Store; Raseman & Cleenewerck's Cigar Store and Wilkins & Hinga's Cigar Store.

Admission at Grounds 25c. - Grand Stand 25c

A newspaper ad heralds the opener of the '06 SML season at new Riverview Park.

**STATIONERY PARK 1920-26
(AKA HARRISON ST. GROUNDS)
(at north end of Harrison St.,
between Walbridge & the river)**

When Kalamazoo joined the revived Central League for the 1920 season, a new downtown ballpark was in order. Property was leased from the Kalamazoo Stationery Company just north of the end of Harrison St. where it intersects Frank St. Harrison Street was paved and extended north past Frank St. to the park entrance. By this time, automobile parking was a necessity and ample space for 500 autos was provided. The interurban railroad from downtown ran north along Walbridge and delivered patrons directly to the main grandstand. In addition, two streetcar lines ran within a few blocks of the park so access to the games was well provided for. Newspaper accounts from 1920 indicate that the covered stand and home plate would be in the southeast corner with center field in the northwest. But period street maps suggest that the main grandstand was on the western edge along Walbridge St. with center field directly east. In 1924 a new steel and concrete grandstand was purportedly built and very possibly the diamond was reoriented to an east-west alignment. Original seating capacity was 2500 but as many as 5000+ fans filled the place on occasion.

Weinmaster of Kalamazoo scores against Grand Rapids in a 1922 game at Stationery Park.

A fine view of the Stationery Park grandstand during a game in the 1920s

SUTHERLAND PARK 1996– (between Mills St. and the Kalamazoo River—where Gibson St. intersects)

⑤

An architect's sketch of the renovated Sutherland Park

Once the site of an earlier ballpark called Riverview Park and later Sutherland Field long before the current renovation, it was the home field for the 1949 & 1951 AABC national champion Kalamazoo Sutherland Paper amateur clubs, as well as home for a time of the AAGBL Lassies in the early fifties. The field had been abandoned and neglected in recent decades until Mayor Annen began a program of restoration and renovation. The property also includes a football/soccer stadium once called Catholic Athletic Association Stadium, which was also renovated and renamed Soisson/Rapacz/Clason Field. The entire complex is now called the Edward J. Annen Jr. Sports & Recreation Facility and includes both parks. The baseball grandstand lies in the northeast corner of the diamond with center field in the southwest. During renovation, a small portion of the old concrete stand behind home plate was retained and refurbished, but all the remaining seating is new. Seating capacity is now 6,279 plus a special picnic deck area along the right field fence. Dimensions are 330' down both foul lines and 395' to dead center.

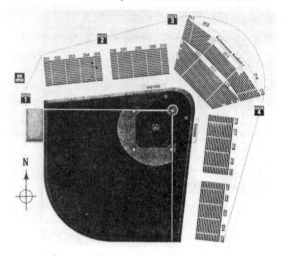

A diagram of the new Sutherland Park layout

A view from the first base bleachers

A view of the playing field

A ground level shot of the new grand-stand and bleacher from outside

LAKE LINDEN

PROFESSIONAL LEAGUE MEMBERSHIP

YEARS	LEAGUE	HOME FIELD
1905	Copper Country-Soo	Lake Linden Diamond
1906	Northern-Copper Country	Lake Linden Diamond

Like most of her nearby Copper Country communities, Lake Linden participated in numerous semi-professional or even fully professional independent baseball leagues that vied for claims to the championship of the region around the turn of the century. A good example of such an alliance was the Houghton County League of 1904, which included the four entries of Lake Linden, Dollar Bay, Calumet, and the Portage Lakes (Houghton & Hancock). Well-heeled backers with money to burn unashamedly recruited professional players from all over to stock their local teams. Lake Linden carried this to the extreme by recruiting an entire team, the crack Ionia independents from the lower peninsula, managed by Joe Ganzell of the famous Ganzell brothers. The Houghton County teams had their own schedule but also took on all comers from all points of the UP during the summer.

Overzealous wagering and an absence of salary limits had ruined competitive baseball in the Copper Country in the 1890s and backers of the renewed baseball interest of 1904 decided to keep the program controlled by entering the new 1905 league into the National Association, making it a fully recognized and protected organization. The name for the new league was to be the Copper Country-Soo League and its members were Lake Linden, Calumet, Hancock, and Sault Ste. Marie. Dr. G. W. Orr was president of the circuit and Dr. Percy R. Glass of Lake Linden was named secretary. Glass was also president, business manager, and field manager of the Lake Lindens. Charles Fichtel's Calumet Aristocrats won the 1905 pennant but Lake Linden was runnerup, only two games behind the Calumets.

In March 1906, after Sault Ste. Marie opted not to rejoin the league, the Copper Country circuit added Houghton and then merged with the nearby Northern League to form the Northern-Copper Country League. Besides the four UP towns, the new circuit included Fargo and Grand Forks (ND), Duluth and Winnipeg. Drs. Orr and Glass were elected VP and secretary of the new eight-team alignment. Outfielder William Foster replaced Dr. Glass as field manager of the Lake Lindens. In a summer plagued by unfavorable weather, controversial umpiring, and failed franchises (Hancock and Grand Forks dropped out in July), Lake Linden finished a distant fifth in the final standings, 20 games behind winner Calumet. But the locals showcased some outstanding players like outfielders Jess Becker, who led the league with a .326 average, Mike Wotell, and Jack Lelivelt. Some losses were recouped by the sale of these stars—Wotell to Toronto, Becker to Cincinnati, and Lelivelt to the Philadelphia Athletics. Lelivelt eventually spent six seasons from 1909-14 with several American League clubs. The Northern-Copper Country League lasted one more year but Lake Linden did not participate.

Joe Ganzell brought his entire Ionia independent club to represent Lake Linden in 1904 competition.

Dr. George W. Orr was an enthusiastic baseball booster and president of the newly formed Copper Country-Soo League.

Another doctor, Percy Glass, was behind the Lake Linden entry in the '05 CC-S circuit. He was also league secretary.

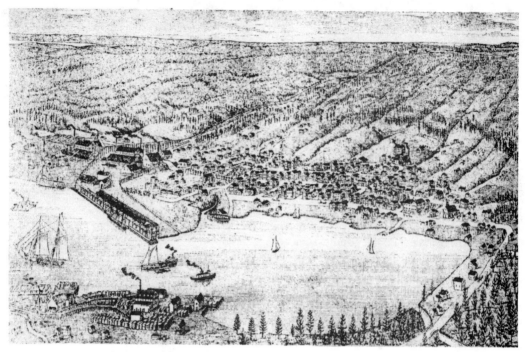

An artist's depiction of Lake Linden in the late 19th century

Jack Lelivelt starred for the 1906 Lake Lindens and wound up in the American League from 1909 to 1914.

THE PLAYING SITE

LAKE LINDEN DIAMOND 1905-06 (location uncertain)

The home field for the 1905-06 Lake Lindens was probably one of two sites where baseball games were believed to be played in the early 20th century. One field was south of the village near the railroad depot and the other possible location was across Torch Lake.

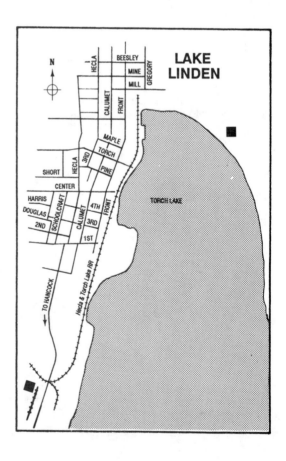

LANSING

PROFESSIONAL LEAGUE MEMBERSHIP

YEARS	LEAGUE	HOME FIELD
1889-90	Michigan State	Capital City Park
1895	Michigan State	Parshall Park (State Lot)
1897	Michigan State	Fairgrounds
1902	Michigan State	Fairgrounds
1907-14	Southern Michigan	League Park (State Lot) (Sundays—Waverly Park)
1921-22	Central	Community Field
1940-41	Michigan State	Municipal Park
1996-	Midwest	Oldsmobile Park

Lansing native Jack Morrissey was the city's "Mr. Baseball" during his time. He was a player, manager, and owner of Lansing teams from 1895 to 1914. He also starred for other Michigan teams and had a "cup of coffee" in the big leagues.

Bud Fowler was a 19th century pioneer for blacks in baseball. He played for Lansing in the 1895 Michigan State League.

Michigan's Capital City participated in its first professional baseball league when it entered the Michigan State League of 1889. Walter Mumby, a native of Corunna, MI and a veteran player/-manager, was hired to manage the Lansing nine. Two years earlier Mumby managed the Big Rapids club in the aborted Northern Michigan League. Other member cities in the '89 MSL were Grand Rapids, Greenville, Jackson, Kalamazoo, and Saginaw. Manager Mumby played shortstop while pitcher Yerkes and catcher Faatz were the team's top battery. Other notable members of the '89 Lansing team included Al Manassau and George Stallings, who joined the team late in the summer after his release by Greenville. The Lansings ended up a distant fifth in the standings but were encouraged to make another run for the State League flag in 1890. C. A. Briggs was the new field boss for the '90 Lansings. Manistee, Muskegon, and Port Huron replaced Jackson, Saginaw, and Greenville in the new six-team alignment. Only a month into the season, the league began to crumble and on June 10 it collapsed for good. Lansing was buried in the MSL basement with a 5-16 record when the end came.

Five years later, Mr. R. N. Parshall obtained a lease from the State Board of Auditors for property to build a baseball field at the corner of Washtenau and Walnut. At the same time, he took on a franchise for Lansing to enter the Michigan State League for 1895. Former Lansing pilot Walter Mumby was the president of the new league. Parshall secured another former Lansing State Leaguer, Al Manassau, to manage his team—to be called "Senators." Other member cities included Adrian, Port Huron, Kalamazoo, Battle Creek (later transferred to Jackson), and Owosso. The Senators fared poorly and finished the 1895 season in fifth place, far in arrears of a strong Adrian club which was reinforced with several talented black stars from the famed Page Fence Giants touring team. Lansing obtained the services of one of Adrian's blacks, Bud Fowler, in late July and he made a fine showing for the Senators with a .333 BA in 30 games. A Lansing boy, 19-year-old John "Jack" Morrissey, made a major contribution to the Senators' cause with a rousing .362 in 77 games. Morrissey later became the city's "Mr. Baseball" with a long career as a player and manager for Lansing and other Michigan towns, plus a brief two-year career with the Cincinnati Reds in 1902-03.

The State League attempted to resume play in 1896 but the whole plan disintegrated before the season started, due in part to Lansing's inability to renew its lease on the so-called "State Lot" grounds. The following year, Lansing made arrangements to play at the fairgrounds and once again the Michigan State League was off and running. John Peck's Senators were in second place, 7-1/2 games behind leader Jackson when the league once again fell apart in late July. Lansing stayed out of Organized Baseball for another five years. The State League idea refused to die and once again was reborn in 1902. Harry Bowie and G. W. Niles entered Lansing into the latest version of the SML, and this time the league survived until late August. Unfavorable weather and other symptoms of instability doomed the 1902 SML from day one and it would be another eight years before it would be attempted again.

Meanwhile, another Michigan-based minor league with better organization, the Southern Michigan League, survived its maiden season intact in 1906. Hometown star Jack Morrissey, still in his prime as a player, assembled a team to represent Lansing as one of the two new expansion clubs for the eight-team SML for 1907. The other seven towns were Tecumseh, Kalamazoo, Battle Creek, Mt. Clemens, Bay City, Flint, and Jackson (until July 15). Arrangements were made to use the old State Lot site on Washtenau Avenue. Morrissey's Senators were consistently mediocre for their first three years in the SML, finishing sixth every season. Pitcher George Pierce and Morrissey himself were the only standouts on the club in those years but the acquisition of pitcher Homer "Slab" Warner and another Lansing product, first baseman Vic Saier, in 1910 propelled the Senators into a tie for the league championship with Kalamazoo. The Kazoos won the pennant outright in a post-season playoff. Hometown hero Saier hit over .300 and led the SML with 175 hits. The following year he was in the major leagues with the Chicago Cubs and became their regular first sacker for the next seven seasons.

Vic Saier had the most productive major league career of any Lansing-born player. He replaced the great Frank Chance as the Chicago Cubs' first baseman in 1911 and was a regular for the next six seasons.

In 1911 Slab Warner returned to Lansing with another spectacular season on the mound, leading the league with 26 victories and 231 strikeouts. But Morrissey's Senators were unable to overtake a strong Kalamazoo club and once again settled for the runnerup spot. The departure of key players Vic Saier and Charles Fox probably cost the Lansing's the 1911 pennant. Morrissey's men faded into the second division with losing seasons in their last two full years (1912-13) in the SML. By 1914, the Lansing franchise was in desparate straits and in early July the team was transferred to Mt. Clemens. It was the end of the SML journey for Lansing and the league itself folded the following year. Outstanding players

during their final years were Jack Onslow, Al "Bull" Durham, T. H. McNellis, and Earl Stimpson. Their nine-year run in the Southern Michigan circuit was Lansing's longest tenure as a member of a professional minor league and the club was owned and managed by Jack Morrissey during the entire period. The Capital City would remain out of Organized Baseball until long after World War I was over.

The great World War put minor league baseball on hold for several years, but in 1920 the class B Central League was revived with four Michigan cities as members—Grand Rapids, Kalamazoo, Ludington, and Muskegon. A successful maiden season encouraged expansion to six clubs in 1921, and Lansing and Jackson were admitted. Lack of an adequate baseball facility had thwarted Lansing's bid to join the league in 1920, but that obstacle was overcome with the construction of a brand new park in the southeast section of the city. Fred J. Blanding was the president of the Lansing club for 1921 and one-time Pittsburgh Pirate Fred Hunter was named first baseman and field manager. The new Senators ended up over .500 with a 65-63 WL record but a whopping 21-1/2 games behind winner Ludington. Lawrence Reno (18-13) and Roy Kauffman (17-13) gave the '21 Lansings some decent pitching but a league-worst 328 errors prevented the Senators from challenging for the championship. Outfielder Charles Miller hit .348 to lead the Lansing offense. Hunter's club slipped to fourth place in 1922, once again with the worst fielding percentage in the circuit. Newcomer Lester Bell led the Lansing regulars with a .329 batting average in 127 games at shortstop. The following year he joined the St. Louis Cardinals and hit .290 in nine seasons in the National League. Over the winter of 1922-23, the Central League lost its key franchises to the Michigan-Ontario League, leaving Lansing out of organized baseball. Minor league baseball in Michigan and elsewhere was losing its popularity by the late twenties and the Great Depression of the thirties prohibited its return until the WWII era.

Fred Blanding was president of the 1921 Lansing club of the reborn Central League.

Les Bell was Lansing's short-stop in 1922. The following year he joined the St. Louis Cardinals and hit .290 in nine seasons of National League play.

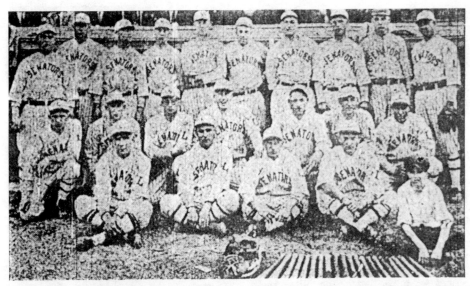

The third place Lansing Senators of 1921. TOP ROW (L to R): Miller, Mgr. Hunter, Weimer, Poorman, Conley, Fannin, Reno, Butler, Main (a 10th player somewhere in this row is unidentified). MIDDLE ROW: Wheat, Vendervoo, Kaufman, Lutz, Kimball, Hibernik, B. Smith. BOTTOM: Thornton, Grimm, C. Smith, Yingling, mascot.

With the return of pre-war prosperity and the evolution of major league farm systems in the late thirties, new minor leagues were springing up everywhere. The St. Louis Cardinals, the leaders of the farm system concept, agreed to sponsor the Lansing entry in the class C Michigan State League for 1940. The six-team circuit also included Flint, Saginaw, St. Joseph, Grand Rapids, and Muskegon. Jess Altenburg, a native of nearby Ashley, MI and one-time Pittsburgh Pirate, was chosen to pilot the Lansing "Lancers." A city-owned Municipal Park on the eastern edge of town was made available for State League games. The Lancers were a good hitting club, leading the league in team batting with a .294 average, but mediocre pitching destined the club to finish dead last in the final standings. Catcher/first baseman Gerald Burmeister was the team's top slugger with 15 HRs, 86 RBIs, and a .360 BA. Norm Petersen and Dick Sisler were close behind with .329 and .322 averages, respectively. Sisler was, of course, the son of baseball immortal George Sisler and attracted much attention throughout the league as a potential carbon copy of his famed father. He eventually made it to the big show for a fairly productive career, but his numbers came nowhere near the feats of father George.

In 1941, the Lansing State League club restored the old nickname "Senators" and once again took residence in the league's basement in both halves of the split season, winning only 35 games all year. Danny Taylor was the new manager, but was replaced by Russ Weuin before the season ended. Once again it was poor pitching and dreadful fielding that kept the young Senators at the bottom of the standings. First sacker Everett Robinson was the only big gun on the offensive

side with a .345 average and 93 runs batted in. Robinson would surface after the war in the 1948-51 Central League as one of Grand Rapids' favorite stars in that league. America's entry into the second World War in late 1941 put the Michigan State League out of business and it was never resurrected after the war ended. For Lansing, it would have to wait another 55 years for a return of professional league baseball.

The son of Hall of Famer George Sisler, Dick Sisler was an outfielder on the 1940 Lansing Lancers. Although he never came close to the feats of his famous father, he played eight seasons in the NL with St. Louis, Philadelphia, and Cincinnati.

With the remarkable success of Grand Rapids' West Michigan Whitecaps franchise in the Midwest League of 1994, other Michigan cities were no longer ignored as sites for new franchises in the midwest circuit and other independent leagues as well. Chicago advertising executive Tom Dickson and other investors had purchased the Waterloo IA Midwest League club in 1991 and ultimately relocated the team to Springfield IL in 1994. The team continued to draw poorly and Dickson looked to Lansing as an ideal location and opened discussions with Lansing Mayor Tom Hollister. After a period of prolonged and often difficult negotiations, a deal was struck for construction of a city-owned downtown baseball park. GM's Oldsmobile Division pledged 1.5 million toward the new park, including the rights to name it Oldsmobile Park. Construction began in 1995 and the Capital City was officially scheduled to become a member of the Midwest League for the 1996 season. As in Grand Rapids, public response was overwhelming as over 400,000 attendance was guaranteed by season ticket sales alone. In keeping with the current trend for catchy nicknames to promote the team's merchandise, the name "Lugnuts" was chosen and soon caught on with even the more skeptical fans. A working agreement with the Kansas City Royals was continued from the Springfield club and the Royals appointed veteran minor league Manager/Coach Brian Poldberg as the new pilot of the Lugnuts. Almost overnight a new rivalry with Grand Rapids was born—not just on the playing field but in the stands, as attendance figures in Lansing show every indication of threatening the Furniture City for class A patronage champions of the USA.

Sherrie Myers and Tom Dickson, managing partners of the new Lansing Lugnuts of the 1996 Midwest League

Brian Poldberg was picked to pilot the Lugnuts, a class A farm club of the Kansas City Royals.

The choice of "Lugnuts" as the new 1996 team identification was somewhat controversial at first, but soon caught on as a clever promotional gimmick for an automotive city.

THE PLAYING SITES

CAPITAL CITY PARK 1889-90 (southeast corner of Washington & Elm Streets)

This park was built in April 1889 for use by the new Michigan State League team. The grandstand for the park was positioned on the northwest corner of the property where Elm intersects Washington. Period newspaper reports describe the grandstand as with "ample accommodations for 500 people... and equipped with all conveniences." A bleacher section with an additional 800 capacity was built along the western (Washington Ave.) edge along the first base line. The property is described as 561 ft. long and 338 ft. wide. As was customary, a high board fence surrounded the grounds. Another newspaper account mentions that the "field will slope a trifle southwest and northeast from the home plate"—apparently a "crowned" feature to facilitate drainage after a rainfall.

A game in progress at the old "State Lot" ballpark, probably around 1910

PARSHALL PARK 1895 LEAGUE PARK 1907-14 (on property immediately south of the Capital Bldg.—bordered by Walnut & Chestnut, Washtenau & Kalamazoo Sts.—called "State Lot")

(2)

This property was first acquired for baseball use from the State Board of Auditors for a rental fee of $75 (for the season) by team owner R. N. Parshall for the State League team of 1895. Its central location was ideal for week day games but the opposition to Sunday baseball inside the city was its main drawback. Being surrounded by residential housing was also a problem as complaining neighbors forced the owners to prevent its usage to the ball team in 1896, thus denying the city of a league team in 1896. The property remained basically dormant for the next 10 years but was used for some sandlot and local high school games. When Lansing entered the Southern Michigan League in 1907, they made new arrangements for this site as a home field—apparently the objections from neighbors had subsided. Jack Morrissey's club made considerable investments in a new covered grandstand and open bleachers along the foul lines. The orientation of the diamond is uncertain, but very likely home plate was in the northeast corner of the lot. This property was commonly referred to as the "State Lot" because it still belonged to the state, but Morrissey's group renamed it League Park. It served as home for the SML club for the seven years of its existence. The

Lewis Cass State Office Building currently occupies the site. Because of the ongoing protests against Sunday baseball, Waverly Park was also used by the SML club for Sunday games during these years.

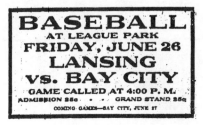

A 1914 newspaper advertisement

FAIRGROUNDS DRIVING PARK 1897, 1902 (on East Michigan between Magnolia & Mifflin)

(3)

Forced out of the State Lot site by complaining neighbors, the 1897 and 1902 State League clubs utilized the existing Driving Park on the city's east side. No photos or map information have been found to provide more precise details about the exact location or orientation of the diamond.

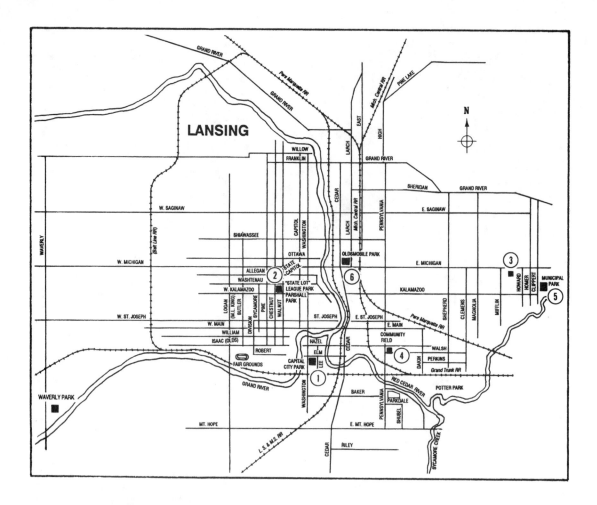

LANSING

N

COMMUNITY FIELD 1921-22
(4) (on Pennsylvania Ave., just north of Potter Park)

Lansing lost its bid to join the Central League in 1920 mainly because they lacked an adequate baseball facility. When the league expanded to six teams for 1921 the Capital City was accepted as a new franchise on the condition that a new ball park would be erected. A lease was arranged with the owners (Lansing Board of Water & Light) for 11 acres of land along Pennsylvania Avenue just north of Potter Park and work began in early 1921 on a modern, expansive baseball park comparable with any in the Central League. No maps or diagrams have been located to suggest the position and orientation of the diamond, but like most new ball parks of the period, it included a commodious, roofed grandstand and bleachers on both sides with a board fence surrounding the field. When the Central League disbanded after the 1922 season, the field was used by local teams for another year, then abandoned for construction of a Power Company warehouse by the owners of the property.

MUNICIPAL PARK 1940-41
(5) (south of E. Michigan, on the east side of Clippert)

Municipal Park was built by the city in 1926 to provide a first class baseball field for local teams after the abrupt demise of Community Field. When Lansing was admitted to the 1940 Michigan State League, the field was upgraded and lights were added. After the final year (1941) of MSL play, the field was retained as a city baseball field and is still used for that purpose today. The current home plate is in the northwest corner of the lot.

OLDSMOBILE PARK 1996- (on Michigan Ave. near downtown between Cedar & Larch)

When principle owner Tom Dickson made a bid to relocate his Springfield IL Midwest League franchise to Lansing in 1995, he persuaded Mayor David Hollister to begin some high-powered and often top secret negotiations to build a state-of-the-art city-owned baseball facility in the heart of Lansing. Eventually a formula for financing the $13 million dollar ball park was worked out and construction began in early 1995. The Oldsmobile Division of GM provided 1.5 million toward the construction costs and obtained the rights to name it Oldsmobile Park. The architect was HNTB Corporation of Kansas City and the principal builder was Clark Construction Company of Lansing. Inspired by current trends of duplicating the nostalgic appeal of the classic parks of yesteryear, Oldsmobile Park combines this flavor with the most modern amenities available for fan comfort and convenience for the teams. Field dimensions are deliberately "quirky" to add to the park's unique personality. The surrounding neighborhood has been partially cleared out and renovated to provide ample parking for anticipated capacity crowds. The latest in electronic message boards, modern lighting, and 26 luxury suites are all part of the Oldsmobile Park experience.

An aerial view of Oldsmobile Park reveals the "quirky" contours of the outfield fence.

An architect's rendering of Oldsmobile Park

113

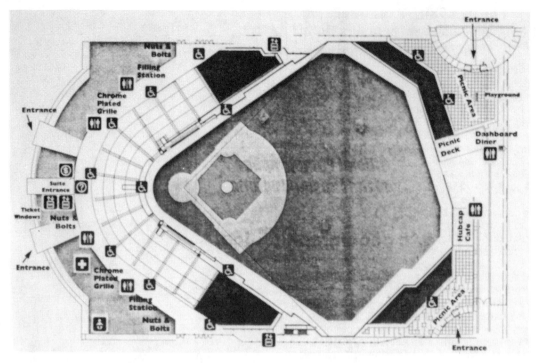

A field diagram identifies many of the features of Oldsmobile Park.

An aerial photo of Oldsmobile Park under construction shows its proximity to the downtown district of Lansing. The State Capitol Building is in the top center.

LUDINGTON

PROFESSIONAL LEAGUE MEMBERSHIP

YEARS	LEAGUE	HOME FIELD
1912-14	Michigan State	Culver Park
1920-22	Central	Culver Park
1926	Central/Mich. State	Culver Park

As with many communities its size, Ludington's opportunity to participate in a professional baseball league was a fortuitous accident of geography. The Michigan State League of 1910-11 was essentially a string of lakeshore towns along the coast of Lake Michigan and considerations for the cost of traveling were always paramount. After two disappointing seasons, the southernmost town of Holland was eager to relocate in 1912 and Ludington, which lies between member cities Muskegon and Manistee, was a logical destination. Team owner Forrest Dickerson (brother of League President Emerson Dickerson) met with prominent Ludington businessman Wilmer Culver and others and obtained pledges for financial backing, including the construction of a new baseball park. Central League veteran player "Mum" Warrender was hired as field manager. Most of the members of the losing Holland club of 1911 were cast adrift (with the exception of star hurler Herb Jewell) as Warrender set about to assemble a competitive roster for the new Ludington "Mariners."

Forrest Dickerson transferred his Holland club to Ludington in 1912.

Ludington businessman Wilmer Culver was behind the new downtown ballpark that gave Ludington a berth in the State League.

The community immediately rallied behind their new franchise and an overflow crowd filled Culver Park for the inauguration of league baseball on May 24, 1912. The fans were rewarded with a thrilling last-inning victory over visiting Boyne City. As the season progressed Warrender's newcomers proved to be a worthy competitor, finishing third in the six-team circuit with a 60-59 record. First baseman Thomas was the team's top hitter with a .339 average for 55 games. Manager Warrender played every game in the outfield and hit a creditable .283. Herb Jewell proved to be one of the league's top hurlers with a fine 19-9 WL record. The 1913 Mariners under new managers Bob Grogan and Harry Arndt were unable to escape the league basement and at season's end a local group purchased the

Mum Warrender played outfield and managed the first OB Ludington team.

The 1912 Mariners who finished third, 23½ games behind Manistee. (L to R): Young, Schafer, Jewell, Sager, Mgr. Warrender, Thomas, Newmeyer, Long, Mathews, Manchester, TeRoller, Varley.

J. B. Smith headed the new group that purchased the franchise from Forrest Dickerson in 1913. He was also president of the new Central League club of 1920.

franchise from owner Dickerson. J. B. Smith headed the Ludington Baseball Association and was the team's new president. Smith proved to be an able executive as he aggressively re-energized community support and played an active role in reassembling a winning roster for the Mariners. Bob Grogan returned as field boss but voluntarily quit in July and was replaced by local favorite, third baseman James "Lil" Sager. The State League of 1914 was struggling to survive and finished the season with only four teams as both Boyne City and Traverse City withdrew late in the season. Muskegon was the eventual winner, but Ludington finished a strong second, only four games out of first. Leo Walker and Dean Bixby led the pitching staff with 22 and 17 wins, respectively. First sacker Carl Tennant's 7 HRs led the State League and his .291 average was tops on the club. Ludington's attendance figures were healthy enough in 1914 to assure the team's return in 1915 but it was a lost cause as the Michigan State League went out of business.

The city's enthusiastic support of the State League team was taken into account when Emerson Dickerson orchestrated a revival of the Central League in 1920. Beginning modestly with only the four Michigan communities of Grand Rapids, Kalamazoo, Muskegon, and Ludington,

Dickerson confidently expected to expand to six or eight clubs as the circuit progressed. J. B. Smith was back as team president and Central League veteran Charles "Punch" Knoll was hired to assemble a cast of players to compete at a class B level. Among the players recruited by Knoll were a pair of hometown brothers, Davey and Danny Claire, who made up the Mariners' keystone combination for most of the season. The 1920 Mariners finished the season at an even .500 (63-63), in third place behind champion Grand Rapids. Outfielder Vince Tydeman hit only .234 but led the league with 11 homers. Bill Shoup was the workhorse of the pitching staff with a 20-11 record, but John Bogart (14-16) led the circuit in strikeouts with 199 and was rewarded with a Detroit Tiger tryout at season's end. Shortstop Davey Claire joined Bogart in Detroit and earned the distinction of being the only Ludington native to play in the big show. Brother Danny actually had a better year at the plate with a .353 average, but it was Davey who got the call.

Punch Knoll, an old veteran of the Central League, was picked to pilot the new 1920 Mariners.

Ludington's own Davey Claire had a brief trial with Detroit in late 1920.

The 1914 Mariners were runnerups in the State League's final season. STANDING (L to R): Sager, Poad, Kirby, Tennant, Asher, Walker, Grogan. SEATED: LeBeau, Murphy, (unknown), Altenburg, Bixby.

A pre-season photo of the 1921 pennant winners. STANDING (L to R): Dodds, Hammond, Shoup, Smith, Johnson, McMenamin, Pasquella, Black, Napier, Beal, Brown. SEATED: Balser, Mgr. Sharp, Burns, Hamel, Nelson, Moore.

The Central League, as planned, expanded to six teams in 1921 by adding Lansing and Jackson. James Sharp was the Mariners' new field boss for '21 and gave the local fans a season to remember by dominating the Central League with an impressive collection of statistics seldom claimed by any league club. For starters, they ran away with the pennant, finishing a full 16 games up on runnerup Kalamazoo. They led all teams in both fielding and hitting, including an awesome total of 73 home runs and a team BA of .303. "Gaty" Hamel led the barrage with 21 HRs, exceeding four of the other clubs' team totals. Catcher Cecil Hammond led the team with a .353 BA, followed by Dan Beal at .334 and "Nellie" Nelson at .320. Napier, McNenanim, and Burns also finished well above the .300 mark. The pitching was equally overpowering with three 20-game winners in Bill Shoup (25), Clarence Brown (22), and Oscar Johnson (22). The only disappointment for the otherwise magnificent 1921 season was the post-season defeat at the hands of a tough London club of the rival MINT League.

In 1922, the Central League adopted a split-season schedule with first and second half winners (if different) to meet in a post-season playoff. Former big leaguer Ambrose "Amby" McConnell was hired to replace Sharp as field manager. Many of the big stars of 1921 had been sold off, but a few key holdovers returned to give the Mariners another winning aggregation for 1922. Ludington still had enough talent to finish with the best overall record but a stronger Grand Rapids club under Josh Devore won the first half championship to earn the right to challenge second half winner Ludington in the playoffs. One factor that reinforced the GR club was the acquisition of Ludington's ace pitcher from the '21 team, Bill Shoup, who also notched 20 victories for his new club. Another unfortunate circumstance hurt the Mariner cause when Manager McConnell was forced to resign in July after a severe injury from a batted ball. Third baseman Andy Woehr finished the season as field boss. Ludington started out well in the post-season series, winning three of the first four, but GR

Mgr. James Sharp gave Ludington fans a team to remember in 1921. He also played third base.

Hard-hitting backstop Cecil Hammond was a fixture on the winning Mariner teams of 1921-22.

Bunny Buffington was a valuable utility man for Ludington in 1921-22.

Mariners' shortstop Hilding "Nellie" Nelson hit .320 and .324 in '21 and '22.

prevailed as new league champions by winning the last three games played. Pitcher Oscar Johnson had another fine year in '22 with a 25-8 record, and newcomer Eddie Wells (13-10) was recalled to the Detroit club at season's end began a 15-year career as a big league pitcher. First baseman Harry Schwab was the big gun on offense with a .359 average but once again most of the regulars hit well over the .300 mark to give the team another lofty average (.293). Enthusiasm for Mariners baseball was still high and the city looked forward to another banner season in 1923, but the fates would turn against them in the following off-season.

Former big leaguer Amby McConnell was the new player/manager for 1922.

First baseman Harry Schwab hit a rousing .359 for the '22 club.

Eddie Wells, a 13-game winner in '22, went on to a 12-year career in the AL, winning 12 for Cobb's Tigers in 1926.

Dick Plummer pitched and played outfield for the 1922 Mariners.

During the winter of 1922-23, four of the larger cities in the Central League were persuaded to abandon that circuit and join the rival Michigan-Ontario (MINT) League for 1923. Because of its size, Ludington was not one of the chosen few and was, in effect, ousted from the baseball map. It was a bitter pill to swallow for the Ludington faithful and accordingly they had to settle for independent baseball for the next three summers. But the MINT adventure for the former Central League members eventually turned sour after 1924 and these towns also went without league baseball in 1925. Emerson Dickerson then took a page from his 1920 book and reinstated the four-team Central League lineup of that year for the 1926 season, and Ludington baseball was back in business. J. B. Smith was once again masterminding the encore of league baseball and the renovation of aging and neglected Culver Park was quickly begun. A new nickname "Tars" was adopted to give the team a fresh identity. One-time Pittsburgh Pirate Ovid Nicholson was given the job of manager and would also patrol the outfield. With a lower class C rating and lesser salary limit, tryouts were staged to attract fresh young talent along with a handful of veteran professionals to assemble a winning combination.

The 1926 Central League season was barely a month along when negotiations for a merger with the struggling four-team MINT League were initiated. Both leagues were a four-team shadow of their former selves and in dire financial straits. With all Michigan towns enlisted, both leagues scrapped their original schedules and began anew on June 15 as the class B Michigan State League. Ludington was 12-12 in the Central and finished in fifth place with a 45-51 record in the reborn Michigan State circuit. Former Mariner Dan Beal had a banner season in both leagues, hitting .360 and then .375 in the latter loop. John Gunderson, Ray Prehn, and Mike Kennedy also hit well over .300. The combined league favored the higher class ex-MINT clubs as Bay City, Port Huron, and Saginaw finished 1-2-3 in the final standings. After 1926, minor league baseball in Michigan faded away for many more years. For Ludington it was a fantastic run, considering the tiny population base that supported the game here for so many summers. Although most personal recollections of that glorious era have all but disappeared, it remains a proud chapter of Ludington's heritage.

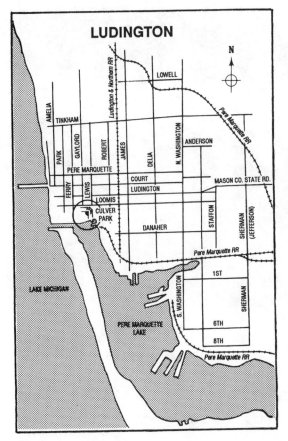

LUDINGTON

CULVER PARK 1912-26
(south of Loomis, where Lewis St. intersects)

When Ludington was accepted for membership in the Michigan State League in early 1912, a suitable baseball park had to be hastily provided—enter prominent local businessman Wilmer Culver to the rescue. A vice president of a local railroad and other enterprises, Culver negotiated a multi-year lease with the Pere Marquette Railroad for downtown property adjacent to the RR ferry docks to be converted into baseball grounds for the new team. He then turned the property over to the city and construction for the new park was underway. The waterfront location was ideal for local fans because of its downtown location and also for visiting groups of followers from nearby Manistee, Muskegon, and Traverse City who very often arrived by passenger ships. The main covered grandstand was in the northeast corner of the grounds directly south of where Lewis Street dead-ended at Loomis. When the park hosted its first Mariner game on May 24, 1912 the park builders discovered an unforeseen flaw in its construction (at least on important dates that attracted huge crowds). The single entrance to the grounds was a narrow passageway directly behind home plate and patrons had to wait patiently to enter or exit the park. During the five year absence of league baseball from 1915-19, the park had suffered some neglect and considerable monies and labor were required to restore it to league standards.

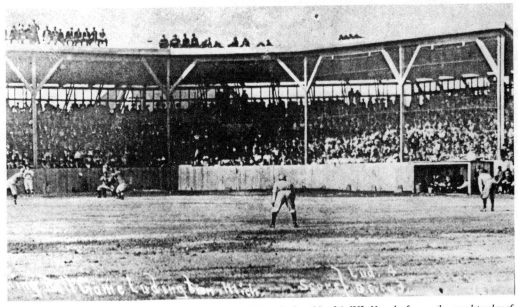

A game action photo of the first professional league game at Culver Park on May 24, 1912. Note the fans on the grandstand roof.

A rare aerial photograph of the City of Ludington looking east, probably taken in the 1920s or 1930s. The Culver Park grandstand can be seen at the bottom of the picture.

A game in progress at Culver Park about 1920. The Pere Marquette grain elevator and car ferry can be seen in the background.

MANISTEE

PROFESSIONAL LEAGUE MEMBERSHIP

YEARS	LEAGUE	HOME FIELD
1890	Michigan State	Parkdale Grounds (Athletic Park) (Recreation Park)
1911-14	Michigan State	Parkdale Grounds

One of the more prosperous lumbering communities along the Lake Michigan shoreline in the late 19th century, Manistee also gave their citizenry some quality baseball teams to root for, both the professional league variety and some pretty "fast" independent clubs. In 1890 the city became a member of the Michigan State League, which also included Grand Rapids, Flint, Port Huron, Muskegon, and Lansing. F. B. Wilson was the president of the '90 baseball association and the field boss was a "war horse" of several Michigan-based professional leagues, catcher John A. Murphy. Home games were played at the old fairgrounds driving park in the Parkdale section of the city. The State League schedule was barely a month into the season when most of the clubs were already in financial trouble. Manistee and Grand Rapids were at the top of the standings in early June when GR abruptly bolted to join the higher class International League. The MSL attempted to make a go of it without Grand Rapids but had to throw in the towel on June 10. Manager Murphy and Manistee's crack battery of pitcher Frank Killen and catcher John McMahon joined the new IL Grand Rapids club, but that league also collapsed a month later. Killen was the prize talent on the local club and finished out the decade in the big leagues, winning 165

games including two 30-game win seasons. McMahon also had a "cup of coffee" with the New York Giants in the early 1890s. After Grand Rapids went under, Manager Murphy came back to Manistee and managed some very good independent teams for several years. Local millionaire lumberman Charles Canfield spent a small fortune bankrolling the Manistee independents in the 1890s and on several occasions they made a claim on the unofficial state championship of the independents.

With minor league baseball enjoying a renaissance of sorts after the turn of the century, one of the many new alignments to surface in 1910 was the reborn class D Michigan State League. Consisting of mostly Lake Michigan shoreline communities, Manistee was a logical but unsuccessful candidate the first year. The following year (1911) the loop was ready to expand from four to six teams and Manistee's renovation of their Parkdale facility made them an overwhelming choice, along with Boyne City, to complete the compact circuit. Charles Bigge was named president of the Manistee club and other important backers included Joseph Baur, P. T. Glassmire, and Dennis Riley. First baseman E. R. Sommerlott was chosen captain and field manager when the season opened but he was soon replaced by outfielder Connie Lewis. Defending champion Cadillac started strong and looked like a cinch to repeat in 1911, but new Manistee Manager Lewis did a yeoman's job in recruiting some new stars and the Manistees began to climb in the race. Outstanding pitching by Ray Williams (25-5 with 169 Ks) and Omer Benn (14-5) were the keys as the locals surged into a virtual three-way tie with Cadillac and Muskegon at season's end. Their brilliant finish

Frank Killen, one of the National League's premier pitchers of the 1890s, played for Manistee in 1890.

J. C. Bigge was president of the new Manistee entry in the Michigan State League of 1911.

Outfielder Connie Lewis took over the Manistee club in early 1911 and quickly assembled a mini-dynasty with three consecutive State League pennant winners the result.

Second baseman Louis Haidt was a star player for Manistee's entire four-year run in the State League.

caught the fancy of Manistee fans during the pennant stretch and they came out to root for Lewis's charges in record numbers. A local favorite was hometown product catcher John Bufka, who had played for Grand Rapids and other Michigan teams in professional leagues. In the final standings, Manistee was 1/2 game up on its two rivals but the final count was protested by Muskegon over an earlier loss they felt should be reversed. A ruling in Muskegon's favor would have cost Manistee the championship, but National Commission Chairman Garry Herrmann ruled against Muskegon and the Manistees were the new State League champions for 1911. Manistee's boosters were ecstatic over their first year triumph and decided to nickname the team "champions" as a fitting tribute.

Connie Lewis was the toast of Manistee and many of his stars returned in 1912. Hurlers Ray Williams and Omer Benn were back, plus second baseman Louis Haidt and third baseman Matt McKillen, as well as outfielder/mgr. Lewis. Traverse City took the early lead in 1912 but Lewis's "champions" overtook them in the end to take their second consecutive pennant. Outfielder Carl Jones led the regulars in hitting with .314 followed by Haidt at .290. Omer Benn (22-7) and Ray Williams (21-9) once again paced league pitchers, with Cummings chipping in with a 16-9 record. The 1913 edition of the Champions came roaring back with yet another winner, this time by a 10-1/2 game margin over second place Traverse City. Several of the team regulars, including McKillen, Lewis, Haidt, Anderson, and Prough, returned to pace Manistee's "hitless wonders"—only Matt McKillen managed to hit over .300 (.302) and the Champions were last in team batting at .246. Grover Prough provided some power with a league-leading 14 HRs. John

Radloff (18-7) and Cummings (17-13) gave the Champions some quality pitching on the way to their third straight State League pennant. In a post-season exhibition playoff with the class C Southern Michigan League winner Battle Creek, Manistee added to her reputation by winning four of five games. The Manistees were living up to their nickname, but their success began to cause some unrest around the league.

After four remarkably successful seasons, the Michigan State League began to show signs of trouble in early 1914. Both Manistee and Traverse City were accused of unethical conduct of their affairs by other league members and only a last-minute transfer of leadership kept both cities from being forced out by league prexy Emerson Dickerson. Connie Lewis was all set to manage the Muskegon club when, at the eleventh hour, the Manistee franchise was saved and Lewis returned as '14 Salt City pilot. But the baseball honeymoon was over in Manistee as their once healthy patronage dwindled to a mere handful of paying spectators. After three seasons of championship teams, a 56-51 record was not up to expectations and on September 8 the franchise was transferred to Belding to finish out the season there. Traverse City and Boyne City had already dropped out, so the troubled circuit completed the schedule with only four remaining clubs—Muskegon finally emerging as the new champion. But the seeds of self-destruction were in place and the Michigan State League did not resume play in 1915. Thus ended Manistee's brief but glorious four-year run as a bona fide minor league city. Local businessmen launched an unsuccessful campaign to finance Manistee's entry in the reborn Central League of 1920, but the proposal failed when local citizenry were unwilling to help bankroll the operation.

The first of three straight pennant winners for Manistee, the 1911 State League "Champions." STANDING (L to R): McKillen, Gritz, Williams, Benn, Mgr. Lewis, Hogan, Thiery. SEATED: Jayes, Conroy, Anderson, Utter, Wilkie, Haidt. Mascot Burns lying down in front.

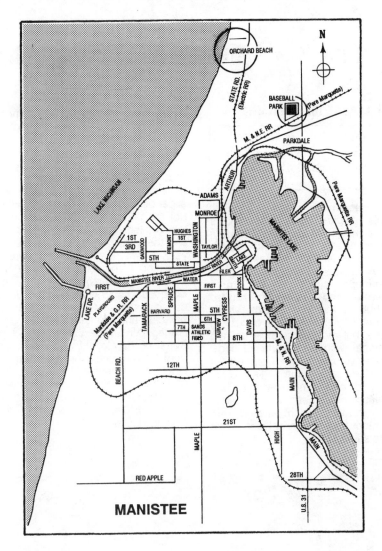

MANISTEE

THE PLAYING SITE

> **PARKDALE GROUNDS 1890, 1911-14 (AKA Driving Park, Athletic Park, League Park, or Recreation Park) (in suburban Parkdale fairgrounds site, north of the city)**

Despite occasional efforts to build a baseball facility in the central city, the fairgrounds site in Parkdale remained as the home field for professional league teams and independent teams for decades. As was the case in so many smaller Michigan communities, the driving park already included a suitable grandstand and outer fence that made the location adaptable for a baseball field. Despite its distance from the central city, the electric railway ran right by the grounds and made public access fairly convenient. Another decent diamond at Orchard

Beach was also available and sometimes used, but it was even more remote than the Parkdale site. When Manistee was admitted to the State League for 1911, the driving park site was essentially rebuilt from scratch with a new grandstand seating up to 800 and additional bleachers for another 600 fans. The original stand used for racing events had burned down several years earlier. No photos or period maps have turned up to verify the exact positioning of the new stands and the orientation of the diamond.

A current view of the site of the old Parkdale Grounds

MARQUETTE

PROFESSIONAL LEAGUE MEMBERSHIP

YEARS	LEAGUE	HOME FIELD
1888-91	Upper Peninsula	3rd St. & Fair Ave.
1892	Michigan-Wisconsin	3rd St. & Fair Ave.

Like everywhere else in the country, baseball became a popular pastime even in Michigan's remote Upper Peninsula. Marquette, the UP's largest city, fielded teams to contend for the championship of the Upper Peninsula as early as the 1880s. So-called Upper Peninsula Leagues were formed among some of the more prosperous towns and usually included Marquette, the hub of the iron district. These "leagues" were not fully professional circuits in the strictest sense, but more accurately defined as semi-professional with a mixture of local amateurs and hired professionals from out of town. The schedule was usually limited to weekend dates and often improvised as the summer progressed. Games with various traveling teams from nearby communities were mixed in so that records of wins and losses were very "unofficial" to say the least.

In any case, Marquette was a member of some form of an Upper Peninsula League from 1888 to 1891. The Marquettes of 1889 under Manager Dan Sullivan finished second to Hancock with a very limited number of weekend games played. In 1890 and 1891 the UP League was closer to a genuine professional circuit with a more expanded schedule, including weekday games. But the teams were still basically made up from talented locals rather than imported professionals and the rosters were fairly consistent from year to year. However, the players were probably well paid and some were very likely "hired guns" to make the hometown team more competitive. Marquette could not claim the UP championship during these years, but they were always a .500 ball club and a feared rival. Ed Douglas was the manager in the last year of this period (1891). Some of the players who represented Marquette from 1888-91 included Mike Birmingham, C. W. Orton, Milt Spencer, Mike Day, Frank Scott, Ed Cull, Paul Craft, Charles Pedroes, and J. J. Hughes. Of this group, only Pedroes advanced to the major leagues, appearing briefly with the Chicago Cubs in 1902.

The Marquette club of 1888 or 1889. STANDING (L to R): Homer Caswell, Milt Spencer, Amby Wheeler, Mike Day. MIDDLE ROW: Mgr. Dan Sullivan, Mike Birmingham. BOTTOM ROW: Charles Myers, Charles Clark, Dennis Cleary, Frank Scott.

James Russell of the Marquette Mining Journal was an important backer of the 1892 W-M League club.

In 1892 Marquette, along with a joint franchise from nearby Ishpeming-Negaunee, became members of the new Wisconsin/Michigan League, a full-fledged professional organization. The border city of Menominee was the third Michigan representative in the six-team circuit, which included the Wisconsin towns of Marinette, Oshkosh, and Green Bay. The prominent men who backed the Marquette entry included James Russell, E. C. Williams, A. H. Holland, and D. W. Kauffman. A popular local player, George Wilbur, was named to manage the Marquettes. Many of the local stars from the '91 UP League club were carried over to the new team, including Manager Wilbur, Pedroes, Hughes, Dixon, Wilder, and Cull. No longer playing in a semi-pro circuit with neighboring towns, the costs of maintaining a competitive roster in a two-state range of operation proved more than Marquette could afford and the team was forced to withdraw on August 5. A losing season (15-26) with a last place club did not help matters and to make things worse for the league's survival, neighboring Ishpeming-Negaunee also was reluctantly dropped because of its easterly location. Marquette's final abdication was an abrupt one, occurring in the 8th inning of their last game with Green Bay. By this time, other teams in the W-M circuit were ignoring the salary limit and signing top players at will in an effort to bolster their rosters. Contract jumping became an epidemic and Marquette shortstop Ryan and outfielder Pedroes walked off the field during that final game to catch a train to their new assignments. This was the last straw for the Marquettes as they disbanded on the spot. It was the end of professional league baseball in the Queen City, but the game continued to remain popular in Marquette in the decades that followed with some very fast teams of the independent variety.

Charles Pedroes of the 1890-91 Marquette club played briefly with the Chicago Cubs in 1902.

NY Giant pitching ace Art Nehf played in Marquette in 1912 under an assumed name prior to his long career in the National League.

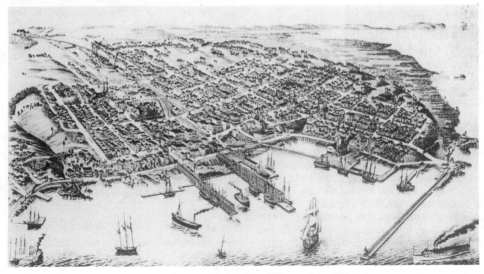

A bird's eye view drawing of Marquette c. 1881

A newspaper ad for a gala Memorial Day opening of the 1890 season in Marquette

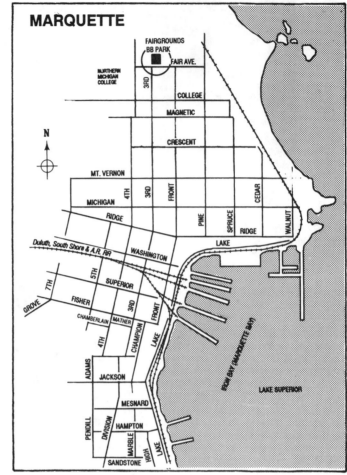

THE PLAYING SITE

FAIR AVENUE GROUNDS 1888-92 (AKA THIRD STREET PARK) (on the fairgrounds site north of town at Fair Ave. & Third Street)

The grandstand built for racing events at the old fairgrounds on the northern edge of Marquette was adapted for baseball use in the 1880s. A long, uphill walk from the downtown area created some inconvenience for city residents, but fortunately there was streetcar service almost directly to the grounds. Unfortunately, no map diagrams or photos from the period have been found to reveal the exact position of the grandstand and playing field. In the years after baseball was no longer played here, the Palestra (whatever that was) occupied the site. Northern Michigan University's athletic field currently takes up the property of the old baseball field and fairground buildings.

Northern Michigan University's athletic field currently occupies the site of the old Fair Avenue baseball grounds.

MENOMINEE

PROFESSIONAL LEAGUE MEMBERSHIP

YEARS	LEAGUE	HOME FIELD
1892	Michigan-Wisconsin	Fairgrounds (Driving Park)
1914	Wisconsin-Illinois (joint franchise with Marinette, WI) (TWIN CITY)	Fairgrounds (alternate home park in Marinette, Wisconsin)

Menominee's location on the Wisconsin border has historically linked its destiny in baseball more with northeastern Wisconsin communities than with its more distant Upper Peninsula neighbors. In fact, its only two adventures in professional baseball involved leagues that were either one half Wisconsin-based or consisting entirely of cities from the Badger State and beyond. In 1892 the Wisconsin State League reached eastward into Michigan's UP to find replacements for several of its defunct 1891 franchises. Marquette, Ishpeming-Negaunee, and Menominee were granted franchises. Baseball fever was high in the Menominee area as neighboring Marinette WI had claimed the Wisconsin League championship the year before. Fred Schultz and Fred Stephenson were the backers of the Menominee entry and W. H. Lucas was named field manager. The year 1892 provided a bumper crop of unaffiliated, skilled players throughout the country and its effect was felt in the minor leagues. The dissolution of the Players League after 1890 and the American Association after 1891 threw these surplus players into the open market to sign with any club that would have them—in many cases they caught on with leagues that were beneath their customary skill levels. This overflow of talent gave the minor league fans some quality baseball, but in the long run it proved to be a curse that undermined the stability of the league. The new Wisconsin/Michigan League was a classic case of such a predicament.

In an effort to bolster their rosters for the pennant chase, W-M League clubs soon discarded their salary limits and started to beef up their clubs with a steady influx of "ringers." Marquette, with a losing team, found themselves unable to keep up and withdrew on August 5. With Marquette out, Ishpeming-Negaunee was reluctantly forced to follow suit. At this time, Menominee was in first place, but the new four-team circuit decided to rewrite the schedule for the balance of the season—then have the winners of the second season play Menominee in a championship playoff. But the "revolving door" of new signings and contract jumping put most of the remaining clubs in financial trouble and they were unable to fully complete the second season, so the post-season playoff never took place. Menominee made the most of their early season success and proclaimed themselves pennant winners, despite the incomplete season. Among the myriad of players who donned a Menominee uniform that summer, a number of them made a name for themselves in the big leagues either prior to or after the 1892 season, including the following: Dick Van Zandt, Willie McGill, Andy Sommers, John Wentz, Frank Pears, Wally Taylor, Harry Burrell, and Harry Truby. Although the above players had little more than a brief tryout in the majors, it was an unusually high number for only one year of a bottom rung minor league town. The bad taste left over from the 1892 Wisconsin-Michigan League fiasco killed interest in organized baseball in the UP for over a decade.

Hank O'Day pitched in the big leagues for seven seasons from 1885 to 1890 before he joined the neighboring M-W Marinette club in 1892. He later became a well-known NL umpire.

Menominee third baseman Dick Van Zandt was one of the many ex-big leaguers that populated the M-W League in 1892.

In 1914 Menominee once again became a member (or half-member) of a professional baseball league when they united with Marinette (WI) to form a Twin Cities franchise in the class C Wisconsin-Illinois League. It was an unheard of display of unity between the rival cities, but the idea was enthusiastically supported on both sides of the river. Neither town made any exclusive claims to the franchise as home games were played alternately in both communities. Newspapers on each side gave generous coverage of "Twins" games and the combined population base ranked with most of the other seven member cities in Wisconsin and Illinois. Charles

Moll was one of the principal backers of the local team and "Red" Wicks was the Twins' field boss. The Twins got off to a good start, reaching first place on June 1, but in the end they were a .500 ball club, finishing fifth, 16 games behind pennant winner Oshkosh. Some memorable Twin City players from the 1914 season were Joe "Shorty" Nagle, Eddie "Rebel" Miller, Sammy Sher, and "Big Jim" Jacks. With minor league baseball's popularity and profitability on the decline, the Wisconsin-Illinois League went out of existence after 1914 and Menominee never again became a participant in organized baseball.

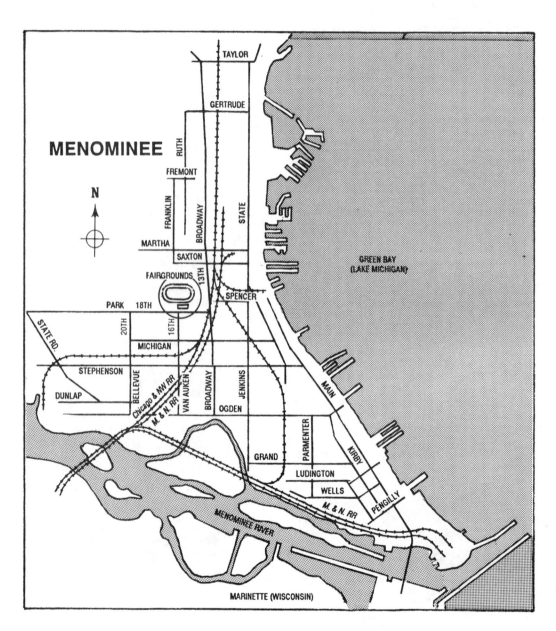

THE PLAYING SITE

FAIRGROUNDS DRIVING PARK 1892, 1914 (on the northwest corner of Broadway & Park— now 13th & 18th Streets)

A rare photo showing the grandstand of the Fairgrounds Driving Park around 1910

The Driving Park grounds at the fairgrounds were already used for baseball games before the Menominee club of the '92 Wisconsin-Michigan League played their home games there. All that was required for league play was to refurbish the playing field up to league standards and modify the race track area as needed. Newspaper reports suggest that the diamond was positioned inside the track oval, but no map diagrams or photos have been found to verify its precise orientation. Like most driving parks, it included a fairly large, straight grandstand that would seat as many as 1000 spectators. A bleacher was also present (at least in 1914) but its location has not been determined. Street names in Menominee were all converted to numbers since the last league game was played there in 1914, so its present location would be just west of 18th and north of 13th. The Emerson Electric Plant currently occupies the site.

The old Fairgrounds site was directly behind the current Emerson Electric Plant on 13th Street.

A 1914 newspaper ad for a W-I League Twin Cities game at the Menominee grounds

MOUNT CLEMENS

PROFESSIONAL LEAGUE MEMBERSHIP

YEARS	LEAGUE	HOME FIELD
1906-07	Southern Michigan	Crocker Field
1912-13	Border	Crocker Field
1914	Southern Michigan (transferred from Lansing)	Crocker Field

The City of Mount Clemens, now just one of numerous contiguous suburbs of the Detroit megalopolis, had a more distinct and remote identity in the early years of the century. Famed for its mineral baths, it was one of the most popular resort areas in the midwest and the constant flow of famous and well-heeled visitors made a major contribution to the town's prosperity. Eager to publicize their community in numerous ways, local baseball enthusiasts assembled some top-notch independent teams to vie for championship honors in state competition. Local hotel owners and other business leaders were the backers of the independents and in 1905 they assembled their finest aggregation of hired professionals to date, winning with regularity. Seth Knight was the manager, but the inspirational leader was veteran first baseman and team captain Walter "Dad" Trombley. The lineup was stocked with top-notch "ringers" and its chief rival for championship honors was the town of Tecumseh, which also fielded a team of well-paid and well-known baseball mercenaries. With much fanfare and heavy wagering involved, the Tecumsehs and the "Bathers" squared off for a late season best-of-nine games playoff to settle the issue. Tecumseh emerged victorious in a closely fought battle that drew the attention of baseball fans all over the region. Mt. Clemens went down fighting and when opportunity knocked to enter a bona fide professional league in 1906, the Bathers were ready and eager to further enhance their reputation as a winning baseball town.

Detroit baseball writer Joe Jackson organized a class D circuit to be called the Southern Michigan League in early 1906 and both Tecumseh and Mt. Clemens were recruited to resume their rivalry on a fully professional level. Other member cities in the new league included Kalamazoo, Jackson, Battle Creek, and Saginaw. Dad Trombley was the obvious choice to manage the new league version of the Bathers. Several key players from the '05 independents were signed on for '06 league play, including Roth, Ort, and Martin. Jackson's well-organized SML enjoyed a successful maiden season and when the campaign was over, Mt. Clemens was the runaway champion, winning by six games over runnerup Kalamazoo. Old rival Tecumseh finished a distant third, which heartened Mt. Clemens fans and partly atoned for their misfortune in 1905. Third baseman Bill Roth led the Bather hitters with a .302 average, but the team's "franchise" player was pitcher Tom McCarthy, who was a minor league sensation with 36 victories.

Despite the most rewarding 1906 season, the management of the '07 franchise was overhauled as A. S. Burkhart took over the club and signed Joe Ganzell, of the famous baseball brothers, to manage the 1907 Bathers. Ganzell, like his more famous brother John, also played first base and already had solid experience as manager of independent and league clubs in various places in Michigan. Dad Trombley stepped down and declared he was through with baseball but, as time would tell, he would later reconsider. As if to reclaim "bragging rights" over arch-rival Mt. Clemens, it was Tecumseh's turn to dominate the

Some key players of the pennant-winning Mt. Clemens "Bathers" of 1906

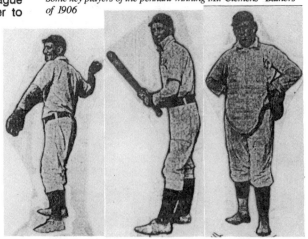

Ort, SS   Roth, 3B   Martin, C

Walter "Dad" Trombley was Mt. Clemens' biggest baseball name in the early 20th century. He played first base and/or managed most of the local entries in league baseball during this period.

A. S. Burkart was owner/-president of several Michigan league clubs, including Mt. Clemens in 1907 and 1912.

Tom McCarthy won 36 games for the '06 champion "Bathers." The following year he won 19 for Newark, then had two disappointing seasons with three NL clubs.

The much-traveled Joe Ganzell was Mt. Clemens' manager in 1907.

SML in 1907 as they captured the league championship by the same margin as the Bathers enjoyed in '06. Mt. Clemens slipped to fourth place with a 51-51 record. Saginaw replaced Mt. Clemens in the 1908 SML lineup and the resort city was out of organized baseball for the next four summers.

Another opportunity for Mt. Clemens to participate in league baseball arrived in 1912 with the formation of the class D Border League. Another Detroit sports writer, E. A. Bachelor, was the organizer of the new circuit which also included Wyandotte, Pontiac, Port Huron, and Windsor ONT. With limited capital available to launch the initial campaign, the Border League set its sights low with Saturday/Sunday dates only. Dad Trombley returned to pilot the new Bathers, but soon yielded the position to Richie LaPointe. Mt. Clemens got some creditable pitching from Louis North and some slugging from Ralph "Moose" Moore, but the Bathers finished third with an 11-15 WL record, nine games behind winning Wyandotte. With disappointing gate receipts and a limited schedule, Border League teams found it difficult to attract first-rate players, but the league resumed play in 1913 with Ypsilanti brought on board to make it an even six members. After a "revolving door" of league presidents created a near fatal anarchy situation, A. L. Ulbrich took charge and vowed to restore order in the second season. Dad Trombley held the option on the use of the Bathers home park, Crocker Field, and his demands for rental fees nearly prevented the locals from getting started. But in the end, it mattered little as the Mt. Clemens club disbanded after playing only 16 games. The Border League itself went out of existence after 1913 and never resurfaced.

One last opportunity to participate in league baseball came unexpectedly to Mt. Clemens in 1914. The Southern Michigan League expanded to 10 cities by adding South Bend IN and Toledo OH. The Lansing club experienced early difficulties and moved to Mt. Clemens to complete the schedule there. The transplanted Bathers proved to be a second division club, finishing seventh in both halves of the split season. The only standouts for the locals were outfielders Helmer (.345) and Spencer (.308). By this time, the SML was on its last legs and reverted to a six-team alignment in 1915—without Mt. Clemens. The league lasted only half a season and disbanded for good after a remarkable 10-year existence. The City of Mt. Clemens was never again a participant in organized baseball.

THE PLAYING SITE

CROCKER FIELD 1905-14 (between Clinton River and Crocker, at Rathbone—now 5th St.)

This location of Crocker Field is suspected but unconfirmed. No information about its location could be found in the Mt. Clemens Monitor of that era. The Detroit Free Press of May 1, 1906 reported "... a much improved park. The grounds, only partially fenced last year, are now completely enclosed... fifty feet is being added to the Mt. Clemens grandstand, which was not large enough to accommodate the patronage last year. The playing field is being wired off to prevent encroachment by the public."

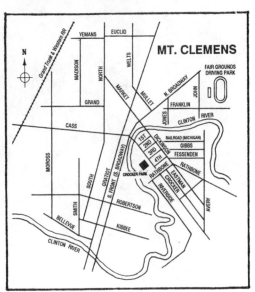

MUSKEGON

PROFESSIONAL LEAGUE MEMBERSHIP

YEARS	LEAGUE	HOME FIELD
1884	Northwestern	Mason's 40
1890	Michigan State	Interlake Park (Sundays—Rosen Bros. Park)
1896	Michigan State	Castenholz Park Driving Park
1902	Michigan State	Driving Park
1910-14	Michigan State	Castenholz Park Recreation Park (Mona Lake)
1916-17	Central	Marsh Field
1920-22	Central	Marsh Field
1923-24	Michigan-Ontario (MINT)	Marsh Field
1926	Central/Mich. State	Marsh Field
1934	Central	Marsh Field
1940-41	Michigan State	Marsh Field
1946-50, 1953	AAGBL (Girls)	Marsh Field
1948-51	Central	Marsh Field

The City of Muskegon has always had a reputation as a great football town and in more recent decades as a hockey town, but it also claims a checkered tradition as a solid minor league baseball town during the periods when the professional game was popular in Michigan. As early as 1883, the prosperity of the lumber business encouraged the locals to recruit a fully professional independent team to take on all comers in the state. The Muskegons won with regularity and the following year (1884) they entered the Northwestern League when the circuit expanded from 8 to 12 teams. It was a big gamble both for the league and for Muskegon, which found itself competing with much larger midwest towns like Milwaukee, St. Paul, Minneapolis, Fort Wayne, and Grand Rapids. L. R. Mann was president of the new Muskegon Baseball Association and local hotel owner Andrew Bradford was named manager. Players under contract included top-notch professionals who later appeared on big league clubs—namely Paul Cook, John Rainey, "Cod" Myers, and William "Rasty" Wright. Manager Bradford, with little or no baseball experience, ultimately yielded managership to a succession of field captains; first John

The 1883 Muskegon independent professional team which entered the Northwestern League the following year. TOP ROW (L to R): Rasty Wright, John Rainey, Jumbo Glasser, Kurtz. MIDDLE ROW: Miller, Mgr. Andrew Fleming, Jones. BOTTOM: Green, Paul Cook, James McLaughlin. Fleming later became Mayor of Muskegon and McLaughlin became a U.S. Congressman.

Rainey, then Charles Cushman, and later Bill McGunnigle. McGunnigle surfaced a few years later as manager of the Brooklyn National League club. As the season progressed, the Muskegons found the going much tougher than the previous year of independent baseball. By early August, the Northwestern League found itself struggling to survive, particularly in the smaller member towns like Stillwater MN, Quincy IL, and Muskegon. First Bay City was forced to relocate to Evansville IN in late July, and shortly thereafter other member cities began to drop out in bunches. Muskegon had a disappointing 23-40 record when they gave it up on August 7. By Labor Day, what was left of the NW League was in total disarray and the league itself closed up shop before completing the schedule.

In the 1890s Muskegon made two more attempts at organized baseball by joining the Michigan State League. The first venture was in 1890 when the six-team circuit included Grand Rapids, Manistee, Flint, Lansing, and Port Huron. E. C. Misner was president of the Muskegon franchise and John Roushkolb was manager. Poor patronage throughout the league created mounting debts and the organization collapsed on June 10, barely a month into the season. The second attempt in 1896 was even more futile as the MSL failed before the season started. The remnants of Muskegon's entry regrouped as an independent team, comprised mostly of local stars with a few top-notch players recruited from Western Michigan towns. These independents called themselves the "Reds" and for the next several summers they were one of the most formidable independent teams in the state. They took on all comers, including exhibition games with the Western League Detroit Tigers and Grand Rapids. Their pitching was the key to their success, led by future big leaguers Frank Kitson and Clarence Currie, plus Frank Barber and Fred "Kid" Luther. By the turn of the century, the Muskegon Reds enjoyed a state-wide reputation as a feared opponent, giving them the confidence to make another try at professional league ball.

Grand Rapids baseball promoters Emerson Dickerson and G. E. Morrison orchestrated another revival of the Michigan State League for 1902 and Muskegon was recruited as one of the six candidates for membership. The success of the independent Reds would hopefully be continued as a bona fide league team and most of the Reds roster was retained, including Captain Archie DeBaker. The new version of the State League would be unaffiliated, not bound by the rules of organized baseball, and this feature would eventually contribute to its ultimate failure. The constant "revolving door" of player rosters, along with a host of other problems, plagued the circuit from the start and once again a full season could not be completed as the MSL folded up on August 20. Grand Rapids, the league's strongest member in terms of fan base, was in last place when it abruptly quit on July 20. Muskegon's chances to climb in the standings were thwarted by the jumping of key players Morrissey and Bufka in July and they were a distant fourth when the league called it quits. For the next seven summers, the city avoided league baseball and concentrated on local factory leagues for baseball entertainment. The independent Reds were revived for a few more years but never recaptured the winning reputation of the pre-1902 teams.

Frank Barber was one of the independent Reds' talented hurlers around 1900. He went on to the higher minor leagues from here.

Lansing's gifted Jack Morrissey, who had a brief trial in the big show, played for Muskegon in 1902.

Arthur "Archie" DeBaker was a prominent player and manager for Muskegon independent and league teams from the 1890s up to the WWI era.

Allegan's Frank Kitson was a star pitcher for Muskegon independent teams in the 1890s. He later won 122 games in the big leagues.

Fred "Kid" Luther, from nearby Hart, pitched for Muskegon and Grand Rapids around the turn of the century.

In early 1910 the Michigan State League was once again revived as a four-team class D circuit consisting of the Western Michigan communities of Holland, Muskegon, Cadillac, and Traverse City. After so many failures in the past, this modest beginning was a qualified success and was profitable enough to make plans for a six-club circuit for 1911. Thomas Jones was the president of the new league in 1910 and Charles Scott headed up the Muskegon franchise. Muskegon's "Mr. Baseball," Archie DeBaker, was the obvious choice to captain and manage, and

Hard-hitting Earl Comstock was a Muskegon favorite during the State League years.

Infielder Johnny Lavan played for the 1910-11 Reds and went on to a 12-year career in the big leagues. He later became a prominent doctor in Grand Rapids.

the old nickname of "Reds" was eventually adopted as team nickname. A few local stars like Earl Comstock and Hans Erickson were signed on, but the majority of players hired were out-of-town professionals. Muskegon finished third but attracted a decent following and was further encouraged by finally playing out a full schedule as a professional league team. Local favorites Comstock (.314) and Erickson (17-9) had fine years to lead the club and the Reds looked forward to an even better year in 1911.

Emerson Dickerson of GR took over as president of the MSL in 1911 and added Manistee and Boyne City to make it a six-team race. C. H. White was the new Muskegon president and DeBaker returned as manager. Most of the 1910 squad were back and the addition of Bill Tierney and Johnny Lavan made Muskegon a serious contender for the league championship. The season ended with Manistee on top but only 1/2 game up on Muskegon and Cadillac. Muskegon, however, refused to concede the pennant and filed a protest over a lost game that they felt should be rewarded to the Reds, thereby giving them the championship. In the end, the matter was settled by National Commission Chairman Garry Herrmann, and he upheld Manistee's claim to the league championship. A bitter disappointment for Muskegon followers, but their thrilling finish gave them another successful season at the gate. Earl Comstock once again had a banner year with the bat, hitting .354 to lead the circuit. Another product of the Muskegon factory leagues, Joe Bomers, was the team's top pitcher with 18 victories.

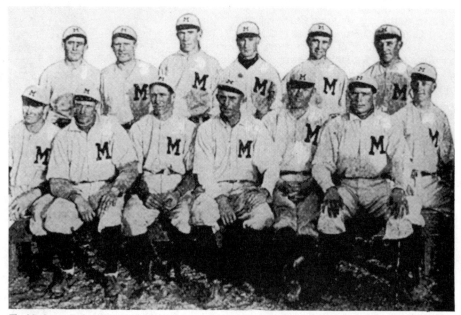

The Muskegon Reds of 1911 lost the State League pennant on a controversial ruling by the National Commission. BACK ROW (L to R): Gerrard, Frind, Brooks, Myron, Lavan, Tierney. FRONT ROW: Ferrin, Oldenburg, Comstock, Mgr. DeBaker, Meyers, LaCroix, Bomers.

Charles W. Marsh, a prominent industrialist, civic leader, and baseball booster, was president of Muskegon minor league teams on three occasions beginning in 1912. His most memorable contribution was spearheading the construction of Marsh Field in 1916.

"Peg" Bemis replaced Archie DeBaker as field boss in 1913. Accordingly, the team adopted a new nickname— "Peglets."

Infielder Sandy Murray came over from the GR Central League club and led Muskegon to its only minor league pennant in 1914.

The only change in the MSL alignment for 1912 was the transfer of the ailing Holland franchise to Ludington. Another significant change in Muskegon's front office was the election of popular local industrialist and team booster Charles W. Marsh as the new president. Marsh would ultimately influence the course of baseball history in the Port City. A new nickname of "Speed Boys" was adopted for DeBaker's 1912 club, but team fortunes went downhill as the Speed Boys wound up a distant fifth. Accordingly, attendance also went down but not enough to threaten the league's survival, and Muskegon was determined to rebound as a contender in 1913 with some new faces. Archie DeBaker stepped down as field boss, replaced by

"Peg" Bemis. The '13 "Peglets" finished third, sparked by newcomers Sid Miller (.359), Carl Dunckel, and pitcher Henry "Chief" Negake. Earl Comstock bounced back from a sub-par 1912 season and hit a solid .291.

The fifth year (1914) of the Michigan State League was a "bad news/good news" scenario for Muskegon fans. The circuit began to show signs of dissension as both Manistee and Traverse City were nearly ousted over some unsavory business tactics. Organizational shake-ups in both towns overcame these early problems and the season started with the same six clubs, but more troubles were in store for the league as the season progressed. Charles Marsh bowed out as team president and infielder Sandy Murray replaced Bemis as field boss. The capable Forrest Dickerson, late of the Ludington club, took over as new business manager of the Port City franchise. Muskegon's "Speed Boys" lived up to their nickname with a league-leading 226 stolen bases and sped to a first place finish, finally ousting three-time champion Manistee from the top spot. New pitcher "Rube" Leiffers was the major contributor with a sparkling 25-8 record. Meanwhile, Manistee fans soured on their losing

Pitcher Abe Bowman won 17 for the 1912 Speed Boys—later had a two-year trial with the Cleveland Indians.

The 1914 Michigan State League champions. (L to R): Umlauf, Tally, Mgr. Murray, Britton, McConnell, Meyers, Watkins, Cypert, Bus. Mgr. Dickerson, Patterson, Comstock, Reynolds, Noble, Lieffers.

team after supporting three straight pennant winners and the beleaguered franchise was transferred to Belding in early September. Traverse City was likewise in financial trouble and dropped out about the same time, a move that forced neighboring Boyne City to follow suit. The MSL finished out the season with four teams and went out of business at season's end. For Muskegon it was a bittersweet finale—their first and only pennant in professional league baseball but the opportunity to defend their championship in 1915 was denied them.

The new manager for the 1916 Central League Reds was Bade Myers.

Young Stanley Raymond Harris, known in later years as "Bucky," had a brief trial with Muskegon in 1916. He was the only Hall of Famer to play for a Muskegon team.

Charles W. Marsh was convinced that Muskegon's five-year run in the State League had established their credibility as a legitimate minor league town. In 1915 one of the city's home fields, Castenholz Park, was dismantled and converted into homesites. Marsh and a group of investors purchased four square blocks of property in the center of town and erected a new, modern baseball park to attract another league team to the Port City. Opportunity knocked the following year (1916) when Muskegon joined Grand Rapids in the prestigious class B Central League. Marsh returned to head up the new CL version of the "Reds" and league veteran Bade Myers was the new field manager. Myers' Reds found rough sledding in the faster Central League, finishing last in the first half and sixth in the second half. A young infielder named Stanley Harris played in 55 games but was let go for his weak hitting—the same "Bucky" who eventually played and managed his way into Baseball's Hall of Fame. Manager Bade Myers feuded with team owners and was replaced by Jimmy Hamilton for the 1917 season. Muskegon finished the 1917 season in a more respectable fourth place, but troubles throughout the league and the advent of World War I forced the circuit out of business for the duration of the war years. One of the few bright spots for the Muskegon team was pitcher Paul Wachtel, who won 19 games and paced the league in strikeouts. Wachtel joined the Brooklyn Dodgers at season's end. Poor patronage and other internal problems cursed the 1917 Central League all summer, not helped by league president Dickerson's abrupt departure in mid-season. For the next two seasons, Muskegon's new Marsh Field hosted local factory league baseball, but another era of league baseball was just around the corner. In a magnanimous gesture, Marsh and his associates turned over the deed to the new park to the City of Muskegon for little or no profit.

The 1916 Muskegon Reds, the newest members of the Central League. TOP ROW (L to R): Hart, McNeil, Covaleski, Whelan, Pres. C. W. Marsh. 2ND ROW: Evers, Mgr. Myers, Textor, Brubaker. 3RD ROW: Wachtel, Stanley, Wagner. BOTTOM ROW: Bratchi, Fisher, Wheatley.

William Heffron was president of the 1920 Muskegon Baseball Club.

Former Chicago White Sox pitching star G. Harris "Doc" White was a stockholder and field manager for the 1920 club, which was nicknamed "White Hopes" for obvious reasons.

Pitcher Freddie Fitzsimmons, shown in his rookie year (1925) with the NY Giants, was a popular favorite on Muskegon teams from 1920 to 1922.

When the hangover of the great war finally faded, Emerson Dickerson made plans to resurrect the Central League for the 1920 season. Unable to entice former out-of-state member cities to return to the fold, he settled on a compact all-Michigan group of the four cities of Grand Rapids, Kalamazoo, Ludington, and Muskegon to launch the league's rebirth. William Heffron was president of the Muskegon entry and former Chicago White Sox pitching ace G. Harris "Doc" White was contracted to manage the Port City franchise. With deference to their new famous field boss, Muskegon fans adopted the novel nickname "White Hopes" for the new team. Unfortunately, Dr. White was unable to escape a last place finish for his White Hopes. But local fans gave the cellar-dwellers decent support, attracted by player/manager White who also played in the field and pitched on occasion. Local former State League favorite Earl Comstock also played part time and hit .272. An 18-year-old pitching prospect from South Bend IN named Fred Fitzsimmons also caught the fancy of Muskegon fans and became a favorite for the next two summers. As planned, the Central League expanded to six cities (still all-Michigan) by adding Lansing and Jackson in 1921. The Muskegon franchise was overhauled for 1921 with Harry Fisher and Isadore Rubinsky taking over club ownership. Dannie Claire of Ludington was hired to replace Doc White and a new nickname of "Daniels" replaced White Hopes. Ludington captured the 1921 flag with ease, but Muskegon overcame a poor start to finish a strong fourth. Bob Berger was the team's top moundsman with a 20-14 record, followed by Fitzsimmons at 14-13. A product of the local factory leagues, Wilbur Swansboro was a pleasant surprise in 1921, hitting .339 to join Comstock (.275) as the home grown heroes. Dannie Claire returned in 1922 and gave Muskegon fans their strongest showing in Central League competition, finishing second in the season's second half. Some fine hitting by outfielder Steve Cozington (.336), Swansboro (.331), "Gaty" Hamel (.327), and Frank Myers (.320) led the offense. Bob Berger with 17 wins, followed by Fitzsimmons with 16, were the top hurlers. "Fat Freddy" Fitzsimmons graduated to Indianapolis the following year and from there he went on to a distinguished major league career, mostly with John McGraw's New York Giants.

Over the winter of 1922-23, the rival Michigan-Ontario (MINT) League had lost support in several of its Canadian cities and made overtures to some of the stronger Central League cities to abandon the CL and join the MINTers. Grand Rapids, Kalamazoo, and Muskegon took the bait and the Central League was thereby dissolved. The new MINT alignment also included Bay City, Saginaw, and Flint, along with the Ontario cities of London and Hamilton. In Muskegon, Charles Marsh returned to the limelight as team president with John "Red" Fisher named as field manager. Returning from the 1922 club were Steve Cozington, Clyde "Buck" Crouse, Tony Welzer, Harry Manush, and Frank Myers. Led by the hitting of Cozington (.320) and Myers (.306), the Anglers made a strong showing in 1923, finishing third with a 73-57 record, the best of the transplanted Central League clubs. Catcher Clyde Crouse left the team in mid-season to join the Chicago White Sox and began a fine eight-year career as a backup for Hall of Famer Ray Schalk. A winning season gave Red Fisher a new contract for 1924 and the Anglers opened the 1924 season at Marsh Field by defeating Josh DeVore's GR club 6-1 before a capacity crowd of 6,000, including Baseball Commissioner Kenesaw M. Landis. With a split-season format, the 1924 Anglers were a disappointment, finishing 7th and 5th in the two halves. Attendance was far short of expectations and the team was losing money, but the caliber of play in the MINT League was arguably the best ever seen in Muskegon. Many of the MINT players ultimately made good in the big show—most notably London's Charley Gehringer. Muskegon's own Bud Clancy got minor league attention with a 40-game hitting streak. Clancy went directly to the White Sox at season's end and enjoyed a productive career in the big show. Other Muskegon MINTers who made it to the majors besides Crouse and Clancy were Tony Welzer, Verdo Elmore, and George Loepp. Unfortunately, insurmountable debts forced Muskegon (as well as Grand Rapids and Kalamazoo) out of the league after the 1924 season.

First sacker John "Bud" Clancy had a sensational season for Muskegon in 1924. He went directly to the major leagues.

Commissioner Landis was the honored guest at the '24 opener.

A determined Emerson Dickerson tried to revive the Central League with the same four Michigan cities of 1920 (Grand Rapids, Ludington, Kalamazoo, and Muskegon) for the 1926 season. Russell Gallagher headed the Muskegon entry and hired Curtis "Buck" Wheat (brother of Hall of Famer Zack) to manage. After a month of disappointing gate receipts, the Central League merged with the four remaining clubs of the MINT League and began the 1926 season anew as the Michigan State League on June 15. It was a bold maneuver to rescue both failing circuits from bankruptcy, but in the end it was a lost cause as debts continued to mount. The former MINT League clubs dominated the new circuit (except for Flint) and the Muskegons finished a lowly sixth in the final count. The only decent crowd at Marsh Field that summer was for an exhibition game with the Chicago White Sox. Minor league baseball was essentially dead in Muskegon and elsewhere in the state after the disappointing 1926 season.

Despite the demise of league ball during the Great Depression, the revival of the independent Reds gave Marsh Field some quality baseball to entertain local fans. Another feeble attempt was made to resurrect the old Central League by Emerson Dickerson in 1934. Cy Boothby, once a star pitcher for Bay City in the old MINT League, assembled a team to represent the City of Muskegon. Some local Reds players, namely Harry Potter, "Shorty" Rojan, and Wilbur Swansboro, were included on the 1934 CL roster, but the remainder were out-of-town professionals. The new league was a disaster all around and lasted barely a month. The only player of note on the Muskegon roster was infielder Alban Glossop, who later had a brief career in the majors. Not until the woes of the Depression began to fade away were the prospects of league baseball reconsidered in Muskegon.

Red Fisher was the new pilot for the '23 MINT Leaguers.

Catcher Clyde "Buck" Crouse went from Muskegon to the Chicago White Sox.

Pitcher Tony Welzer of the '22-'24 club also had a two-year trial with the Red Sox.

With the nation's economy on the upswing in the late thirties, new minor leagues began to emerge all over the U.S. Flint's Thomas Halligan, with financial support assured by major league clubs, organized a class C six-team version of the Michigan State League for the 1940 season. The Detroit Tigers, following the new trend of widespread farm systems pioneered by the St. Louis Cardinals, agreed to sponsor a team in Muskegon. Grand Rapids, Lansing, St. Joseph, Flint, and Saginaw were the other member towns in the new circuit. The parent Tiger organization would be the principal owner of the Muskegon club and they appointed catching prospect Jack Tighe as manager. The old favorite nickname "Reds" was revived to identify the young Tiger farmhands. The Detroit organization provided funds to upgrade Marsh Field, including two new open bleacher sections. Local high school baseball coach Harry Potter was named business manager. To further sweeten the pot, the Tiger club agreed to visit Marsh Field each summer and give local fans a close-up look at their big league heroes. Tighe's Reds barely missed the final playoff spot, but the eager youngsters gave their followers an exciting brand of competitive baseball. Part-time backstop Harvey Riebe led the team in batting with a .348 while Clarence Gann was one of the circuit's top hurlers with a 16-3 WL record and a league-leading 2.80 ERA. As promised, the parent club arrived at Marsh Field on June 17 and entertained a big crowd of 4,453 fans.

The popular Jack Tighe returned to manage the Reds in 1941 and once again Muskegon fell short of playoff contention. But Tighe's aggressive style of managing along with several outstanding new prospects kept the local followers entertained all season. The most exciting player on the '41 Reds was shortstop Johnny Lipon, who feasted on State League pitching for a league-leading 35 HRs to go along with a .359 BA and 115 RBIs. He also had a 28-game hitting streak. Second baseman Adam Bengoschea was not far behind Lipon's numbers with a .352 average and 106 RBIs. Left-hander Frank "Stubby" Overmire, a West Michigan product, was the Reds' ace pitcher with a 12-4 record. Third baseman Gordon Howerton and first sacker Johnny McHale rounded out the stellar Muskegon infield. Manager Tighe also contributed with a .351 in 70 games behind the plate. World Series hero Buck Newsom was the star attraction when the parent Tigers came back to Marsh Field in June before another capacity crowd. Unfortunately, the advent of WWII put the State League out of business for the duration, and Muskegon fans settled for independent baseball during the war years.

The parent Detroit Tigers picked catching prospect Jack Tighe to manage the Reds of 1940-41.

The Muskegon Reds of 1941. STANDING (L to R): Lipon, Clark, McHale, Moceri, Weinschreider, Howerton, Latter, Fisher, Steger. KNEELING: Steinrede, Lis, Overmire, Mgr. Tighe, Bengoschea, Radulovich, Scott.

Frank "Stubby" Overmire joined the Reds from WMU in June 1941 and won 12 games.

Shortstop Johnny Lipon was a minor league sensation with the 1941 Muskegon State Leaguers.

In 1946 Muskegon was awarded a franchise in the wartime-inspired All American Girls Professional Baseball League. The novel version of competitive league baseball (actually a hybrid blend of softball and hardball) soon caught on and attracted a good following among local fans. Unlike the previous years of men's baseball, the girls had the advantage of night games with lights finally installed at Marsh Field in 1946. The "Lassies" surprised everyone by setting attendance records in their first years of play. The 1947 club won the regular season championship before an amazing total of 140,000 paid attendance—far more than any men's team had ever drawn in any season. An exciting pennant race was the big attraction but having a local girl, Donna Cook, on the team was an added bonus. The '47 Lassies lost out in the post-season playoffs, but the league's most valuable player that year was Muskegon's pitcher/outfielder Doris Sams. After 1947, the Lassies were forced to share the local fan base with men's league baseball when the Central League Clippers also used the Marsh Field facility beginning in 1948. Attendance tapered off in the following years for both clubs and reached crisis proportions by early 1950. Unable to recapture the magic of 1947, staggering debts forced the Lassies to relocate to Kalamazoo in June 1950. After the Central League folded in 1951, Muskegon tried to revive AAGBL baseball with the relocated Belles in 1953, but it was another financial disaster and failed to complete the season. The doomed AAGBL went out of existence the following year.

Perennial AAGBL All-Star Doris Sams pitched and played outfield for the Lassies.

Muskegon's 1947 regular season champions. STANDING (L to R): Mgr. Wamby, Lenard, Warren, Barringer, Vonderau, Watson, Fisher, Sams, Bergman, Maguire, chaperone Hannah. SEATED: Siegfried, Johnson, Applegren, Warwyshyn, Stolze, Reeser, Cook, Pryer.

Meanwhile, back up to 1948 and the rebirth of the class A Central League. Flint's veteran baseball patriarch T. J. Halligan was the principal architect of the postwar version of the CL, organized in February 1948. The six teams awarded franchises included Muskegon, Grand Rapids, Flint, Saginaw, Dayton OH, and Fort Wayne IN. Veteran baseball promoter John "Jake" Outwin headed up the Muskegon entry, which was partially owned and sponsored by the Chicago White Sox. Another long-time Muskegon baseball booster Ray Maihofer was named secretary-treasurer and the parent White Sox chose ex-catcher Benny Huffman as field boss. The traditional nickname "Reds" was considered for a time but in the end a contest was staged with the winning entry "Clippers" adopted. For the new Clippers, the good news was that they finally had the opportunity to play under the lights—installed at Marsh Field only two years earlier. The bad news was that they had to compete with the successful girls' team, the Lassies, for the entire summer and there were only so many fan dollars to spread around in a community the size of Muskegon. Although the divided patronage cost both teams, each managed to attract about 80,000 fans apiece in 1948. The Clippers finished the '48 season in third place and were quickly eliminated by Dayton in the first round of the playoffs. Dick Lane was Muskegon's most productive hitter at .333 and he wrote minor league history by hitting five home runs in a game at Fort Wayne on July 3. Muskegon led the Central League teams in batting with four regulars well over .300. Lanky Bill Evans was the Clippers pitching ace with 17 victories and a league-leading 187 Ks.

Former Yankee pitching great Red Ruffing was the White Sox' choice as Muskegon pilot in 1949. Except for outfielder Bill Higdon's league-leading .330 BA, 1949 was a forgettable year for the Clippers as they finished 1-1/2 games out of the cellar and saw their attendance fall sharply to 46,560. Newcomers Alex Grammas (.327) and Jim Busby from the '49 squad later enjoyed fruitful big league careers. After the disappointing season, the parent White Sox announced their intentions of abandoning Muskegon in favor of Colorado Springs as their class A farm club. The idea of losing their CL franchise was unthinkable to local stockholder John "Smitty" Vanderplow and he immediately swung a deal to buy out the White Sox share of ownership to keep the Clippers in Muskegon. He then negotiated a working agreement with the New York Yankees to supply players for the 1950 season. The Central League also came to the rescue by stocking the new organization with some quality players from other CL teams, plus providing them with a first rate field boss in Bob Finley, former Saginaw pilot. Unfavorable weather and a horrendous start by the team caused local fans to lose interest early and even a miraculous turnaround came too late to re-energize any meaningful fan support. Other distractions such as the Korean War and a sensational summer by the Detroit Tigers also diverted attention from the Central League race. The arrival of new players, notably Loren Babe, Johnny Mackinson, Elston Howard, and Frank Barnes, seemed to turn the team around in mid-summer and they surged forward into a second place finish behind a strong Flint Club. Pitcher-turned-outfielder Jim Greengrass (.336), Loren Babe (.335), Ed Krage (.328, 19 HRs), Lou Urcho (.306), Bob O'Neal (.301, 20 HRs), and Ron Bowen (.297, 24 HRs, 128 RBIs) were the heart of a virtual minor league "murderers' row" that vaulted the 1950 club into contention. They disposed of Dayton in the first round of the playoffs but could not overcome a talented Flint club in the final series. Despite the heroic finish, Marsh Field attendance improved only slightly over 1949 but Yankee support assured another season of baseball in Muskegon for 1951.

Jake Outwin was Clippers' president in 1948-49.

Outfielder Dick Lane hit five HRs in a 1948 game at Fort Wayne.

Smitty Vanderplow took over the club in 1950.

The first blacks to play in the Yankee system, Elston Howard (seated) and Frank Barnes, signing 1950 Muskegon contracts.

The 1950 Muskegon Clippers. STANDING (L to R): Bundemay, Pres. Vanderplow, Barnes, Krage, Greengrass, O'Neal, Bowen, Howard, (trainer), (clubhouse boy), G. M. Sarade. SEATED: Logue, Rich, King, Consoli, Mgr. Finley, Mackinson, Carlson, Babe, Urcho, Braun.

Bob Finley was the 1950 field boss of the Clippers.

Future Yankees' star Elston Howard was a Clipper in 1950.

Insurmountable debts from the 1950 season forced owner Vanderplow to surrender control of the 1951 Clippers to a community group which included the local Chamber of Commerce. Former big leaguer Jimmy Gleeson replaced Finley as manager, but several of the big bats from 1950 were back, including Ed Krage, Ron Bowen, and Jim Greengrass. Once again the Clippers started slowly, but the arrival of speedy outfielder Nino Escalera a month into the '51 season seemed to spark the club and they went on a late season winning rampage. Greengrass led the charge with a sensational .379 season but everyone contributed as the team batting average was a lofty .295 when the regular season ended. Dayton had surged to a huge early lead but the red-hot Clippers almost overtook them, finishing only 2-1/2 games behind. The loss of pitching ace Frank Barnes (15-6) to Toronto in late summer might have prevented them from catching Dayton. But unfortunately it all came to naught as the entire Central League was on the verge of extinction. Mounting losses forced the league to cancel the playoffs and ultimately go out of business. The sensational surge of the Clippers went virtually unnoticed as only 45,000 fans came out to support the team. Interested observers were convinced that Muskegon had enough momentum to breeze through the post-season playoffs and give the city a rare championship. But the reality of it all was that minor league baseball was finished in Muskegon—indeed in the State of Michigan as four decades went by before it resurfaced in Grand Rapids. Its recent success there and elsewhere in Michigan has fostered hope that Muskegon may once again become a member of a professional league.

Jim Greengrass had two fine years with Muskegon in '50 and '51. He later played five seasons in the NL.

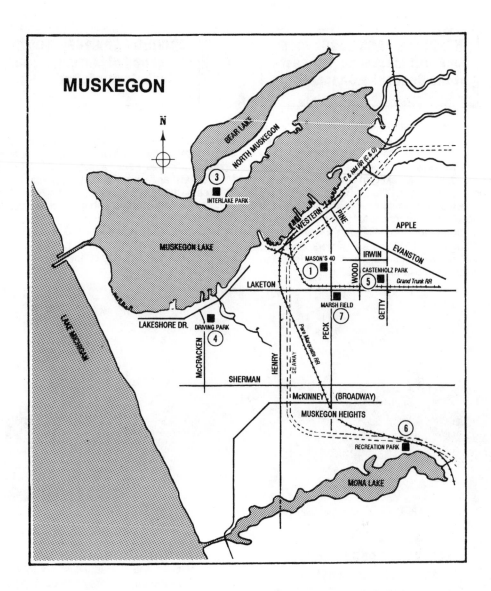

MUSKEGON

(map labels:) BEAR LAKE · NORTH MUSKEGON · INTERLAKE PARK · MUSKEGON LAKE · LAKE MICHIGAN · LAKESHORE DR. · DRIVING PARK · McCRACKEN · SHERMAN · HENRY · SEAWAY · Pere Marquette RR · PECK · McKINNEY (BROADWAY) · MUSKEGON HEIGHTS · RECREATION PARK · MONA LAKE · WESTERN · PINE · LAKETON · MASON'S 40 · MARSH FIELD · IRWIN · WOOD · CASTENHOLZ PARK · GETTY · APPLE · EVANSTON · Grand Trunk RR · C & NW RR (C & O) · ③ ① ④ ⑦ ⑤ ⑥ Ⓝ

THE PLAYING SITES

① **MASON'S "40" 1880s (general vicinity of today's Hackley Stadium)**

Mason's 40 was an open area just south of downtown Muskegon that was suitable for such outdoor activities as picnic outings and baseball games. Its precise location is undetermined but it was known to be close to Jefferson Avenue and St. Jean's Church. It served as the city's principal ball field up to 1890.

② **ROSEN BROS. DIAMOND–1890 (location unknown)**

This "mystery" baseball field was mentioned as a favorite spot for local baseball around 1890. Rosen Bros. was a prominent clothing store in Muskegon and a sponsor of amateur baseball teams. Because of its name, very likely it was built by the local merchant—probably around 1889. It served as an alternate home for the 1890 Michigan State League team. At this writing, its exact location is still unknown.

INTERLAKE PARK 1890
③ (in North Muskegon just east of the Bear Lake Channel)

North Muskegon's Interlake Park was a popular spot for weekend outings by Muskegon area citizens in the 1890s. Regular ferry service from downtown Muskegon made the park accessible by water across Muskegon Lake. The exact location of the baseball field is uncertain, but we know it included a small covered grandstand. It served local amateur teams for years and was an alternate home for the Michigan State League team of 1890. By 1900 the entire park area was converted to residential plats and was referred to as Interlaken in subsequent decades.

DRIVING PARK 1896-1902
④ (west end of Muskegon, near today's McGraft Park)

In the late 19th century, harness racing and bicycle racing were popular pastimes and almost every community had a driving park. Muskegon's Driving Park was near Lakeshore Drive between McCracken and the Ruddiman Creek Lagoon. The ready-made grandstand and open track area made it suitable for baseball games and even high school football. Home games of the independent Reds of the late 1890s and the 1902 State League team were played here. By 1910 the property was converted to residential plats.

The old Driving Park was also home field for local baseball around the turn of the century. The grandstand is visible in the background.

CASTENHOLZ PARK 1896-1914
⑤ (on east side–just west of Getty St. and north of Laketon)

The Castenholz brothers, who owned a meat packing plant along Getty Street, were also baseball enthusiasts. About 1896, they built a baseball field on property they owned just across

Getty. The field occupied a vacant lot at the corner of Dale and Superior just south of Nims Street. The Pine Street trolley line carried patrons to within a block of the park. A small roofed grandstand, bleachers, and a wooden fence around the grounds were park features. It was the home field for local independents and Michigan State League teams for 20 years until the property was made into residential lots in 1914.

Castenholz Park on the city's east side served Muskegon baseball for two decades.

RECREATION PARK 1910-14 (on the northeast shore of Mona Lake–south of the city)

Recreation Park was a combination picnic grounds, pavilion, and amusement park that included a first-rate baseball diamond. For most of its years, it was ranked with rival Castenholz Park as one of the two most popular diamonds in the Muskegon area. Despite its distance from the central city, the interurban railway went directly to the park, making it easily accessible for local patrons. The State League teams of 1910-14 shared home dates with Castenholz Park up to 1914, when the dismantling of Castenholz made Recreation Park the exclusive home field. Its distance from any protesting neighbors made it preferable to Castenholz and Sunday dates were often scheduled there. This particular Mona Lake diamond is not the site of the present day diamond at current Mona Lake Park, but believed to be further east near the end of Mona Lake.

A game in progress at Mona Lake's Recreation Park

MARSH FIELD 1916- (southeast corner of Peck & Laketon–in the center of the city)

When Castenholz Park was razed in 1914, local industrialist and baseball booster Charles W. Marsh and a small group of investors purchased four square blocks in the heart of Muskegon and constructed a modern baseball park to make up for the loss of the Castenholz facility. Clearing the land was begun immediately in early 1916 and construction of the roofed grandstand was rushed to completion for the opening of the 1916 season. The architect was Harry Boyle & Co. of South Bend IN, and the contractor was Nelson & Mayson. The park complex included a picnic area and a children's playground. Three years later Marsh deeded the facility over to the City of Muskegon with the stipulation that it could not be used for any purpose other than a recreational field. Accordingly, Marsh Field has survived to this day as the principal baseball park in Muskegon. In the 1930s a concrete box seat section and dugouts were added to the front of the wooden grandstand structure. In 1940 the Detroit Tigers, owners of the Michigan State League franchise, invested in additional open bleachers and other improvements. Light towers were installed in 1946. Marsh Field's glory years were the late forties when the old park offered baseball all summer long with two professional teams: the AAGBL Lassies and the Central League Clippers. The decaying grandstand was torn down in 1957, replaced by makeshift open bleachers. With league baseball gone for good, the park was kept alive mainly through the dedication of local baseball enthusiast Les David. His widow and other family descendants still maintain the field for local amateur baseball. No longer the handsome and stately structure it once was, the nearly "sandlot" appearance belies its heritage as a monument to so many baseball memories that are an indelible feature of the city's history.

10-year-old Marsh Field was filled to capacity in 1926 when the Chicago White Sox played an exhibition game with the locals.

A fine aerial photograph of Marsh Field looking east in the 1930s. The old Grand Trunk railway station across Laketon Avenue can be seen on the extreme left.

The familiar main entrance structure for the grandstand

The fully-roofed grandstand was filled to capacity on this night in 1949 to pay tribute to Clippers' owner Jake Outwin.

In 1940, the pennant-bound Detroit Tigers came to Marsh Field to play their local farm team youngsters. (L to R): McCoskey, Fox, York, Greenberg, Higgins, Mgr. Del Baker, Shea, Croucher, Nelson, Averill, (unknown), Miller, Sullivan.

Still used for local baseball, Marsh Field is arguably the oldest minor league park in Michigan, serving the city continuously since 1916.

A current bronze plaque pays tribute to the park's benefactor and namesake Charles W. Marsh.

Widow of the park's savior in recent decades, Mrs. Les David (center) and granddaughters Lu (left) and Penny still operate concessions and other routine operations at Marsh Field.

PROFESSIONAL LEAGUE MEMBERSHIP

YEARS	LEAGUE	HOME FIELD
1910	Indiana-Michigan	Wayne & 8th Sts. (LaPierre Park) (Springbrook Park)

In 1910, a record 51 professional minor leagues started play as league baseball became a national epidemic. Of these, 18 were first-year leagues and one of the newcomers was the Indiana-Michigan League, a class D loop of smaller towns in Southwest Michigan and northern Indiana. It was a low-budget league that hoped to survive a summer of weekend games on the strength of its convenient travel connections, since all the member towns were on an interurban railway route. Originally planned as an eight-city circuit with four teams in each state, the I-M League settled on six teams when Benton Harbor and Goshen defaulted at the eleventh hour. Niles, Dowagiac, and Berrien Springs represented Michigan versus the Indiana towns of Elkhart, Gary, and Ligonier. The man behind the Niles entry was local businessman and baseball enthusiast Fred "Bunny" Marshall. Marshall was also named secretary-treasurer of the League. The I-M was to be a fully accredited class D league and game results were to be published regularly in the Chicago newspapers and elsewhere. Owner/Manager Marshall also arranged and financed a new baseball park to be built in the downtown area. With a salary limit of $250 per month, the I-M League found it difficult to attract quality professionals and in most cases settled for the best available talent that could be found in the immediate locality.

The Niles "Blues" opened the season at Gary on May 8 with an 8-1 drubbing at the hands of the Hoosier City. After another loss at Dowagiac, Manager Marshall conspired with Chicago baseball writer Ring Lardner, a native of Niles, to recruit some talented "ringers" to beef up the Blues lineup for their home opener against Berrien Springs on May 22. Lardner persuaded legendary University of Chicago football star Walter Eckersall to accompany some top-notch Chicago semi-pros plus a pair of reserves from the big league Chicago Cubs (under assumed names) to play for the home team. The result was a one-sided 8-2 victory over their rival city and a rousing send-off for local fans. Although the maneuver was legal under league rules (except for the unproven use of contracted major leaguers), after June 1 Marshall was forced to play his less-talented roster for remaining games after some loud protests from Berrien Springs. Rivalries were intense and fan support was encouraging in the early weeks of the season, but fading interest and mounting debts soon forced Gary and Ligonier to withdraw, leaving only four cities to challenge for the I-M pennant. The season ended on August 25 with Berrien Springs as the champion and Niles finishing third with an 8-10 record. Like Halley's Comet, the 1910 Indiana-Michigan League came and went and was not seen again by local fans. Niles settled for independent baseball in the years following.

University of Chicago grid-iron legend Walter Eckersall accompanied Lardner's "ringers" to Niles in 1910.

Fred "Bunny" Marshall was Niles' biggest baseball booster and president/manager of the 1910 I-M League club.

Famed writer Ring Lardner was a Niles native and an overzealous booster of the 1910 club. He arranged a devious scheme to "stock" the Niles team with out-of-town "ringers" for an early game with Berrien Springs.

Chicago Cub pitcher A. J. Carson was one of the "unknowns" recruited in Lardner's 1910 caper.

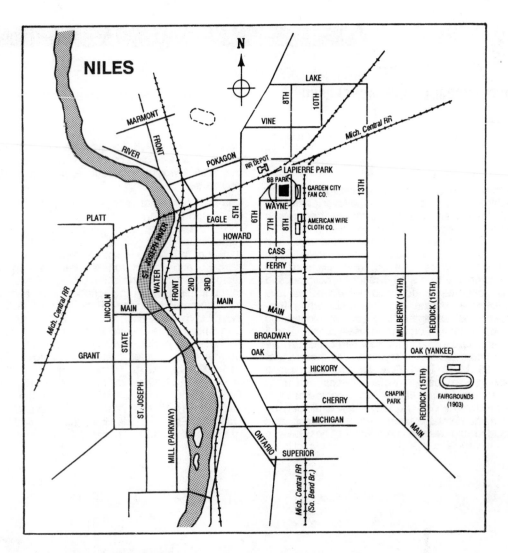

THE PLAYING SITE

LAPIERRE PARK (AKA SPRINGBROOK PARK) 1910 (north side of Wayne St., between 7th & 8th)

In early 1910, owner Fred "Bunny" Marshall of Niles' new Indiana-Michigan League club obtained a lease for some vacant property on 8th Street directly west of the Garden City Fan Company. Work began immediately on a suitable diamond and grandstand with a surrounding high-board fence. Not much else is known about this ballpark, since no photos or map details have been found. Presumably it became the site for local and independent teams in Niles for years afterward, but its ultimate demise is also unknown at this writing. Even its official name (if it had one) is uncertain, but since the original property was called LaPierre Tract, the baseball site was sometimes referred to as LaPierre Park.

OWOSSO

PROFESSIONAL LEAGUE MEMBERSHIP

YEARS	LEAGUE	HOME FIELD
1895	Michigan State	Athletic Assn. Grounds (Howard & Washington Sts.)

Owosso, like all other communities its size in Michigan, took to baseball in the latter part of the 19th century and assembled independent teams to compete against neighboring towns. In 1889, the Owossos joined Corunna, St. Johns, and Ovid in an amateur circuit called the Clinton/Shiawasee League and claimed the championship with a 13-8 record. Their first and only opportunity to participate in a fully professional league came in 1895 when they entered the Michigan State League, competing against Adrian, Port Huron, Kalamazoo, Battle Creek, and Lansing in the six-team circuit. Walter H. Mumby, of nearby Corunna, was president of the '95 MSL. Fred Craves, and later Frank Wicking, were managers of the Owosso "Colts" in the reborn State League, an organization that featured some first-rate player talent judging by the many names that enjoyed later careers that included big league experience. The Owosso club included some last names (full names have not been found to verify their identity) like Donovan, Gleason, and Brashear that may indeed have surfaced later in the big show. For certain, Isaac "Ike" Butler, who played briefly with the AL Baltimore club of 1902, was a member of the 1895 Owossos although appearing in only one game.

The Michigan State League season, after a good start, soon experienced financial difficulties in most of the member cities and the first to go under was Battle Creek, which transferred to Jackson in early August. A month later both Owosso and Port Huron withdrew, leaving four teams to finish out the schedule. The Colts were in fourth place when the schedule was reworked to accommodate the Battle Creek-Jackson switch. When Owosso finally called it quits on September 3, their overall record was 35 wins vs. 46 losses. Adrian, with the help of some borrowed black stars from the hometown Page Fence Giants, was the "class" of the league at the finish with a 57-30 overall record. Alfred Kern and Frank Haynes were the best pitchers on the Colts' staff with 11-10 and 7-10 records, respectively. Outfielder Eddie Shields hit an amazing .442 in 28 games for the Owossos, followed by

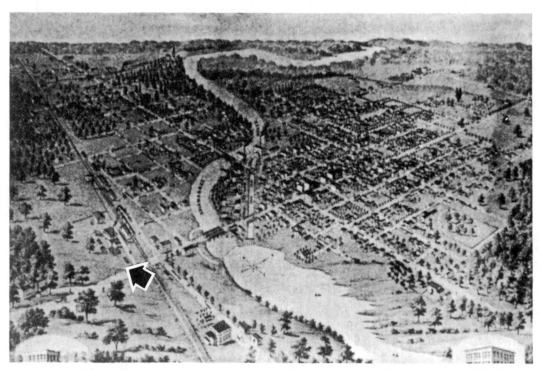

A bird's eye drawing of Owosso in the 1880s, looking northwest. Arrow indicates the ballpark site.

Bloomington at .347 and Donovan at .308. Owosso made another bid to join the 1896 version of the State League, but the circuit disintegrated before the season could get underway. Although occasionally considered for league franchises in subsequent years, the city never again participated in Organized Baseball.

Owosso native William Graham pitched for the St. Louis Browns in 1908-10.

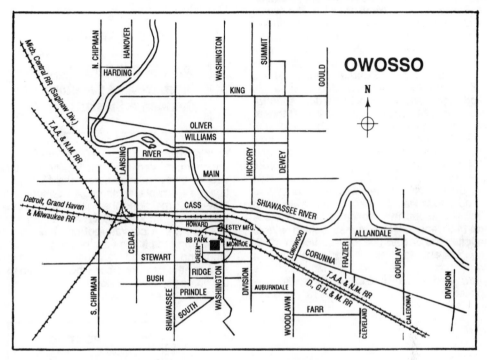

THE PLAYING SITE

ATHLETIC ASSN. GROUNDS 1895 (on Washington just south of the railroad tracks)

Built to accommodate the 1895 State League team, newspaper accounts describe the location as follows: "The grounds are situated just south of the Estey Factory and are about 450 x 550 feet... the grandstand will probably be placed in the northeast corner of the ground and will be next to the main entrance from Washington Street." No photographs or other descriptive details have been found to provide a clearer picture of this ballpark.

A current photo of the 1890s ballpark site, now occupied by Marco's Pizza and the Magnetek factory

PONTIAC

PROFESSIONAL LEAGUE MEMBERSHIP

YEARS	LEAGUE	HOME FIELD
1912-13	Border	Wisner Park

With successful new minor leagues springing up in all corners of the country, Detroit baseball scribe E. A. Bachelor orchestrated the formation of the Border League of 1912. All of the towns involved were in or near the Detroit area—specifically Pontiac, Mt. Clemens, Port Huron, Wyandotte, and Windsor ONT. It was to be a limited class D circuit with a minimal salary limit and a short schedule of Saturday-Sunday games only. If successful, a more expanded schedule and additional franchises would be discussed for the next year of operation. The Pontiac "Moose" franchise was managed by a Mr. McIntosh. On May 30, 1912 Pontiac's Mayor Lounsbury threw out the ceremonial first pitch at Wisner Park and the "Moose" aggregation opened the Border League season with a 3-2 victory over Port Huron. Bill Harper was the winning pitcher and shortstop Zerkle was the batting hero with three hits. Pontiac ended the season in second place with a 14-9 record, 4-1/2 games behind winner Wyandotte. The Border League encored in 1913, adding Ypsilanti to make it an even six, but halfway through the season Mt. Clemens withdrew and once again the schedule was completed with only five teams. The 1913 season also continued its abbreviated season of weekend games only and newcomer Ypsilanti unseated Wyandotte as BL champs, winning by 1-1/2 games over the runnerup Alkalis. Pontiac settled for fourth place with a 13-18 record. Discouraged by disappointing fan support and a general waning interest in minor league baseball, the Border League went out of business after the 1913 season.

THE PLAYING SITE

> ### WISNER PARK 1912-13 (northwest of downtown at Oakland & Summit)

At this writing, the location of Wisner Park is still unconfirmed. Very likely the facility was already in use for local baseball before the 1912-13 Border League team played there. A newspaper item in May 1912 mentions the following improvements underway: "Improvements are being made at Wisner Park. A canvas roof has been put on the stands and the fences are being bolstered up... a long strip of canvas was hung along the fence to shut out the gaze of those who preferred to watch the game from the outside."

Elijah "Bumpus" Jones from nearby Oxford pitched for Detroit in 1907 and 1909.

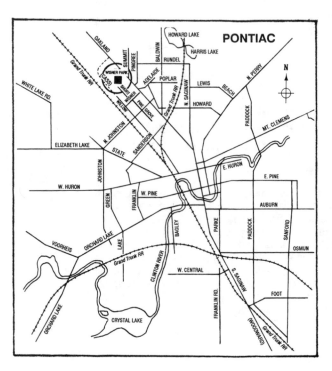

PORT HURON

PROFESSIONAL LEAGUE MEMBERSHIP

YEARS	LEAGUE	HOME FIELD
1890	Michigan State	Athletic Club Grounds
1895-97	Michigan State	
1898, 1900	International	Recreation Park (Driving Park)
1912-13	Border	Athletic Park (Sundays– Driving Park)
1921-22	Michigan-Ontario (MINT) (joint franchise with Sarnia)	Watkins Park (also games played in Sarnia)
1926	MINT/Mich. State	Watkins Park

Michigan's "Tunnel City" held franchises in numerous minor leagues from 1890 to 1926. Their first adventure in organized baseball was in 1890 when they joined the six-team Michigan State League at the eleventh hour, replacing Jackson. The officers of the new Port Huron baseball club were Phil Axman, president; D. J. Stephenson, secretary; Phil Truesdell, treasurer; and George Brown, David McArron, H. J. Boyce, Charles Runnells, directors. Veteran professional Joe Walsh was named field manager. The 1890 State League season was barely underway when it was already floundering—Grand Rapids abruptly quit to join the International League in early June and both Flint and Port Huron withdrew about the same time. With only three teams left, the MSL was forced to close. Port Huron was in fourth place (11-13) when the end came. It was a bitter disappointment for local boosters, who were confident that Manager Walsh had sufficient talent to challenge for the championship. Two local players with big league experience, Fred O'Neil and "Medicine Bill" Mountjoy, were fan favorites. Other players with major league backgrounds included Steve Dunn and John Morrison.

In 1895 opportunity knocked again for Port Huron when they re-entered the Michigan State League along with Adrian, Battle Creek, Kalamazoo, Lansing, and Owosso. Joe Walsh returned as manager of the new MSL "Marines." Like 1890, this version of the State League struggled at the gate as Jackson replaced Battle Creek in early August. By Labor Day, both Port Huron and Owosso threw in the towel and the league managed to complete the season with the four remaining clubs. For the Port Hurons, it was a losing proposition both on the field and at the turnstile as fans lost interest in a last place team. But the '95 MSL was a hitter's league as the entire circuit averaged over .300. Infielder Art Sippi led the Port Huron barrage with a .382 BA, followed by Downs (.379), and George Ganzell (.377). The 1896 State League collapsed before a game was

played but G. H. Brown and A. L. Goble put together another Port Huron entry for the 1897 MSL. Local baseball booster David McArron was the new field boss for '97. But once again the State League began to disintegrate as Bay City replaced Kalamazoo and Flint took over the vacant Bay City operation in early July. Both Lansing and Jackson abdicated on July 26 and the league itself was finished within a week. Port Huron was a distant fifth in the final season totals and once again was unable to complete a full season of professional league baseball.

Determined to find a home for Port Huron in league baseball, David McArron entered the city in the International League of 1898. It was a six-team circuit of towns in eastern Michigan and Ontario, Canada. A veteran of the minor league baseball wars, John A. Murphy, was recruited to assemble a winning combination but once again the Port Hurons were in last place when their new league also collapsed in early July. The Ontario members of the '98 IL went over to the Canadian League in 1899, but another Michigan-Ontario combination was assembled by Detroit Free Press Sports Editor H. O. "Bo" Needham to resurrect the International League for the 1900 season. Needham was also behind the Port Huron entry and he selected Pat Flaherty to manage the Tunnel City team. Burt Cady and David McArron were once again among the backers of the Port Huron club. Grand Rapids, after being unceremoniously snubbed by Ban Johnson's new plan to go "major" with his Western League, reluctantly joined the lower class International and was the catalyst for the collapse of the IL when they pulled out abruptly in late June. For the fifth time in five tries, Port Huron was once again a victim of an aborted league. With the team in last place when the IL folded on July 4, it marked the end of league baseball in Port Huron for another dozen summers.

With the renewed nationwide popularity of minor league baseball that took place around 1910, it was not long before the waters would be tested again in Port Huron. The game was as popular as ever in the Tunnel City and Port Huron was serenaded to enter another Michigan-Canada circuit to be called the Border League in 1912. It was the brainstorm of another Detroit sportswriter, E. A. Bachelor, and included the southeastern Michigan communities of Port Huron, Mt. Clemens, Pontiac, Wyandotte, and Windsor, ONT. Operating on a minimum budget, the league would play a short season of weekend games only to test its survival capabilities the first year. With little monies in its treasury, it was unable to attract first-rate professionals and the rosters were mainly the "cream" of local talent. But they managed to complete their brief schedule, a first for any Port Huron league team. The bad news was that Manager Bowen's Port Hurons finished dead last, but the league was solvent enough to operate again in 1913 with Ypsilanti added to make it a six-team circuit. Except for the withdrawal of Mt. Clemens in mid-season, the Border League once again fulfilled their schedule without going bankrupt. Port Huron, paced by ace pitcher George Mueller, finished third behind leaders Ypsilanti and Wyandotte. Over the following winter, meetings were held to continue the operation under the new name Eastern Michigan League, but the plans never materialized and the Border League faded out of existence.

After so many disappointments in league baseball, Port Huron was not eager to repeat the past but another opportunity surfaced unexpectedly in early 1921. The class B Michigan-Ontario (MINT) League, begun in 1919, approached Port Huron as a candidate to replace the struggling Battle Creek franchise in that circuit. William H. "Watty" Watkins, a renowned former manager and baseball executive in the higher leagues, was by this time a resident of Port Huron and he quickly seized the opportunity to bring organized baseball back to the Tunnel City. The neighboring Canadian city of Sarnia was invited to participate and the new franchise was to be identified as the Port Huron-Sarnia "Saints." Home games would be divided between Port Huron's Watkins Field and Sarnia's ballpark. "Hump" Pierce was the Saints' field boss and led them to a tie for 5th place in the final combined standings with a 58-63 record. Catcher Bill Kelly took over for 1922 with the same end result—5th place. Pitcher Jack Glasier's sensational finish, winning 10 straight games with an ERA of less than one, was too little, too late to make the

Saints a contender. Outstanding players for Port Huron in the 1921-22 years were Ted Kaylor, Burleigh Horne, and second-sacker Getsie. Disappointing fan support for second division teams made Port Huron a marginal MINT franchise and when the league regrouped over the winter by enticing several Central League towns to participate in 1923, Port Huron was dropped from the circuit.

W. H. "Watty" Watkins had a long career in professional baseball as a player, manager, and executive before he settled in Port Huron. He was behind the city's 1921 MINT League club and the home field was named in his honor.

Base Ball

WATKINS FIELD
SUNDAY
PORT HURON-SARNIA VS. LONDON
Game Called 3:30 P. M.

AT SARNIA SATURDAY
GAME CALLED 4:00 P. M.

A 1922 newspaper ad for the Port Huron-Sarnia joint franchise home games, played in both cities

The 1922 Port Huron Saints pose before the Watkins Field grandstand. The players are unidentified.

By 1925 the MINT League was in a life and death struggle to survive as the three Canadian cities withdrew at season's end. Attempting to stay alive with only four Michigan franchises, Port Huron was welcomed back as the fourth member. James Edson headed the 1926 franchise and John Carlin was named manager. The new Saints got off to a roaring start, led by Frank Tubbs' splendid pitching, and they took the top spot in the early going. But disappointing gate receipts and other problems caused the resignation of league prexy T. J. Halligan in early June. The circuit was floundering badly when they found a formula that they hoped would be their salvation. They merged with the equally unstable rival Central League to be reborn as the Michigan State League on June 15. When the MINT League schedule was finalized on June 13, Port Huron was in first with a 20-10 record. The new MSL proved to be a mismatch as the ex-MINT clubs (excepting Flint) dominated the final standings, the difference in classes (B versus C) being difficult to overcome by the ex-Central Leaguers. The powerful Bay City Wolves ran away with the pennant with Port Huron the runnerup, eight games behind the champions. Pitcher/outfielder Tubbs was a major contributor, batting .430 in 41 games. Earl Stimpson and Ivan Phippen led the regulars with .338 and .310, respectively. Lou Brower and Reynolds Kelly were the only '26 Saints to reach the big show—Kelly pitched one game for the Athletics in 1923 and Brower played shortstop in 21 games for the 1931 Detroit Tigers. After 1926, Port Huron never again entered Organized Baseball. The great "Watty" Watkins lived out his days in the border city, dying there in 1937.

THE PLAYING SITES

ATHLETIC CLUB GROUNDS 1890s (location uncertain— possibly the same as later Watkins Field)

(no photo or descriptive data found)

RECREATION PARK 1898-1913 (believed to be at the fairgrounds Driving Park location at Elmwood and 13th)

Although its location is uncertain, Recreation Park was built in 1898 for the Port Huron International League club. An 1898 newspaper item states that "the grandstand has been turned around and the grounds are being leveled," suggesting that a grandstand already existed—for race track viewing? The park was officially opened May 9, 1898 with an exhibition game between Port Huron and London, Ontario. Center fielder Carnahan of the Port Hurons had the honor of hitting the first home run in the new park during that game. If Recreation Park and the Driving Park are the same site, it was also used for some Sunday dates during the 1912-13 Border League season.

Earl Brown was a starting pitcher for the '26 Saints.

Pitcher Frank Tubbs was 16-1 and hit .430 for Port Huron in 1926.

Shortstop Lou Brower of the '26 Saints later played briefly for the Detroit Tigers.

BASE BALL
HAMILTON
—vs—
PORT HURON
TODAY

Tuesday's Game 4 o'clock. Wednesday's games (Decoration Day). 2 games for one admission. First game called at 2 o'clock.

Since the last game the Port Huron team has been strengthened by the addition of Pitcher Bartelt, Second Baseman Healey and Fielder Hudson.

ADMISSION 25 CTS.   CHILDREN 10 CTS.

A 1900 newspaper ad for a home stand of the International League club vs. Hamilton

ATHLETIC PARK/WATKINS FIELD 1912-1926 (on the south end of town, along the St. Clair River at 24th & Moak)

③

The site known as Athletic Club Grounds had been used for baseball games since the last century and was refurbished for league play when Port Huron entered the Border League of 1912. An alternate location for some Sunday games was arranged at the old Recreation Park fairgrounds site. When long-time baseball executive W. H. Watkins succeeded in gaining admission for Port Huron in the Michigan-Ontario League of 1921, the park was once again remodeled and named Watkins Field in his honor. Since the 1921-22 team was a joint franchise with neighboring Sarnia, home games were also played in the Canadian city. The main grandstand was believed to be in the northwest corner at the intersection of Moak and 24th Streets. Currently, the ballpark site serves as a parking lot for the Prestolite factory on 24th Street.

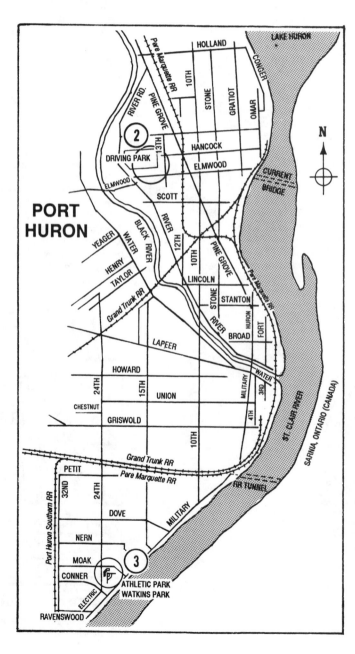

REED CITY

PROFESSIONAL LEAGUE MEMBERSHIP

YEARS	LEAGUE	HOME FIELD
1887	Northern Michigan	Reed City Baseball Grounds

With a population of about 2500 inhabitants, the Village of Reed City enjoyed the distinction of belonging to a legitimate professional baseball league in 1887—a claim that many Michigan towns several times its size cannot make. The Northern Michigan League of '87 was arguably the most compact league geographically and with possibly the smallest total population base to draw from of any minor league in the USA. The member cities of Reed City, Evart, Greenville, Big Rapids, and Ionia were all no more than a short train ride apart and the average population of the five communities was around 4,000—ranging from Evart's 1600 to Big Rapids' 6500. But the rabid rivalries between these neighboring towns encouraged the formation of the Northern Michigan League and the competition was spirited to say the least. W. A. Higbee was Reed City's owner/president and was also league president for a time, succeeding Thomas Malone of Ionia. William Slosson, another one of the Reed City backers, was also field manager of the local nine. League teams were a mixture of the best hometown talent plus whatever mercenaries from elsewhere their modest budgets could afford. The schedule was limited to weekends and holiday dates. Once underway, overzealous partisanship led to wild accusations and unsportsmanlike conduct by everyone involved, including fans and newspapers in all member towns. Evart finally withdrew in the aftermath of a protested game

and the circuit soon disintegrated when Big Rapids and Ionia also gave it up. With only Reed City and Greenville left, Reed City proclaimed themselves champions with an 11-8 record, but it was a pointless boast as the NM League was effectively dead. In the final statistics published later that year in the Detroit Free Press, J. M. Springer and E. E. Vance of the Reed Citys were among the circuit's top batsmen, with averages of .503 and .425. Despite the brief and stormy life of the Northern Michigan League, it put towns like Reed City on the Michigan baseball map and helped foster the growing popularity of baseball in the region.

THE PLAYING SITE

> **REED CITY BASEBALL GROUNDS 1887 (believed to be at the north end of Higbee St., near the waterworks site)**

No information has been found to verify the site of the baseball grounds nor its descriptive details. One game account mentions a batted ball ending up in the pond, which suggests its proximity to the waterworks pond of the Hershey River. Another possibility might be the fairgrounds site on the south side of town.

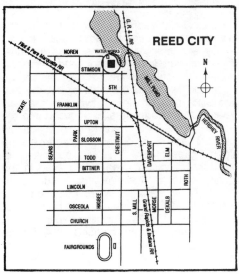

This building, part of the water works next to the baseball grounds, still stands today at the corner of Higbee & Noren.

SAGINAW

PROFESSIONAL LEAGUE MEMBERSHIP

YEARS	LEAGUE	HOME FIELD
1883-84	Northwestern	(West Saginaw)
1888	Saginaw Valley	(unknown)
1889	Michigan State	(unknown)
1890	International (joint franchise with Bay City)	(unknown)
1893	Ohio-Michigan	Union Park Grounds
1896	Interstate	Union Park
1897	Michigan State	(unknown)
1898, 1900	International	Athletic Park (Carrolton-W. Saginaw)
1902	Michigan State	Athletic Park
1906	Interstate Assn.	Athletic Park
1906	Southern Michigan	Athletic Park
1908-15	Southern Michigan	Recreation Park (renamed Burkart Park '09—later renamed Opportunity Park)
1919-25	Michigan-Ontario (MINT)	Opportunity/Aces Pk. Aces Park
1926	MINT/Mich. State	Aces Park
1940-41	Michigan State	Fairgrounds Park
1948-51	Central	Saginaw Stadium (Veterans Park)

Saginaw's 1883 Northwestern League champions. TOP ROW (L to R): W. H. Hawes, Mgr. Arthur Whitney, Thomas Forster. 2ND ROW: John Arundel, John Clarkson, W. H. Hunter. 3RD ROW: W. H. McGunnigle, Milton West, John Mansell. BOTTOM: Fred Nichols, W. H. Robinson, Malcolm McArthur.

The City of Saginaw ranks behind only Grand Rapids as one of Michigan's most prominent participants in minor league baseball through the years. From 1883 to 1951 the city was represented in no less than 10 different professional leagues and offered Saginaw fans league teams to root for in 32 summers during that time period. It all started when Arthur Whitney's "Old Golds" joined Bay City and Grand Rapids as .Michigan's representatives in the eight-team Northwestern League of 1883. The remainder of league members were from comparable towns in Ohio, Illinois, and Indiana. The league played an 84-game schedule and the final standings placed Saginaw in second place, only two games behind Toledo. However, at season's end, Toledo announced its intention to join the higher class American Association, so the NW League awarded the championship to Saginaw, still a member in good standing. The Old Gold's winning record was in no small measure due to the contributions of some first-rate players on the payroll, including John Clarkson and Bill McGunnigle.

With a successful season under their belts, the Northwest League overestimated their drawing power by expanding to 12 members in 1884, reaching westward into Minnesota and Wisconsin for four new franchises there. Minneapolis and St. Paul seemed like solid candidates, but the NW League also threw in tiny Stillwater in the new alignment. Milwaukee was also seduced into the expanded circuit, as were the questionable choices of Terre Haute, IN and Muskegon, the 4th Michigan representative. The winning battery of pitcher John Clarkson (who also played in the field) and catcher John Arundel returned to bolster Saginaw Manager W. A. Dier's pennant prospects. J. J. Rust also returned as president of the Saginaw entry in '84. Traveling expenses and poor attendance soon plagued the league treasuries and most franchises had trouble meeting the payroll, resulting in player desertions and low morale. Bay City withdrew on July 22, transferring to Evansville, IN. In short order, other clubs began to drop out like dominoes. Saginaw called it quits on Aug. 13 despite a fine 40-14 WL record, good enough for third place. Their "franchise" player, the great John Clarkson, had already gone to the Chicago National League club to launch a Hall of Fame career there. What started out in 1883 as a solid minor league organization had self-destructed in '84 by way of overzealous expansion.

Hall of Famer John Clarkson played for Saginaw in 1883-84. He won 327 games for three NL clubs from 1882 to 1894.

After a revival of semi-pro league baseball in the local Saginaw Valley League of 1888, Saginaw was eager to test the waters of a fully professional circuit when they joined the Michigan State League in 1889. John A. Murphy was the manager of the Saginaw entry. The '89 State League managed to play out a full schedule with only Kalamazoo transferring to Flint at the end. Paced by the pitching of Wheaton, Abbott, and future big leaguer Fred Schmidt, Saginaw held the top spot all summer long but Jackson went on a late-season tear and ended the season in a virtual tie for first. The Jacksons, without consulting League Secretary D. Z. Curtis, padded their final week with make-up games to give them enough wins to surpass Saginaw, but the league refused to recognize these games and Saginaw was declared the official champion of the 1889 State League.

The successful '89 season encouraged Saginaw to join forces with neighboring Bay City and enter the higher class International League for 1890.

The joint franchise would be aptly called the "Hyphens." The IL was essentially a Michigan-Ontario alliance, with Detroit as the other Michigan representative. W. A. Pettapiece was the president of the Hyphens franchise and the manager was Malcolm McArthur. Unfortunately, the circuit collapsed on July 7 with Saginaw-Bay City in first place. Saginaw avoided organized baseball adventures for the next three summers until the 1893 Ohio-Michigan League beckoned. This extension of the Ohio State League proved to be another financial failure, with Saginaw and Bay City as the only Michigan representatives. Saginaw, piloted by an '89 local favorite, Fred Popkay, was 5-15 when both Michigan cities dropped out on June 14. Three years later (1896) Saginaw entered the class B Interstate League, a far-flung circuit that extended as far east as Pennsylvania and West Virginia. George Black was the manager and the '96 Saginaw lineup included future big leaguers Charles Hemphill and his brother Frank. After Ft. Wayne (IN) jumped out to a huge lead, the league decided to split the season into two halves, hoping to make it more competitive. For Saginaw, it didn't help as they finished with the circuit's worst record, 41 wins vs. 72 losses.

In 1897, Saginaw opted to keep their competition closer to home and decided to re-enter the Michigan State League. The officers of the Saginaw franchise were William H. Saltonstall, W. F. Pearson, and J. P. Sheridan. George Black returned as field boss, but was later replaced by William Phillips. The "Lumbermen" were in 4th place when the State League suddenly fell apart in late July. Determined to find a league home for Saginaw, the city rehired George Black as manager and re-entered the Michigan-Canada based International League for 1898. But once again they failed to complete a season as the IL went "belly up" in early July. After sitting out the 1899 season, Saginaw was brought back into the International when Woodstock, ONT owner Fred Eddy transferred his franchise here for the 1900 season. But it was like 1898 all over again as Eddy's Saginaws had to abort when the IL once again collapsed in July. One noteworthy player on the 1900 Saginaw roster was catcher "Red" Kleinow, who went on to a major league career of some distinction.

George Black led Saginaw to a last place finish in the 1896 Interstate League.

John "Red" Kleinow, catcher on the 1900 Saginaw club, played eight years in the big leagues.

Like the proverbial cat of nine lives, the Michigan State League reappeared in 1902 and Saginaw joined Battle Creek, Flint, Muskegon, Grand Rapids, and Lansing to make yet another attempt to survive beyond a partial season. Saginaw's C. F. Baker was named secretary of the revived circuit and veteran minor leaguer George "Doggie" Miller was named manager of the Saginaw club. But once again the league was cursed with instability and poor patronage. Saginaw was the first to cave in, transferring operations to Jackson in mid-July. Miller's bunch were having a fair season, in second place when the team was relocated. The MSL survived another month with four teams but finally called it a season on August 20 with Battle Creek on top. It would be another four years before Saginaw would attempt league baseball again.

With the popularity and profitability of minor league baseball on the upswing in 1906, Grand Rapids newspaperman and baseball booster Emerson Dickerson quickly assembled a midwest alliance of eight towns to form the Interstate Association, a class C loop whose Michigan members (Saginaw, Bay City, and Flint) would rival the newly formed Southern Michigan League. Once again, this new loop failed to attract a sufficient following and all three Michigan towns dropped out by early July. Bay City and Muncie, IN were the first casualties on May 18 and Saginaw gave it up a month later. The better organized SML had a more successful first season and soon after the demise of their Interstate Assn. rival, they took on the vacated territory of Saginaw as a sixth member of that organization. Catcher Clarence Jessup was named manager, replacing Clyde McNutt of the IA team. The new Saginaws wound up in last place in their "second season" of 1906 and did not rejoin the SML in 1907.

A. S. Burkart became president of the Saginaw club in 1908 and gave the city two consecutive pennant winners. The home field was renamed in tribute to him.

Billy Smith replaced Hayes as Saginaw manager in 1909.

Saginaw re-entered the Southern Michigan League in 1908 and began the most glorious period of baseball in the city's history—eight consecutive years of professional baseball for Saginaw fans, and it started with the most

memorable seasons of all with consecutive championships. A. S. Burkart, late of the Mt. Clemens SML team, was the guiding hand in assembling the 1908 Saginaws. Bruce Hayes managed and played second base. When the '08 season ended, Saginaw was the new champion of the SML with a record of 72-52, three games up on 2nd place Kalamazoo. The spectacular season was blemished somewhat in early September when the grandstand of the home park was completely destroyed by fire. But no games were lost to the schedule as play was resumed before the charred ruins, with owner Burkart admitting fans at no charge. The team's success and Burkart's popularity resulted in the renaming of the rebuilt field as Burkart Park in 1909. Billy Smith was the new field boss in 1909 and led Saginaw to a second consecutive SML pennant in a thrilling finish over runnerups Flint and Jackson. Saginaw hurler Ed Kusel was the ace of the '09 staff, tying Elmer Criger of Jackson for league honors with a 22-7 record. Saginaw was the toast of the Southern Michigan League, but it would be all downhill after 1909.

Outfielder Frank Gilhooley went from Saginaw in 1910 to a nine-year stay in the big leagues.

Former big league backstop Malachi Kittredge was the new field boss in 1911.

Billy Smith returned in 1910 to defend Saginaw's SML championship but had to recruit a whole new lineup as many of the '08-'09 stars moved on to higher assignments. The magic was clearly gone as Saginaw nosedived into the 1910 SML cellar, a full six games behind seventh place Jackson. A Saginaw man, Judge James P. Bowen, replaced Jackson as SML president in 1911. Another team overhaul was in order for 1911 as ex-major league catcher Malachi Kittredge was appointed new manager. To honor their new field boss, the team adopted a new nickname—"Kittens." The hitting of J. W. Hopkins and Joe Kutina elevated the Kittens to a more respectable fifth place finish, but Kittredge was not rehired to lead the 1912 club. Walter Hartwell was the new field boss, but mother nature dealt both Saginaw and Bay City fans a cruel blow by forcing both teams out in mid-season—both cities victimized by torrential flooding of the Saginaw River that inundated their ballparks and so disrupted their home schedule that they abandoned the 1912 campaign. But neither city had abdicated their membership in the SML and

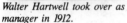
Walter Hartwell took over as manager in 1912.

Future Hall of Famer Jess Haines won 17 games for the 1914 pennant-winning Ducks.

both returned to the fold in 1913. Former big leaguer "Ducky" Holmes was signed to catch and manage the Saginaws for 1913. In keeping with the prevailing fad of adopting team nicknames that identified with the current manager, the 1913 club was christened "Ducks"—an ironic choice after the floods of 1912. Misfortune struck again in May 1913 when Burkart Park, the Ducks' home field, once again was leveled by fire, but play continued as the grandstand was quickly reconstructed. The new Ducks, paced by the pitching of Hal Schwenk, finished in the middle of the pack with a 60-65 WL record. Schwenk joined the St. Louis Browns at season's end and his battery mate, catcher Jack Snyder, later caught on with the Buffalo Feds and Brooklyn.

Ducky Holmes was back as pilot in 1914 and gave Saginaw its third Southern Michigan pennant. The league had expanded to 10 cities and adopted a split-season format to match up first and second half winners in a post-season championship playoff. This formula ultimately helped Saginaw gain the playoffs, as they finished far behind first half winner Bay City with a mediocre 38-39 record. However, the second season was a different story as the Ducks caught fire and captured the other playoff spot with an impressive 52-16 record. The combined standings of a full season would have put Saginaw six games behind Bay City and virtually tied with Battle Creek for second. The Ducks were blessed with sensational pitching from Walter Scott (26-10), John Jones (23-11), Russ Robbins (20-16), and Jesse Haines (17-14). Newcomer Haines was only five years away from a Hall of Fame career with the St. Louis Cardinals. Harring (.364), Stupp (.322), and Leber (.303) were the leading Saginaw hitters. The Ducks won the first three playoff games from Bay City, then suffered three consecutive setbacks before capturing the 1914 SML pennant in the final game. Clutch pitching by Haines in the dramatic 7th game held Bay City in check after Saginaw scored the game-winning run in the top of the 10th. From there they added to their laurels by defeating Michigan State League champion Muskegon in an interleague playoff. Disregarding the higher league teams in Grand Rapids and Detroit, Saginaw was the "king" of professional league baseball in the State of Michigan for 1914. The SML returned to an eight-team alignment in 1915, but the appeal of minor league baseball was inexplicably on a downward trend by this time and mounting losses forced the league to disband on July 5. It was never resurrected and thus ended a memorable run of Saginaw league baseball after eight years and three championships.

Catcher Ducky Holmes led his "Ducks" to a pennant in 1914.

The 1914 champions of the Southern Michigan League. STANDING (L to R): Tate, Plate, Olsen, Robbins, Jansen, Jones, Scott, Haines, Mgr. Holmes. KNEELING: Harring, Foley, Manning, Trainer Eiferlee, Bashang, Stupp, Leber.

Outfielder Earle "Greasy" Neale hit .332 for Saginaw in 1915. He went on to an eight-year ML career but gained greater fame as a football coach in the NFL.

When the World War finally ended, the American public began to clamor for a revival of league baseball. One of the first new leagues to emerge in 1919 was the Michigan-Ontario (MINT) League, organized by former Southern Michigan League founder Joe Jackson. Saginaw, Battle Creek, Bay City, and Flint were the Michigan entries in the class B circuit, the remaining four being Ontario cities. Frank "Buzz" Wetzel was the Saginaw manager and he picked up where the SML left off in 1914 by leading his team to the championship with a 78-32 record, 3-1/2 games up on second place Hamilton, ONT. Saginaw fans were ecstatic over their new champions but the bottom fell out in 1920 when the Saginaws plummeted to the league cellar. The Canadian cities had strengthened their rosters over the winter and the Ontario half of the league took over the entire first division. The following year (1921) some semblance of balance was restored and Saginaw, led by the pitching of Claude Gillenwater, climbed into a 5th place tie with newcomer Port Huron-Sarnia. Flint's T. J. Halligan took over the MINT League in 1922 and Saginaw surged back to respectability by winning the first half of the split season. They slipped to under .500 in the second half and lost to Hamilton in the post-season playoffs, but Saginaw fans had to be pleased and optimistic about their return to the first division. Pitcher

Herman Schwartje was the circuit's top winner with 23 victories. Frank Wayneberg finished out the season pitching 47 consecutive innings without allowing an earned run.

Buzz Wetzel's 1923 club made another strong showing, finishing a close second to a powerful Bay City club. By this time, the pendulum of strength had swung back over to the Michigan teams of the MINT, with the two remaining Ontario cities (London and Hamilton) winding up deep in the second division. Outfielder Al Bashang was the new manager for 1924 and his club had a good first-half season, finishing a close second to Flint. But in the second half, the Saginaws slumped to sixth, eliminating themselves from playoff contention. Third baseman Yoter was the club's top hitter with a .337 average and Wayneberg led the mounds- men with a 15-6 WL record. In 1925 the two Canadian teams from Hamilton and London took all the honors, while Saginaw finished a distant third. The 1926 MINT League was a misnomer as the circuit became a four-team all-Michigan loop when the three Ontario cities had bowed out. The diminished MINT found interest waning as the season progressed, but found new life by merging with the four-team Central League, which was likewise struggling at the gate. Since both leagues were all Michigan towns, the new combination rechristened itself the Michigan State League and started a new season on June 15. The difference in class (the MINT was B, the Central C) became apparent as the top three clubs were ex-MINTers. Bay City ran away with the pennant, with Saginaw finishing third. The "Aces" were managed by former big league backstop Les Nunamaker, who also played numerous positions and hit .324 in 83 games. Sid Dyer and Frank Matuzek were Saginaw's top slab artists. Unfortunately, the early season merger was not the salvation hoped for as disappointing patronage forced the MSL out of existence for another 14 summers.

The Saginaw Aces of 1919 or 1920. The players and the year are unconfirmed, so this group is either a pennant winner (1919) or a cellar dweller (1920)—take your pick.

The end of the Great Depression in the late 1930s saw a national revival of minor league baseball. Another factor that encouraged many more leagues to form was the growth of farm systems by the major league clubs. Former MINT League President T. J. Halligan was instrumental in organizing a class C Michigan State League for the 1940 season. The six communities of Saginaw, Flint, Lansing, Grand Rapids, Muskegon, and St. Joseph were lined up as members and all but St. Joseph had big league sponsors. The Philadelphia Athletics would be the parent club of the Saginaw entry and would be responsible for supplying player talent. James "Ike" Bearinger was team president and Tex Avery was the first "Athletics" field boss. A new ballpark was put in order on the fairgrounds property. 1500 fans came out on May 20, 1940 to welcome the return of league baseball and watch the locals pull out a 6-5 victory over Grand Rapids. After catcher Hank Camelli took charge, the Athletics went on to a winning season, finishing a strong second behind a talented Flint club. Reb Wright (15-8) and Jim Schelle (12-6) provided steady pitching, backed up by the bats of Camelli (.345 and 13 HRs), outfielder Bill Fuchs (.315), and utility man Frank Gunkel (11 HRs). Saginaw eliminated Grand Rapids in the first playoff round and squared off to take on St. Joseph, upset victors over Flint, in the championship round. But mother nature denied the Athletics an opportunity to claim the final prize when a seemingly endless stretch of heavy rains forced the league to cancel the playoff finals.

For 1941, the Saginaw club switched affiliation to the Chicago AL club and henceforth became the "White Sox." Bill Prince was the new pilot but was later succeeded by first baseman Whitey McMullen. The '41 State League adopted a split-season format to match up first and second half winners in the post-season playoffs, but the idea backfired when the powerful Flint club won both seasons to nullify a playoff. For Saginaw it mattered little, since they finished a distant fifth in both halves. Only outfielders Stan Platek (.320, 17 HRs) and Hal Cromer (.298) had productive seasons for Saginaw—not enough to offset a mediocre pitching corps. Gate receipts were adequate enough, if not spectacular, to guarantee a repeat season in 1942, but the attack on Pearl Harbor put the State League out of business. Among the Saginaw stalwarts of the MSL years, only Hank Camelli emerged as a bona fide major leaguer with five journeyman seasons in the National League from 1943 to 1947.

Outfield stars for the '41 club were Hal Cromer (L) and Stan Platek.

Jim Schelle was a steady hurler in 1940-41.

Ike Bearinger was club owner in two leagues in the 1940s. *Hank Camelli was Saginaw manager in 1940 and 1950.*

Wheeler scoring on his HR in the 1940 home opener.

The 1941 infield (L to R): Andy Kreevich 3B, Mike Lazorchak SS, Dan Snell 2B, Whitey McMullen 1B

With the war over and the nation's economy in high gear, minor league baseball was once again a healthy business in the late 1940s. Former State League founder T. J. Halligan set his sights higher and assembled a class A edition of the Central League for 1948. The six-team circuit would be comprised of the four Michigan towns of Saginaw, Flint, Grand Rapids, and Muskegon plus Dayton, OH and Ft. Wayne, IN. Ike Bearinger once again headed the Saginaw organization and, accordingly, the team nickname would be "Bears." Former Detroit GM Jack Zeller was a VP and Bob Finley was hired as field boss. Unlike the other CL clubs, Saginaw would operate as an unaffiliated independent. The '48 Bears wound up only a game out of the CL basement with a 55-85 record. Second baseman Lou Farotto (.325) was the team's best hitter, along with outfielder Ralph Rhames (.319), and catcher/manager Finley (.311). A local high school phenom, 19-year-old Bob Buhl, made a creditable professional debut with the hometown Bears, winning 11 games on the mound. Saginaw's independent status had proved to be their undoing by 1949 as their inability to recruit top prospects on their own gave them another losing club in their second CL season. Lou Farotto had another fine season to top the last place Bears in hitting, and new sluggers "Timber" Dahlberg and Ron Bowen were crowd pleasers, but decent pitching was nowhere to be found.

Hank Camelli, the popular catcher from the 1940 State League club, was hired to replace Bob Finley as manager in 1950. But the patience of the Saginaw fans finally faded as another last-place club caused attendance to drop to crisis levels. The phenomenal popularity of minor league baseball in the post-war years was already in decline and having a perennial loser only worsened the situation in Saginaw and elsewhere. An organizational overhaul in the Saginaw franchise began in mid-1950 when Ike Bearinger

Hometown product Bob Buhl won 11 games for the '48 Bears. Five years later he began a splendid 15-year career in the National League, winning 166 games for three teams.

Bob Finley was Bears' boss in '48-'49.

Saginaw's 1948 infield included (L to R): Ev Robinson 1B, Lou Farotto 2B, Charles Aickley SS, Joe Janet 3B, George Ogorek (utility)

Saginaw's Jimmy Wallace was one of the Central League's best pitchers in 1950.

Lou Farotto homered on opening day 1948 at Alumni Field.

R. Lee Gilbert became the new president in 1950, succeeding Ike Bearinger.

Saginaw native Ed Albosta pitched creditably for the hometown team in 1950-51.

stepped down, turning the club over to a new group headed by R. Lee Gilbert. Bert Niehoff replaced Camelli as field boss for 1951 and a new nickname of "Jack Rabbits" was introduced to escape the identity of the Bears' losing years. The changes bore fruit in the '51 season as the team surged into playoff contention with a third place finish and an accompanying jump in attendance. The '51 Jack Rabbits were a far cry from the previous Bears with solid pitching, good defense, and dependable hitting. Saginaw native Ed Albosta led the hurlers with 19 victories and third baseman Oscar Khederian hit .326 to lead the offense. But Saginaw's rebound as a solid Central League franchise was all for naught as the league

itself was in a state of bankruptcy that drove it out of business. Its despair was so severe that it abandoned the post-season playoff and, as in 1940, a recharged Saginaw club lost another opportunity to claim a league championship for the city. It was the "last hurrah" for organized baseball in the city, but hope springs eternal as rumors abound in various Michigan cities with the current revival of minor league baseball in the state. Saginaw's fine tradition as a minor league town makes it a serious candidate for a future franchise in any new league with Michigan connections.

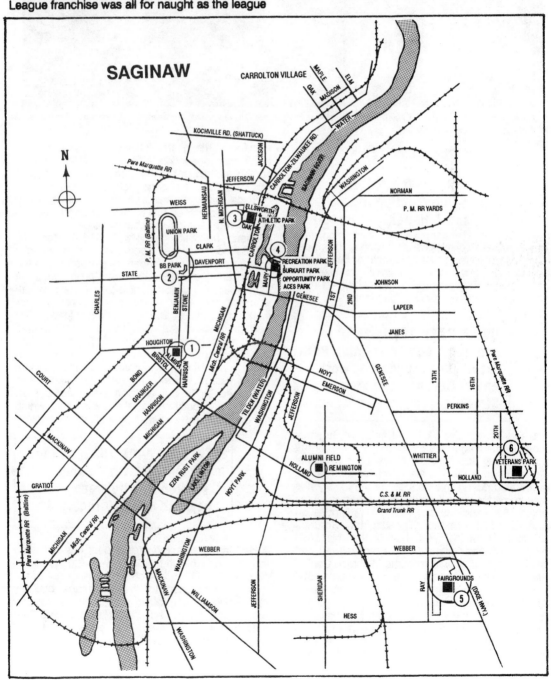

A detailed aerial view drawing of Saginaw looking northwest around 1893. The blackened area near the top shows the area destroyed by a monstrous fire of that year.

THE PLAYING SITES

WEST SAGINAW GROUNDS 1880s (intersection of Harrison & Houghton Streets)

This baseball facility was on property that now includes either the General Hospital or Bliss Park, at least in this general vicinity. Its use by professional league teams is not certain—it may have been used only for local baseball.

UNION PARK 1880s-1900 (on southeast corner of Union Park racetrack grounds—at west end of Davenport at Stone Street)

The use of this site as home field for Saginaw professional league teams in the 19th century is not precisely documented. Newspaper accounts did not always identify the exact location of the home field during this period, but very likely this was home for most if not all of the league teams of the 1880s and 1890s. The Bay City Tribune on April 27, 1883 reported: "The Saginaw Grounds are located on the west side of the river, two blocks from the Saginaw City street railway and within five minutes walk from the Michigan Central depot. The field is a very large one, probably 500 x 500 feet. The diamond lies east and west." Another newspaper account in 1909 recalled that "the grounds upon which this team (the 1883 NW League champs) played were about three blocks directly east of the late Gov. Bliss' home, near what is now Clark Street." Other 1883 items

mention some of the following park features: a telephone connection, a high board fence, a wire screen on the front of the grandstand, open seats (bleachers) under construction, and a special carriage gate for carriage ticket holders. The Saginaw Courier of July 5, 1883 reported that "the extensive structure, capable of holding twelve or thirteen hundred people..." Other features mentioned were a scoreboard and special scorers and reporters' quarters (press box) in the grandstand just behind the home plate screen. In early 1896, the Union Park facility (or a new site adjacent) was entirely rebuilt with a new grandstand, bleachers, and surrounding fence. The new grandstand was said to hold 1000 people and the new bleachers 500 more. The grandstand was to occupy the southeast corner of Union Park. A high fence was erected on the northern and western sides. The park entrance was described as in the extreme southeast corner, apparently directly behind the grandstand, which ran parallel to the eastern boundary of the park.

ATHLETIC PARK 1902-06 (on west side of river—along Carollton Rd., between Ellsworth & Oak Streets)

A detailed description of this park has not been found. It was home for Saginaw league teams in 1902 and 1906. In July of 1902, the owner of the grounds attempted to disrupt league play by maliciously tearing down part of the fence and grandstand when the State League club had defaulted on rent due. The fence was hastily repaired with volunteer help and the games proceeded.

RECREATION PARK/BURKART PARK/OPPORTUNITY PARK/ACES PARK 1908-1926 (on west edge of Saginaw River at Davenport & Mary Sts., just north of the Genesee Bridge)

This facility, which opened in 1908 as Recreation Park, lived a turbulent and glory-filled life as the home of Saginaw baseball through the 1920s. It survived numerous name changes, reconstructions, floods and fires, and was the stage for some of the most memorable moments of league baseball in this city. It was also home for many amateur and interscholastic contests, including football. The precise orientation of the diamond and grandstand are not recorded, and possibly may have changed from time to time through the life of the field. When new owner A. S. Burkart gave Saginaw a championship team in the first year (1908) of Southern Michigan League competition, and followed it up with another flag in '09, he became a folk hero among the city's baseball boosters. At the end of the 1908 season, the home park was totally gutted by fire, but the games went on and Burkart further endeared himself to local fans by charging no admission to games played immediately after the fire. He immediately set about to rebuild the park and it was fittingly renamed for him in 1909. The new edifice had all the features of its predecessor and more, and was ranked with Detroit's Bennett Park as among the state's finest. A huge new grandstand included a spacious row of box seats along the front of the main stand, replete with opera chairs. Perhaps its proudest moment was June 3, 1909 when a capacity crowd participated in all the pomp and circumstance surrounding the raising of the 1908 pennant.

Misfortune struck again at Burkart Park in 1912 when the Saginaw River left the park hopelessly inundated, so much so that Saginaw (as well as neighboring Bay City) had to withdraw from the SML pennant race in July. The following spring another disastrous fire consumed the grandstand (now called Opportunity Park) and temporarily disrupted the league schedule. But once again, the park was rebuilt as the season progressed. After league baseball returned to Opportunity Park in 1919, the outdated name "Opportunity" soon gave way to a rechristening—the new name "Aces Park" was adopted to acknowledge its newest tenant, the Saginaw Aces. Evolutionary improvements took place periodically through the park's final year as a home for league baseball (1926). After its abandonment, the old park's dignity was totally stripped as it ended up as the site of the city's Davenport Street dump.

FAIRGROUNDS PARK 1940-41 (on fairgrounds property in southeast part of city at Webber & Dixie Hwy.)

The grandstand for racing events at the fairgrounds was adopted for baseball games when Saginaw entered the Michigan State League in 1940. Significant improvements, including improved drainage, light towers, and new dugouts were added by the State League club. The fairgrounds and grandstand are still in existence today.

A view of Fairgrounds Park in early 1940, still under construction

SAGINAW STADIUM/VETERANS MEMORIAL STADIUM 1948-51 (southeast of downtown at Holland and 20th Streets)

(6)

When Saginaw signed on for Central League play in 1948, arrangements were hastily made to build a suitable playing field on the property of current Veterans Memorial Park, southeast of downtown. The project proved to be more difficult than anticipated and it was over a year before the facility was finally completed to acceptable standards. Progress was so slow in early 1948 that home games had to be played at Saginaw High School's Alumni Field. Once play had commenced at the new Saginaw Stadium, both fans and players found fault with the facilities. Drainage was woefully inadequate and numerous rocks in the outfield made it hazardous for the players. Fans also complained about no covered grandstand and a poor view at best from the open bleachers. The absence of lavatories and sidewalk ramps only added to the inconvenience for patrons. By 1949 major improvements took care of most of the complaints, but it would be another year before the major goals of construction were met. The whole experience tested the patience of Saginaw fans who still

came out to support losing teams on a field that fell far short of expectations. In 1951, the City of Saginaw took over the park from the Saginaw Stadium Corp. and renamed it Veterans Memorial Stadium.

A workman applies finishing touches to a new gravel track along the box seats at Saginaw Stadium in 1949.

The San Antonio Stadium (above) was built from the same plans as Saginaw Stadium, but the roof was never added to the Saginaw version.

A view of the playing field from the first base side

An aerial view from 1951

ST. JOSEPH

PROFESSIONAL LEAGUE MEMBERSHIP

YEARS	LEAGUE	HOME FIELD
1940-41	Michigan State	Edgewater Park

The twin cities of St. Joseph and Benton Harbor made reputations as baseball towns in their own unique way. Benton Harbor never presented a team in a professional league—the closest they came was in the Indiana-Michigan League of 1910 when they dropped out because of the lack of a suitable playing field. But the City of Benton Harbor later became famous in baseball circles as the home of the popular House of David traveling team. Meanwhile, St. Joseph was represented by a crack independent club sponsored by the hometown Automotive Specialties Mfg. Co., known throughout the state as the St. Joe "Autos" or "Auscos." When the class C Michigan State League was formed in 1940, the Autos were given an opportunity to add to their winning credentials by competing in a full-fledged minor league. Edgewater Park, the home of the independent Autos, was already a first-rate grounds and needed little upgrading. The Auto Specialties firm would continue to sponsor the league club, with Clayton Williams as chief officer. Although all of the other State League clubs (Muskegon, Grand Rapids, Flint, Lansing, and Saginaw) would have working arguments with big league teams, St. Joseph chose to remain independent from farm club status. Second baseman Elmer Kirchoff also served as field manager.

The talent-laden Flint Gems won the 1940 State League regular season in a breeze, finishing a dozen games up on second place Saginaw. The Autos finished third with a 52-51 record, which qualified them for the post-season playoff. St. Joseph surprised everyone by upsetting Flint in the first round, then saw their chances of a championship go literally "down the drain" when torrential rains canceled the final series. Despite finishing behind Saginaw in the standings, the Autos could at least lay claim to a co-championship on the basis of their standing in the playoff picture. Herb Nordquist (11-2) and Ed Schumaker (14-8) topped the St. Joe pitchers. Shortstop Tom Woodruff appeared in only 27 games but hit a sensational .404 and was picked on the State League all-star team for his achievement. Other key members of the Autos hit parade were Jim Russell (.343), Norm Snyder (.339), and Chet Manning (.328). First baseman Manning was also the league's top base stealer, with 40 to his credit.

The Michigan State League changed its schedule to a split-season format in 1941, which would match up first and second half winners in a single playoff series. Flint spoiled the party by taking both halves and it was another opportunity lost for St. Joseph in post-season play. The Autos played steady ball all season, finishing second in both halves. Elmer Kirchoff was back as '41 pilot, as were Norm Snyder and catcher Stan Bazan. Snyder had another banner season, hitting .320 with 27 HRs and 115 RBIs. Bazan also chipped in with a .320 season, as did outfielder Stan Platek.

The 1940 St. Joe Autos. STANDING (L to R): Woodruff, Snyder, Meredith, Manning, Bazan, Martin, Russell, Nordquist. KNEELING: Pacotti, Edelman, Martin, Schumaker, Rotoni, Mandjack, Mgr. Elmer Kirchoff.

Newcomer Joe Morjoseph, who would resurface after the war in the Central League, hit .308 in 96 games. Another new arrival, first baseman Hank Arft, hit .303 and would become a regular with the St. Louis Browns. Other 1941 Autos who eventually made it to the big show were pitchers Al LaMacchia and Marlin Stuart. The Autos looked forward to another chance at the MSL flag in 1942 but WWII put the state league out of business. And so ended little St. Joseph's two-year stint as a member of organized baseball.

Marlin Stuart from the '41 Autos threw a perfect no-hitter for Toledo in 1950. He also had six years in the AL as a relief pitcher for four different clubs.

Hank Arft hit .303 for the '41 club and eventually played for the St. Louis Browns.

THE PLAYING SITE

> ### EDGEWATER PARK 1940-41 (north of downtown, across the St. Joseph River)

Built at a cost of $30,000, Edgewater Park was arguably the finest diamond in the Michigan State League of 1940-41. Beautifully landscaped with ample parking due to its isolated location, it had all the latest features of the best minor league parks of the day. The covered grandstand included a double tier of 44 box seats circling the home plate area. Ample open bleachers extended down both foul lines. The latest in lighting facilities made this park a "jewel" for summer evenings.

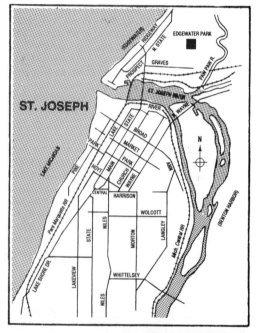

A fine aerial view of Edgewater Park

SAULT STE. MARIE

PROFESSIONAL LEAGUE MEMBERSHIP

YEARS	LEAGUE	HOME FIELD
1905	Copper Country-Soo	Brady Field (Sundays-Country Club Grounds)

The city of the locks took to baseball as a popular pastime as much as any of the other Upper Peninsula towns, but its top teams around the turn of the century were always of the independent or semi-pro variety. Local boosters with money to spend attracted talented prospects from points distant to give local "cranks" a brand of baseball a notch above that of comparable towns in the lower peninsula. The 1904 independents showcased future big leaguers Eddie Cicotte and William "Jap" Barbeau in their games with other UP towns. With baseball interest high and local economies generally prospering in the Upper Peninsula, the Copper Country communities of Calumet, Hancock, and Lake Linden persuaded Sault Ste. Marie to join them in the formation of a recognized class D professional league for the 1905 season. The circuit would be called the Copper Country-Soo League and would be fully bound by the National Agreements, with forfeiture funds deposited and other limits enforced to maintain stable competition. A. L. Ferguson was named president of the Soo club, with W. B. Earle as field manager. The league adopted a full 100-game schedule, a big gamble to test the appetites of baseball followers in the north country. Brady Field would host the majority of home dates with Sunday games played at the Country Club Grounds.

Little Barbeau returned from the 1904 team to hold down the third base position for the Soos. Other fan favorites were M. O. "Kid" Taylor and Manistee's John Bufka. The '05 Copper Country-Soo League completed their season on Labor Day with Calumet on top and Sault Ste. Marie on the bottom. The league was a modest success, but the Soo franchise became a liability because of its distance and its poor performance on the field and at the gate. The following winter, the Copper Country members merged with the nearby Northern League and the Soos were not included in the new alignment. And thus ended Sault Ste. Marie's brief one-year representation as a member of Organized Baseball.

William "Jap" Barbeau was a Soo favorite in 1904-05. He went directly from here to the Cleveland AL club.

Pitcher Eddie Cicotte had a long career in the big leagues, abruptly cut short by his involvement in the 1919 "Black Sox" scandal. He pitched in Sault Ste. Marie in 1904.

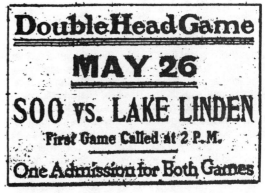

Double Head Game
MAY 26
SOO vs. LAKE LINDEN
First Game Called at 2 P.M.
One Admission for Both Games

A newspaper ad for a Copper Country-Soo doubleheader in 1905

171

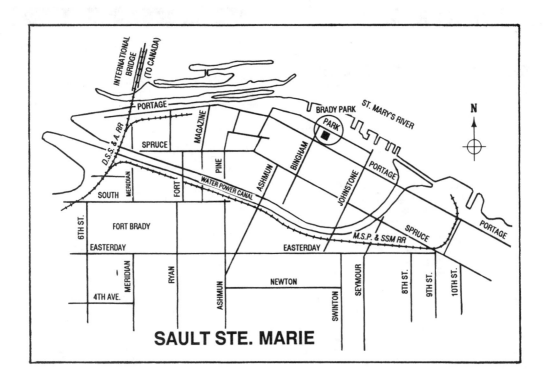

SAULT STE. MARIE

THE PLAYING SITE

> ### BRADY FIELD 1905 (on Portage between Bingham & Brady Streets)

After the original Fort Brady was relocated further into the city, the old Fort property was used as a public park, including a baseball diamond on where now stands the River of History Museum (the former Federal Building). The 1905 Copper Country-Soo League team played the majority of home dates there, but also played Sunday games at the Country Club Grounds (whereabouts unknown). No photographs or other descriptive details of Brady Field have been found. Shortly after the demise of the '05 Soo Club, the baseball diamond was closed and the new Federal Building erected on the site.

The old Federal Building, now the River of History Museum, occupies the site of Brady Field.

TECUMSEH

PROFESSIONAL LEAGUE MEMBERSHIP

YEARS	LEAGUE	HOME FIELD
1906-08	Southern Michigan	Athletic Park

Tiny Tecumseh, with a population of 3000, was a hotbed of independent baseball after the turn of the century. First-rate professional players and some very talented locals gave Tecumseh fans a representative team that ranked with the best in the state in the post-1900 years. Their winning ways came to a grand climax in the fall of 1905, when they met their most serious challengers for the championship of the independents, Mt. Clemens, in a series of playoff games. With no other Michigan-based minor league in the lower peninsula at that time, this much-publicized playoff attracted statewide attention—even more than the major league pennant races. Horace R. Brewer was manager of the Tecumsehs and the team president was J. L. Anderson. The lineup was laced with some of the best known "hired guns" in the area, including captain "Bo" Slear and second baseman Charley Wagner. A local boy, Harvey Teal, was the ace pitcher. Enthusiasm which bordered on hysteria was rampant in both cities and a purse of $500 for the winning team was held by Detroit Free Press Sports Editor Joe Jackson. The best-of-nine series went the distance with Tecumseh taking the final game at Mt. Clemens to claim the championship and the $500 pot.

Sportswriter Jackson was so captivated by the success of this competition that he was inspired to enlarge upon it and perpetuate it in an organized professional league in 1906. The new circuit would be called the Southern Michigan League and, in addition to Tecumseh and Mt. Clemens, would include Kalamazoo, Jackson, Battle Creek, and Saginaw. Brewer was back to manage the new professional league version of the Tecumsehs, to be called the "Indians." Many of the 1905 regulars also returned—namely ace pitcher Teal, captain Slear, second baseman Wagner, first baseman Beasley, and outfielder Preston. Much to the dismay of Tecumseh followers, Dad Trombley's Mt. Clemens bunch got a measure of revenge from the previous year by running away with the SML pennant, with Tecumseh finishing third. A 17-year-old Wisconsin lad, infielder Fred Merkle, made a good impression with local fans and would be back in 1907.

A successful maiden season encouraged the Southern Michigan League to expand to eight clubs in 1907, adding Lansing and Flint with Bay City replacing Saginaw. Preston, Wagner, Slear, Merkle, and Teal, the nucleus of the '06 club, all returned and this time it was Tecumseh's turn to replace hated rival Mt. Clemens as champions of the SML. Harvey Teal and newcomer Tom Railing each recorded 21 victories to pace the Indians' pennant chase. Fred Merkle tied for the league lead with six home runs. Young Merkle found himself in the big show at season's end and the following year. Playing with John McGraw's New York Giants, he was a key figure in an exciting pennant race with the Chicago Cubs. Despite a long and distinguished major league career, Fred was forever cursed with the infamous "Merkle Boner" in 1908 that lost a crucial game for the Giants and forced a post-season playoff game which went to the Cubs.

Horace Brewer managed both the '05 independents and the SM League club.

The 1905 independents. TOP ROW: Pres. J. L. Anderon, Ellerby, Beasley, Mgr. Brewer. MIDDLE: Gillen, Teal, Smith, Bell, Slear, Wagner. BOTTOM: Preston, Striker, Krouse. Many remained on the League team the following year.

Tecumseh was back for another SML pennant chase in 1908, but was forced to reassemble a winning club with new faces and the result was a fourth place finish. Saginaw was the new champion as Mt. Clemens had dropped out after 1907. Tecumseh fans began to lose interest after savoring the winning combination of '05 and '07, and over the following winter the franchise was transferred to nearby Adrian. At least Lenawee County was still represented in league baseball, and four years later earned another SML flag when Adrian copped the prize. For Tecumseh fans, the memories of the great seasons of 1905 and 1907 would be fondly recalled for decades to come.

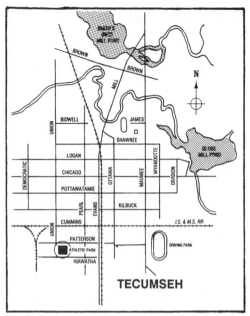

Bo Slear was a key player on Tecumseh clubs of 1905-07.

The NY Giants' Fred Merkle played for the Indians in 1907.

THE PLAYING SITE

ATHLETIC PARK 1905-08 (Patterson & S. Union Streets)

Not much detailed information has been found on this park—its origins and its final demise still a mystery. The orientation of the diamond is also uncertain, but the surviving photograph on this page confirms the existence of a small fully-roofed grandstand and a covered pavilion on the first base side. The site is currently a vacant lot.

The Athletic Park location today is an empty lot.

A rare photo of Tecumseh's home field

TRAVERSE CITY

PROFESSIONAL LEAGUE MEMBERSHIP

YEARS	LEAGUE	HOME FIELD
1910-14	Michigan State	League Park (Fairgrounds)

Traverse City's only participation in a professional minor league was a five-year run in the class D Michigan State League of 1910-14. When first conceived by Grand Rapids newspaperman and baseball promotor Emerson Dickerson in early 1910 it was referred to as the West Michigan League, which was a more geographically correct title since indeed the member towns were in the western part of the state along the Lake Michigan shoreline. This also clearly distinguished it from the Southern Michigan League of that era, but by the time the season opened it was officially christened the Michigan State League. It was a four-team alignment consisting of Traverse City, Cadillac, Muskegon, and Holland, with plans to expand to six or eight in 1911. Traverse City, under the leadership of W. C. Hull, was already assembling a fast independent team and was ready to convert this effort into a league club.

The "Resorters," under Henry Collett and later H. Thacker, made a strong challenge for the 1910 MSL pennant, finishing only three games behind Cal Wenger's Cadillac champions. A mid-season slump was Traverse City's undoing and they were unable to overtake Cadillac after that. Outfielder Pfeiffer was TC's top batter with a .309 average. A local boy, 18-year-old Anthony "Bunny" Brief from the nearby Remus/Big Rapids area, made a promising debut in the TC outfield and would become a fan favorite in the years following. Another Michigan product, pitcher Larue Kirby from Eureka, joined Brief as another homegrown star who played several seasons in the Resort City. Both Brief and Kirby later had short stays in the big show.

Boyne City and Manistee joined the State League in 1911 to make it a six-team circuit. Newcomer Manistee edged out Muskegon and Cadillac in a thrilling finish while Traverse City wound up a distant fourth despite a winning record. Most of the key players from 1910 had returned under new Manager W. W. Hawker. Local favorites Brief and Kirby had splendid seasons, but attendance went down as fans were unhappy with team ownership. J. J. Corcoran replaced James Kehoe as team president during the season. For 1912, Jimmy Hamilton was hired to manage and play third base and he assembled the strongest squad yet to represent TC in the State League. Once again paced by stalwarts Bunny Brief (.353) and Larue Kirby (18-3), the Resorters compiled a fine 79-40 WL record but were unable to overtake a potent Manistee club in the pennant chase. Manager Hamilton made a strong contribution, hitting .305 in 92 games. Major League scouts were monitoring the State League talent closely in 1912, and the signing of pitchers Kirby and Smith by the NY Giants and Brief by the St. Louis Browns before the season was finished might have spoiled Traverse City's bid to catch Manistee, which finished only four games up on the Resorters.

Emil Frisk from nearby Kalkaska played in the majors around the turn of the century.

The 1910 Resorters. BACK ROW (L to R): Williams, Dunckel, Brief, Elder, Talbot, Kirby, Dull. MIDDLE: Moore, Graham, Tierney, Mgr. Thacker, Westerman, Frind. FRONT: Pfeifer, Zook, Geiser.

A financially successful 1912 season made the Michigan State League one of the more solid minor leagues in the country and the same six teams (Ludington had replaced Holland in 1912) looked ahead to another banner season in 1913. The Resorters had lost many of their key players to the higher leagues and found themselves buried in last place for the entire first half of the season. But they suddenly went on a winning rampage and wound up the season in second place. However, the perennially strong Manistee champs were once again too far out in front to catch. The pitching of Holmquist, Collins, Seager, and Kiefer developed into a formidable rotation but it came too late to overcome the disastrous start. First baseman Bruce Evans led the hitting department for the locals with a robust .327.

The 1914 State League season began with the expectations of another successful campaign but ended up in shambles. Despite a yeoman's effort by outfielder Gil Patterson (.314), woeful pitching dispatched the Resorters into last place and attendance plummeted to disastrous levels. Neighboring Boyne City, in deep financial straits and facing a player mutiny, was forced out by League President Dickerson on August 30. In an effort to salvage the season and cut travel costs for the four remaining clubs, Traverse City, with a pitiful 22-76 record, was also dropped the next day. The once healthy dynasty of three-time champion Manistee also fell by the wayside and finished out the schedule in Belding. Muskegon ended up as the new MSL champ, but it proved to be the State League's last gasp of life as the circuit did not resume play in 1915. Thus ended Traverse City's five-year saga of professional league baseball—a few good teams and some exciting players to entertain the fans but, alas, no pennant winners.

A Michigan boy, Larue Kirby was a pitching standout for the 1910-12 Resorters. He later played in the Federal League of 1914-15 as an outfielder.

Another local product, outfielder Bunny (or Bundy) Brief, was a TC favorite in 1910-12. He went on to a lengthy career in the higher professional leagues, including four seasons in the big leagues.

The 1912 runnerups. TOP ROW (L to R): Smith, Riley, Brief, Kirby, Chase, Krueger, Sharrock. MIDDLE: Evans, Davis, Mgr. Hamilton, Brier. BOTTOM: Seegar, (mascot), Matt.

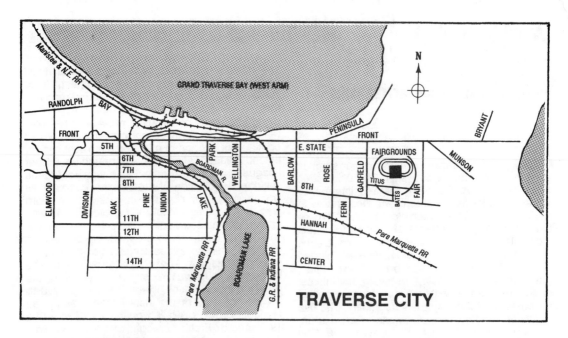

TRAVERSE CITY

THE PLAYING SITE

LEAGUE PARK 1910-14 (at fairgrounds site on east end of town)

In May 1910, the Traverse City Driving Park Association gave the local State League baseball club a big boost by offering free use of the fairgrounds driving park for home games. A baseball diamond of sorts already existed on the grounds, but numerous repairs and improvements were quickly underway to bring the field up to acceptable league standards. The fairgrounds site, east of downtown, was convenient for local patrons and included a ready-made spacious grandstand suitable for baseball. The large race track occupied the southern half of the fairgrounds and very likely the main grandstand was positioned on the north side of the track. But no photographs or detailed maps have been found to confirm this. The Civic Center currently occupies the site.

A more contemporary aerial photograph of Traverse City looking east clearly shows the old fairgrounds and race track near the top of the photo (arrow).

A current view of the Civic Center grounds which also includes a baseball diamond, but not in the same location as 1910

WYANDOTTE

PROFESSIONAL LEAGUE MEMBERSHIP

YEARS	LEAGUE	HOME FIELD
1912-13	Border	Alkali Park

Following the successes of other minor leagues in the Michigan area after 1910, Detroit sportswriter E. A. Bachelor solicited interest by some of the larger suburbs of the Detroit area in forming a fully recognized, low-budget "Trolley League" with qualified professionals and the best local talent available to stock the teams. Detroit owner Frank Navin, who could have easily nipped the idea in the bud based on territorial rights, gave the plan his blessing, believing that interest in suburban teams only whetted fans' appetites for baseball of the major league variety. The five cities of Pontiac, Mt. Clemens, Port Huron, Windsor ONT, and Wyandotte were the final candidates chosen and the circuit would be called the Border League. With each community within a short train ride from each other, travel costs would be negligible and no hotel costs were required. A short schedule of Saturday, Sunday, and Holiday dates only was adopted.

The downriver town of Wyandotte was an ideal candidate, since it already had a fine ballpark available and had supported strong independent teams in prior years. The Michigan Alkali Company had generously provided the field (Alkali Park) on its riverfront property and would continue its support of a league team as it had for the independent Alkali clubs. Although the Border League was fully accredited as a signatory to the National Association of Professional Leagues, its limited operation made it in reality a semi-pro league. Very few established professionals with career potential would be attracted to such a league and the rosters were made up primarily of marginal minor league prospects and crack semi-pro players from the Detroit area. The Wyandotte club was mostly a carryover of the previous independent Alkalis, but they proved to be the "cream" of the new Border League as Manager Brown's Alkalis won the 1912 flag with a 19-5 record. Frank Loranger of Wyandotte was the league's top hitter with a .376 BA. Key players from the previous Wyandotte independents who continued with the Border League club included Captain Charley Boettner, A. H. Woodruff, and Teddy Moxson. The City of Wyandotte paid tribute to their champions by staging a banquet in their honor and showering the players with gifts and mementos.

The Wyandotte independent team of 1907 had several players who played with the 1912-13 Border League club: Stephen Orr (top row, 2nd from right), Ted Moxson (kneeling, 2nd from left), Benny Woodruff (kneeling, 3rd from left), Charles Boettner (kneeling, 2nd from right).

With a modestly successful maiden season under their belt, the Border League overcame some shuffling of leadership and added Ypsilanti to the 1913 alignment. A slightly larger schedule was adopted but the basic low-scale operation was continued. Woodruff and Loranger were back to carry the Alkalis to another winning season, but newcomer Ypsilanti edged them out for the 1913 pennant. The Alkalis finished at 24-13 with hurler Frank Manning responsible for almost half of the team's victories with a 10-win season. Unfortunately, most of the Border League clubs finished in the red and could not be bailed out by the sale of top players to the higher leagues as in other full-schedule minor leagues. A futile attempt was made in early 1914 to continue the circuit another year but it was abandoned soon afterward.

Aloysius "Wish" Egan, one-time big league player and later legendary chief talent scout of the Detroit Tigers, made his home in Wyandotte.

THE PLAYING SITE

ALKALI PARK 1912-13 (on the south end of town between Biddle and the Detroit River)

The Michigan Alkali Company was always a dominant presence in Wyandotte and indeed was the guiding economic force in the growth of the downriver community. The company owned a good portion of the city and generously sponsored baseball and other recreational activities, since it was the town's principal employer. Alkali Park was built by the company on its plant no. 1 site on the south shore of the Detroit River in 1901. The new park was inaugurated on May 16, 1901 with a game between the Wyandotte Alkalis and Detroit College. No photos of the park have been located, but a period street map shows a grandstand in the northwest corner along the railroad tracks and Biddle Street.

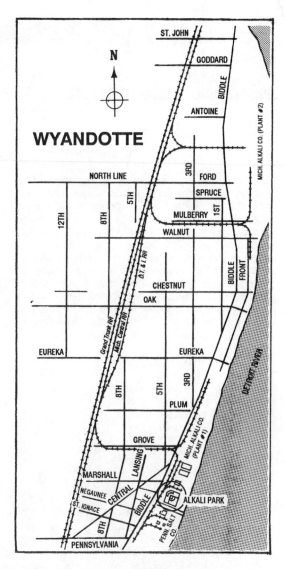

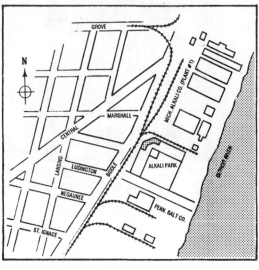

YPSILANTI

PROFESSIONAL LEAGUE MEMBERSHIP

YEARS	LEAGUE	HOME FIELD
1913	Border	Recreation Park (Fairgrounds)

The town of Ypsilanti was a member of a recognized professional minor league one year only (1913) but like Berrien Springs in 1910, both cities can make the claim that they never participated in a minor league pennant race that they didn't win. The Border League of 1912-13 was essentially a semi-pro "trolley league" connecting the southeastern Michigan towns of Mt. Clemens, Pontiac, Port Huron, Wyandotte, and Windsor, ONT. Ypsilanti joined this circuit in 1913 as its sixth member. With a short schedule of only weekend and holiday dates, it ranked at the bottom of the minor leagues that were members of the National Association. Most of the players hired were marginal youngsters with little hope of a full-fledged pro career, plus the cream of semi-pro talent in the region. The Ypsilanti franchise was hastily assembled in April 1913 by M. K. Phillips and William Varney. Very little has been recorded about the player roster but the newcomers were able to compile a 24-10 record to edge out defending champion Wyandotte for the league championship. Jack Shafer of Ypsi was the league's top batter with a .395 average. Other local players who made key contributions were Carl Stimpson, Ralph Bell, and Otto Gallant. Pitcher Bell finished with a perfect record of 6-0 to lead the Border League in that category. After 1913, the Border League was never heard from again, nor were most of the players.

The 1913 Border League champions. BACK ROW (L to R): Percy Wilson, Tennison, B. Gaseon, Carl Stimpson, Jack Shafer, Otto Gallant, Ed Standish. FRONT ROW: Crossman, Leo Hammerschmidt, Robtoy, Mgr. Pierce.

THE PLAYING SITE

> ## RECREATION PARK –1913
> ## (on fairgrounds site, West
> ## Congress & Oakwood)

This ballpark location is unconfirmed for the 1913 Border League team, but is very likely where they played. Like so many towns its size, Ypsilanti had a driving park as part of its fairgrounds facilities and a ready-made grandstand and outer fence made it adaptable for league baseball. No photos or detailed map information have been located, nor has any descriptive information been found in period newspapers.

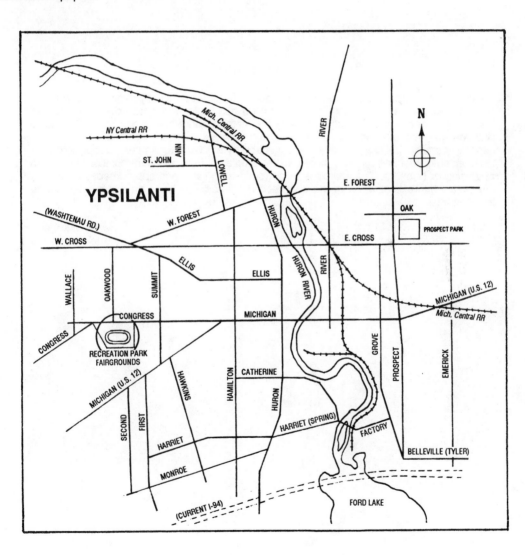

POSTSCRIPT

It is my sincere hope that this volume on Minor League baseball in Michigan is not the end but the beginning of more detailed research on this topic. Trying to cover the baseball history of 43 communities in all corners of the state in about one year's time is bound to produce erroneous educated guesses and important missing information. It will be especially gratifying if local historians are inspired by this work to dig more deeply into their local baseball past and develop more detailed studies of their own communities in the form of articles or booklets. The search is a "bottomless pit" and perhaps someday in the not too distant future another more thorough and more accurate book on this subject will be forthcoming.

Marc Okkonen
Muskegon 1996

INDEX